A CONSERVATIVE ENVIRONMENTALIST

A Conservative Environmentalist

The Life and Career of Frank Masland Jr.

THOMAS G. SMITH

The Pennsylvania State University Press
University Park, Pennsylvania

Library of Congress Cataloging-in-Publication Data

Names: Smith, Thomas G. (Thomas Gary), 1945– author.
Title: A conservative environmentalist : the life and career of Frank Masland Jr. / Thomas G. Smith.
Description: University Park, Pennsylvania : The Pennsylvania State University Press, [2024] | Includes bibliographical references and index.
Summary: "Explores the works of Frank E. Masland Jr., a wealthy Pennsylvania carpet-maker who was both a prominent twentieth-century conservationist and a political conservative, and his cross-party efforts to expand the national park system, preserve wild country, and protect the environment"—Provided by publisher.
Identifiers: LCCN 2024008510 | ISBN 9780271097527 (hardback) |SBN 9780271097534 (paper)
Subjects: LCSH: Masland, Frank. | Conservationists—United States—Biography. | Conservatives—United States—Biography. | National parks and reserves—United States—History—20th century. | Conservation of natural resources—United States—History—20th century. | LCGFT: Biographies.
Classification: LCC S926.M34 S65 2024 | DDC 333.72092 [B]—dc23/eng/20240329
LC record available at https://lccn.loc.gov/2024008510

Printed in the United States of America
Published by The Pennsylvania State University Press,
University Park, PA 16802–1003

The Pennsylvania State University Press is a member of the Association of University Presses.

It is the policy of The Pennsylvania State University Press to use acid-free paper. Publications on uncoated stock satisfy the minimum requirements of American National Standard for Information Sciences—Permanence of Paper for Printed Library Material, ANSI Z39.48–1992.

GPSR Authorized Representative: Logos Europe, 9 rue Nicolas Poussin, 17000 La Rochelle, France, contact@logoseurope.eu.

For Sandra, as always

CONTENTS

ILLUSTRATIONS (AFTER PAGE 128)

ACKNOWLEDGMENTS

Many hands have made for lighter work in crafting this biography of Frank Masland Jr. Fortunately, most of the heavy research lifting was done before the COVID pandemic disrupted our lives, including accessing libraries. For help, both pre- and post-COVID, I am especially grateful to Frank Masland IV, who chatted with me about his grandfather, provided access to private papers and family photographs, and was ever gracious in responding to my email queries. At Dickinson College, Jim Gerencser, Debbie Ege, and Melinda Triller Doran of Special Collections proved exceptionally friendly and accommodating. I worked closely with Debbie Ege, who went out of her way to help, took a keen interest in my project, and never seemed to tire of my requests for more materials and information. The archivists at the Cumberland County Historical Society in Carlisle also provided a warm welcome and a strong helping hand. I also appreciate the time and effort of individuals who communicated with me by email and telephone and the help of a park ranger who gave me a guided tour of Kings Gap, a former Masland company retreat that is now a Commonwealth of Pennsylvania environmental resource center.

At Nichols College, where I am now a professor emeritus, I have been buoyed by colleagues Andrea Becker, Maureen Butler, Paul Lambert, Don Leonard, Alan Reinhardt, and Edward Warren. Jim Douglas, Rosalba Onofrio, and Cindy LaFortune have provided research and technical help. For financial support I am indebted to Robert Kuppenheimer, a Nichols alum whose generosity helps fund faculty research and attendance at conferences.

Editor Kathryn Yahner of Penn State University Press encouraged and patiently guided this project during its initial and formative stages. After she left to pursue other opportunities, Maddie Caso deftly shepherded the book to publication. And Suzanne Wolk served as an exacting, gracious, and exemplary copyeditor.

The suggestions and insights offered by the anonymous readers improved this book immeasurably, and I am deeply in their debt. And a fellow historian, Tom Martin, whom I've never met, shared his expertise on Otis "Dock" Marston and Colorado River running.

Throughout the text, along with the terms "Navajo" and "Diné," I have used the word "Indian," as it was the accepted usage of the time.

I am indebted to the editors of the following publications for giving me permission to use portions of previously published material: "The Canyonlands National Park Controversy, 1961–1964," *Utah Historical Quarterly* 59 (Summer 1991): 216–42; "John Kennedy, Stewart Udall, and New Frontier Conservation," *Pacific Historical Review* 64 (August 1995): 329–62; and *Stewart L. Udall: Steward of the Land* (Albuquerque: University of New Mexico Press, 2017).

My family, including my sister, Janet, and a cluster of in-laws living along the Susquehanna River in upstate New York, have furnished welcome and often comic diversions. So have old friends. My four children, their spouses, and my eight grandchildren provide joy, laughter, stress relief, and unstated reminders about what is important in life. My wife, Sandra, my high school sweetheart, is unstinting in her love, good humor, support, and practical-mindedness. She has tried to save me from myself and from mistakes in this book. My lapses, within and apart from this book, are my own.

Introduction

On a scorching, sunny forenoon in mid-July 1948, Frank Masland Jr., a wealthy textile titan from Carlisle, Pennsylvania, stood at the river's edge anticipating his first raft run through a raucous rapid on the Colorado River. Nearly fifty-three years old, he was the only novice among four male and two female passengers who had hired acclaimed boatman Norman Nevills and his small crew to pilot them for several days on four oar-propelled wooden boats through dozens of rapids with no contact with the outside world. Masland's heart raced as he heard the rumble of the downstream cataract. "Never had I heard anything like it," he later wrote. Lurching through the flume safely was exhilarating. "It was thrilling beyond words—the roar, speed, power and force of the water, the height of the waves, depth of the holes, the sudden pitch, wild rush and tossing." Besides being invigorating, connecting with the stark beauty and isolation of the entire 277-mile length of the Grand Canyon for three weeks was emotionally and spiritually enriching. That maiden voyage, Masland said later, served as a turning point in his life: it transformed him into a champion of untamed rivers, wilderness areas, and national parks. Subsequent river and pack trips to the rugged canyon country of the American Southwest and other primitive areas around the world deepened his commitment to the preservation of nature.[1]

Masland fits the profile of an early and mid-twentieth-century conservationist. Born into a prominent family, he was white, male, Protestant, well educated, socially connected, and raised in a strongly religious and Republican household. He had the time, money, and inclination to experience nature—hunting, birding, fishing, hiking, yachting, riding horses, playing polo, joining sportsmen's clubs, and spending summers at a youth camp in the Maine woods. In middle age, however, he showed few signs of becoming an ardent advocate for nature conservation. He had no notion that he would dedicate the remaining third of his life to the National Park Service and the cause of conserving public lands.[2]

A champion of the national parks and wilderness, Frank Masland is the most influential preservationist no one has ever heard of. Well known among the conservation community during his lifetime, he is largely forgotten today. Neither a politician, nor a writer, nor an orator, his influence derived from his explorations of pristine nature and his nearly three decades as an unpaid member of the national park system's prestigious Advisory Board and counselor to Interior Secretary Stewart Udall. Deeply committed to preserving nature, he was involved in nearly every major environmental issue in the post–World War II era.

Masland deserves our attention for several reasons. First, he played an integral role in numerous national park issues—defining boundaries, exploring unknown regions, naming landscape features, recommending new additions to the park system, and using his influence with the Department of the Interior to protect public preserves from commercial intrusions. Second, he championed federal protection of a sizable portion of the desert and canyon country of the American Southwest well before the Sierra Club and other mainstream conservation groups took an interest in that desolate region. His most enduring legacy is the establishment of Canyonlands National Park in 1964. Just as John Muir is linked to the establishment of Yosemite National Park and George Bird Grinnell is associated with the creation of Glacier National Park, Masland can be identified with achieving congressional park designation for Utah's canyon lands. Although he loved the American Southwest and served as an aesthetic pioneer for its federal safekeeping, his influence ranged from Pennsylvania to Florida and all the way to Africa. Third, as a conservative for nature, Masland was both unique and broadly representative of a general trend. He was unique as one of the few industrialists and ultraconservatives who gave unstinting support to the federal preservation of public lands and most environmental regulations. He was also representative of a time (1964–76), termed "the Green Years" by writers Gregg Coodley and David

Sarasohn, when bipartisan coalition building and environmental concern enabled Republicans and Democrats to cooperate as stewards of the earth. Though fervently conservative in his politics, Masland believed that efforts to preserve nature should be free from political partisanship. Masland's long life (1895–1993) also provides a vantage point from which to track the evolution of the twentieth-century American environmental idea through the lens of a conservative Republican.

Like many young men of his social station in the early 1900s, Masland doubtless was transfixed by Jack London's *Call of the Wild,* Edgar Rice Burroughs's *Tarzan of the Apes,* and other adventure stories in which young heroes confronted the wild. The popularity of those raw nature stories, along with the rise of out-of-doors roughing-it groups like the Boone and Crockett Club, Sons of Daniel Boone, Camp Fire Club, and Boy Scouts, has been called the "wilderness cult" by historian Roderick Nash.[3] Masland would join the upscale Boone and Crockett Club, Explorers Club, Appalachian Mountain Club, Cosmos Club, and Sierra Club. Throughout his middle age he sought to unplug from the modern world and to test his mettle, at least temporarily, in primitive nature.

For decades, writers have used "conservation," "preservation," and "environmental protection" interchangeably as catch-all terms to describe the relationship of humans with the earth and the oversight of its grandeur and bounty. Additionally, these terms have been applied to specific approaches to the environment, "conservation" being primarily resource-based; "preservation," place-based; and "environmental stewardship," human-based. During the first half of the twentieth century, the so-called wise-use or progressive-conservation stage, federal bureaucrats led by President Theodore Roosevelt and the first chief of the US Forest Service, Gifford Pinchot, worked to prevent the despoliation of finite public resources through efficient use. In the immediate post–World War II decades, conservation organizations emphasized the preservation of sublime landscapes, national parks, and wilderness areas. In the century's last three decades, environmentalists focused on the interconnectedness of all living things, the dangers to human health posed by pollution and other quality-of-life issues in urban areas, and the pursuit of environmental justice for the poor and communities of color.[4]

There was overlap and interplay among the various approaches. During the early twentieth century, Pinchot, Roosevelt, and other mainly Republican reformers of the Progressive era decried the unregulated and wanton waste of forests and other public resources while emphasizing the need for their efficient use. Experts in the federal bureaucracy, they maintained, could scientifically administer public resources, saving them from commercial depredation and managing their use wisely, including setting aside some scenic and scientifically significant natural places, like Yellowstone and Yosemite National Parks, for posterity or later use. As historian J. Brooks Flippen has aptly put it, traditional conservationists "were not preservationists. They sought to protect nature for, not from, man; they did not seek to remove a resource from use but rather to manage it properly to ensure perpetual use." This wise-use, utilitarian, or efficiency method, which Pinchot dubbed "conservation," generally dominated until the postwar era.[5]

At the same time, though less prominently, an aesthetic or preservationist approach to awe-inspiring landscapes gained support. While not forsaking the wise use of natural resources, early twentieth-century nature writer and Sierra Club co-founder John Muir and J. Horace McFarland of the American Civic Association championed the preservation of wild and breathtakingly scenic places such as California's Yosemite Valley for their aesthetic value, recreational opportunities, intrinsic worth, and spiritual uplift. Such natural "temples," Muir insisted, should be left nearly inviolate, Muir preferring permanent protection to delayed commercial use. But when the two approaches conflicted, aesthetic value generally gave way until the 1950s and 1960s, when the preservationist perspective took precedence.[6]

The first major clash between the conservation and preservationist viewpoints began in 1908 over a proposed dam in the Hetch Hetchy Valley of Yosemite National Park. San Francisco's political leaders, whose city had recently been ravaged by an earthquake and fire, sought a dependable supply of water from the proposed reservoir. Progressives like Pinchot and Roosevelt supported the proposal, insisting that it was the most efficient and wisest use of a watershed resource. Muir and McFarland opposed it on aesthetic grounds, arguing that once a scenic landscape had been established as a national park it must not be violated and urging the city to seek an alternate site for a reservoir. The battle dragged on until 1913, shortly after Muir's death, when Congress approved the dam.[7]

John Muir has rightly achieved legendary status as the sage of aesthetic and wilderness preservation. But as historian Robert Righter has demonstrated, Muir was not as fully committed to the wilderness principle as some have made him out to be. The Hetch Hetchy clash, Righter argues, was essentially over whether the protected valley would be used for water storage and hydroelectric power for the city of San Francisco or for recreational tourism. Wilderness protection was never at issue. Muir and other opponents of the dam favored the construction of hotels, restaurants, and roads to accommodate tourists who sought a sublime natural setting for outdoor activities, spiritual nourishment, and relief from the evils of the city. Dam proponents maintained that a reservoir would not mar the integrity of the park or discourage recreational use. Preservationists claimed that a dam built for a city's water supply would likely be off-limits to the public, mar the wholesomeness of the natural setting, and set a precedent for future commercial intrusions into national parks.[8]

Upset over the loss of the Hetch Hetchy Valley, preservationists worked for the establishment of a single federal agency to administer, protect, and promote the national parks. McFarland helped draft a bill, and in 1916 Congress enacted a revised version of it, creating the National Park Service (NPS) within the Department of the Interior. The NPS was authorized to promote and administer existing and future units—parks, monuments, and reserves—to conserve their scenic, wildlife, and scientific value and "to provide for the public enjoyment of the same in such manner as will leave them unimpaired for the enjoyment of future generations." It often became difficult for the NPS to balance the conflicting goals of public enjoyment (recreational use) and scenic preservation (aesthetics). To what extent should the NPS permit roads, restaurants, and lodges within the park? And would a dam that produced an artificial lake for public benefit violate the objective of leaving parks unimpaired? When Frank Masland became an active conservationist in the early 1950s, he identified with the aesthetic outlook of Muir and McFarland. In his three decades with the NPS, Masland insisted that once a federal preserve had been established, it should remain off-limits to man-made intrusions apart from a minimal number of roads, campgrounds, scenic pullouts, and trails.[9]

Though always present, the preservationist perspective was strengthened in the 1930s with the birth of the Wilderness Society, an organization dedicated to the preservation of roadless national forest areas for the protection of natural ecosystems and for human uses like camping, fishing, hiking, and other nonmotorized pursuits. President Franklin Roosevelt's New Deal, with its federal dam building, soil conservation, tree planting, and clutch of new national parks and monuments, struck an acceptable balance between resource use and preservation.

The preservationist idea gained political and public ascendancy in the three decades following World War II. The booming tourist and recreation industry triggered public demand for more national parks. Nature lovers reevaluated the works of John Muir and enthused over the ecological messages of Aldo Leopold's *Sand County Almanac* (1949), Joseph Wood Krutch's *Desert Year* (1952), and Sigurd Olson's *The Singing Wilderness* (1956), which stressed the intrinsic worth of wild nature and the obligation of humans to practice stewardship, not dominion, of the earth. Preservationists managed to stop plans to build massive federal hydroelectric dams in the West that would have intruded upon Dinosaur National Monument and Grand Canyon National Park. They also battled successfully for congressional legislation protecting wilderness. Masland was deeply committed to this perspective.

The human-based approach, generally referred to as ecological, environmental, or "the New Conservation," gained acclaim and currency in the century's last three decades and beyond. Hundreds of thousands of readers were alarmed by the publication in 1962 of *Silent Spring*, Rachel Carson's dire warning about the use of pesticides. The following year, Secretary of the Interior Stewart Udall warned readers in *The Quiet Crisis* that their health, quality of life, and survival as a species were at risk from environmental degradation and technological arrogance. The new wave of environmentalists, which included politicians, bureaucrats, scientists, writers, and citizens at the grassroots level, sought political, legal, and individual action to remedy threats to the planet and to humankind. These threats included overpopulation, disappearing open space, urban and rural blight, pollution of air and water, hazardous chemicals and toxins, nuclear and industrial waste, rampant consumerism and runaway technology, and numerous other ills. This wave of environmental reform crested in the late 1960s and 1970s, and except for major backlashes from the Right during the Reagan and Bush presidencies, it prevailed for the remainder of the century. Masland was cautiously supportive of that outlook.[10]

Throughout his lifetime, Masland was guided by his bedrock conservative principles—Protestant Christianity, free-enterprise capitalism, individual rights and initiative, anti-statism, moral order, states' rights, traditional family values, opposition to labor unions, and concern, bordering on paranoia, regarding the internal and external threat of communism. He was perhaps the only person in America who supported the agendas of both the John Birch Society and the Sierra Club. The contradiction between his anti-statism and his support for strong federal authority over the public lands makes for an intriguing narrative.

Today, the concept of a "conservative conservationist" appears oxymoronic, but, as historians Brian Drake and J. Brooks Flippen have explained, this was not necessarily the case in the mid-twentieth century, when a bipartisan Congress, robust economy, and nonpartisan conservation groups produced landmark achievements. Unlike conservative members of Congress Barry Goldwater, John Saylor, and a few others, Masland was not an elected official beholden to a political constituency. And he was one of the few US industrialists to commit totally to the protection of wilderness.[11]

During his long life—he lived nearly one hundred years—Masland used his voice, influence, experiences with nature, and considerable wealth to champion environmental causes virtually without restraint. Despite holding some extreme and at times outlandish political views, he was respected by most conservationists, including the unabashedly liberal Democrat Stewart Udall, perhaps this nation's most influential interior secretary and environmentalist. Masland worked closely with Udall, especially for the establishment of Canyonlands National Park. He also helped establish the boundaries of Everglades National Park, becoming a regular winter visitor and informal lobbyist for its protection. Masland served happily as an Interior Department insider during the administrations of Dwight D. Eisenhower, John F. Kennedy, and Lyndon B. Johnson as the bipartisan conservation movement surged. While he never voted for a Democratic president, he was able to support their conservation agendas while disdaining their generally liberal economic and social policies.

In preserving nature, Masland believed that he was doing his duty as a conservative, a patriot, and a Christian. As a conservative, he held that only the federal government could be trusted to preserve American natural beauty, wilderness, and public resources from commercial and recreational depredation. He separated himself from most conservatives by consistently supporting preservation over the commercial use of resplendent public lands. As a patriot, he believed that the nation's natural bounty, majestic landscapes, open space, and wilderness made Americans exceptional and that the Republic would hardly be worth saving if those resources were depleted. As a Christian, he favored stewardship, not dominion, over the earth. Connecting with nature, he maintained, provided spiritual nourishment.

Pleased by bipartisan support for environmental causes in the postwar decades, he was disgusted when President Nixon politicized the Park

Service by naming his campaign manager as its director, and he was appalled when the president undercut the environmental program that he had initially promoted. President Reagan further damaged the cause by appointing anti-environmentalist James Watt secretary of the interior. When conservatives turned against environmentalism during and after the Reagan presidency, Masland, in jarring contrast, refused to join what historians James Morton Turner and Andrew Isenberg have termed the "Republican reversal."

During the middle decades of the twentieth century, Masland rafted western rivers, explored the remote and largely unmapped Utah and Arizona canyon country, served on the boards of national and state conservation organizations, chaired the influential national park system Advisory Board, evaluated pristine natural areas at home and abroad for national park status, counseled and took inspection tours with Secretary of the Interior Stewart Udall, partnered with Lady Bird Johnson in her goal of American beautification, advised Pennsylvania governors William Scranton and Raymond P. Shafer on environmental issues, and served as Pennsylvania's fish commissioner.

Frank Masland is worth knowing because he was a rare industrialist whose business became the business of saving nature for future generations. To date, however, his contributions at the national, state, and local levels have gone unheralded by the academic community. I hope that this narrative will show that Masland merits recognition as a passionate Republican conservative for nature.

CHAPTER 1

A Family of Weavers, a Boy of Privilege

Frank Masland had textiles in his blood. A family of weavers, the Maslands traced their lineage to Nottinghamshire, England, where, in the 1770s, John and Elizabeth Masland served as caretakers at Annesley Hall, a castlelike estate hardly an arrow's flight from Sherwood Forest. Owing to hard times in the English textile industry, John and Charles Masland, the great-grandsons of the family founders, migrated to North America. In 1837 John married, spent some years at the Lowell mills in Massachusetts, became a US citizen, and then relocated to Germantown, a main hub of the Pennsylvania textile industry. For two decades, he worked making men's stockings and underwear. Though married, the father of eight children, and fifty-four years old in 1861, he joined the Union Army, participating in several battles before being medically discharged in late 1862.[1]

His sons James and Charles—or C. H., as Charles was called—also joined the Union cause. C. H. served in the 6th Pennsylvania Cavalry, experiencing action during the Peninsula Campaign and the Battle of Antietam before contracting typhoid and serving the remainder of his three-year stint performing guard duty at a Philadelphia hospital. In April 1864, four months prior to his discharge, he married Annetta (Nettie) Meyer. The union produced six surviving sons.[2]

Like many of his ancestors, C. H. entered the textile trade, launching a family business after the war that would eventually be led by his grandson Frank Elmer Masland Jr. C. H. and his brother James leased yarn-dyeing houses before earning enough money to acquire the Allegheny Dye Works in the Kensington section of Philadelphia. After a falling-out with James, C. H. became the sole proprietor in 1875. Realizing that he could make more money manufacturing carpets than dyeing yarn, he sold the Allegheny Works and purchased the Amber Carpet Mill at 1732 Lieb Street in Kensington. A business partnership with his sons Maurice and Frank marked the start of C. H. Masland and Sons in 1886. By investing in more than two hundred power looms and new multistory buildings, the partners expanded their workforce, product line, and sales through catalog houses and by hiring the New York City sales agency W. J. Sloane to market Masland rugs to retail department stores like Gimbels, Marshall Field's, and Jordan Marsh. Two more brothers were added as executives, and in 1907 the partnership was reorganized as a corporation, with C. H. serving as CEO and sons Maurice, Charles Jr., Frank, and John Wesley functioning as executives and principal stockholders.

With C. H. observing from the sidelines, the brothers expanded the business until World War I, when a shortage of raw materials and a series of labor union strikes crippled production. Expecting sales to improve after the war but frustrated and embittered by disruptive labor strife between 1915 and 1919, they searched for nonunion manufacturing opportunities outside Philadelphia. Selecting a new factory site in Carlisle, they entrusted their relocation to Frank Masland Jr., the son and nephew, respectively, of company treasurer Frank Sr. and president Maurice Masland.[3]

For the next seven decades, the business in Carlisle grew, especially under the direction of Frank Jr., who replaced his uncle Maurice as head of the company. As president from 1930 until 1960, and then as CEO for another decade, Frank Jr. guided Masland and Sons through the Great Depression and transformed it into one of the largest carpet manufacturers in the world. Like his father and his uncle Maurice, he was a conservative Republican, a devout Methodist, a philanthropist, and a fierce opponent of labor unions. But he also became an all-in preservationist and passionate advocate for planet Earth whose outlook on the natural world was partially shaped during his formative years in the small Pennsylvania towns of Bustleton and Carlisle.

Born at home on December 8, 1895, in a row house on East Allegheny Avenue in Kensington, Frank Elmer Masland Jr. inherited a life of splendor. In 1896, the family moved to the small but upscale rural community of Bustleton (now a residential neighborhood of Philadelphia), where Frank Sr. and his wife, Mary, bought a twenty-three-room house on fourteen acres of land. They raised two sons, Frank Jr., then an infant, and the soon-to-be-born Robert Paul. The house included a formal dining room and fifty-by-thirty-foot drawing room with two fireplaces. In a vast upstairs playroom, Frank and Paul (as he was called) kept worms, frogs, bugs, turtles, and other wild creatures. "We boys were free as the wind and badly spoiled. . . . We lived graciously," Frank Jr. recalled. "Life was a bowl of cherries." In addition to the spacious home and lawn, the boys had access to a barn, a stable of thirty racehorses, a carriage house, and open pastures where they romped with their pony, horses, bicycles, and St. Bernard dogs. The household maintained two maids, a horse trainer, a gardener, a coachman, and, later, a chauffeur. The village of five hundred residents sported a bank, school, general store, train station, barber shop, tavern, drug store, three churches, and a doctor. From childhood, Frank Jr. took pride in the entrepreneurial initiative of his family and the cooperative spirit of his community. There was no federal assistance for financial success or social uplift. There was no government safety net, he remembered proudly. Charity came from family or community members, not Washington, DC. "There was no Social Security, no Medicare or Medicaid, no Blue Cross and Blue Shield, no Big Brother. A person was a person and not a number." For Frank Jr., Bustleton served as a model for idyllic small-town America.[4]

Raised in a strict evangelical Methodist household, Frank attended church twice on Sunday and prayer meeting on Wednesday evening. Card playing, dancing, drinking, and theatergoing were considered sinful and were forbidden. As an adult, Masland indulged in many activities his mother and other strict Methodists had considered sinful, but he attended church regularly, lived a morally upright life, and actively supported Methodist outreach, refugee work, and the YMCA.

Although the family rarely vacationed, it lived large, especially Frank Sr.; his great-grandson Frank IV remembered him as an imposing figure and "a bit of a dandy." He joined the best country clubs, yachted, bought trotting and pace horses for racing, and regularly purchased new Hudson, Buick, and Cadillac automobiles. Frank Jr. seldom spoke of his mother, perhaps because his parents divorced, but he wrote admiringly, though not warmly, about his father as ruggedly independent, adept at business, and generous toward the poor, the YMCA, and the Methodist Church.[5]

His admiration for his father notwithstanding, Frank said little about their personal relationship. Growing up, he appeared to have spent more quality time with his uncle Maurice than with his father. When his mind turned to

Maurice, he remembered fondly "the many good times we had together, the horseback rides where we would arrange to meet, ride for hours and then head for our respective homes. They were good days, days when life was simple." He did not express similar sentiments concerning his father.[6]

Although he wrote little about her, he was devoted to his mother and blamed his father for divorcing her. Mary Masland was an austere woman who disapproved of horse racing, drinking, and her husband's fast lifestyle. Frank Masland Sr. began a relationship with Minnie Thomas, the Bustleton housekeeper, prompting a separation and eventual divorce in 1927. Frank Sr. and Minnie married the following year and moved to Lake Worth in West Palm Beach, Florida. Frank Sr.'s moral lapse may account for his son's adherence to a strict moral code and his abhorrence of divorce, sexual liberation, and pornography.[7]

As a youngster, Frank Jr. initially attended a public elementary school in Bustleton, but his parents transferred him to a private school for grades 7–12. From the train station at Bustleton, young Frank rattled by rail to nearby Philadelphia, where he attended the Friends' Central School. He took part in the football and debate teams and served as treasurer of the junior class and vice president of the senior class, which consisted of fifteen boys and forty-two girls. According to the school yearbook, *The Record,* his goal was to graduate, his chief characteristic was "laziness," and his favorite activity was going to Philadelphia.[8]

His trips to Philadelphia usually meant visiting the family mill in Kensington. Being born on Carpet Row in the mill district, he later reminisced to his sons, was perhaps a "prenatal influence" because he learned to weave as a youth. "The clatter of looms was always music to my ears and the smell of wool being dyed attar of roses." Besides wandering through the mill, his out-of-school activities included roaming the family fields by foot and on horseback, swimming in creeks, hunting, fishing, sailing off the New Jersey shore, where the family maintained a yacht, playing tennis and polo, and attending a summer camp in Maine.[9]

Masland's love for the natural world derived early on from his experiences at Camp Minnewawa on Little Sebago Lake in North Windham, Maine, where he spent two months each summer from age ten to age eighteen. He swam, tented, fished, hiked, and learned to canoe, including one memorable paddle down the remote Allagash River in northern Maine. "My love for nature developed," he recalled. "It became a part of me that has meant more to me than anything but my family ever since."[10]

Besides sylvan Maine, he also was shaped by his rural surroundings in Pennsylvania, a state that has proved to be fertile ground for growing nature writers and avid conservationists. In the twentieth century alone it produced Gifford Pinchot, J. Horace McFarland, Howard Zahniser, Rachel Carson, John Saylor, Edward Abbey, Annie Dillard, Maurice Goddard, Frank, John, and Jean Craighead, and Frank Masland Jr.

Founded by William Penn in 1690 as a haven for English Quakers, Penn's Woods also attracted Scots-Irish, Germans, and other mainly European groups that pushed aside Delaware, Susquehannock, Iroquois, and other aboriginal people. The colony played a leading role in the drive for independence and, following statehood, helped propel the transportation and industrial revolutions. It also was a haven for nature lovers, even after the mighty industrial machine invaded the garden in the nineteenth century. Centrally located along the Atlantic Coast, the Keystone State abounds with nature's blessings, including a moderate climate, copious rainfall, teeming wildlife, abundant forestlands, rich farmland, and a multitude of opportunities for hunting, fishing, camping, birding, boating, and hiking. It also possesses plenty of underground and surface water, including Lake Erie to the northwest and three major river systems: the Delaware on the eastern border, the Susquehanna in midstate, and the Monongahela-Allegheny-Ohio in the west. The Appalachian Mountain chain coils southwesterly from the northern border to the southern state line and continues into several southern states. The Appalachian chain and its subranges, such as the Allegheny to the west, Pocono to the northeast, and Blue Ridge to the south, yield timber, iron ore, and coal and include the Marcellus Shale, with its deep pockets of natural gas.

The state's natural bounty enabled it to become an industrial, agricultural, and political powerhouse well before Masland's birth in 1895. Tucked into the state's southeastern and southwestern corners, respectively, Philadelphia and Pittsburgh were the two main hubs of commerce, industry, and learning, while Harrisburg, nestled along the Susquehanna River, served as the state capital. In population, and thus in congressional political clout, Pennsylvania trailed only New York until it was overtaken by California in 1960 and then Texas and Florida.

Industrial growth brought numerous problems—unhealthy and unsafe workplaces, noise, labor strife, crowded cities, polluted air and streams, and disfigured landscapes. But the state retained much of its open space and bucolic beauty, and early in the twentieth century concerned citizens' groups like the American Civic Association and women's garden clubs worked to sanitize and beautify cities and to revitalize and preserve decimated forests and wildlife.

The Maslands, like other families of means, found relief from urban problems in rural summer retreats and in estates in communities like Bustleton outside Philadelphia. As a young man, Frank Masland Jr. found comfort and a sense of place, to borrow a phrase from author and poet Wendell Berry, in the Cumberland Valley of the Appalachian Mountains. Edward Abbey, like Masland and Berry an anti-statist nature lover, also had an attachment to Appalachian country. Cupped between North Mountain on one side and South Mountain on the other, the 544-square-mile valley crouched serenely in south-central Pennsylvania. Its wooded hillsides were free of the shaved, disfigured, coal-mined mountainsides to the northeast, and its streams and air were not fouled by smokestack emissions and waste runoff from industrial centers like Pittsburgh. In south-central Pennsylvania, dairy herds, weathered barns, and neat farmhouses dotted the landscape, and the fertile valley carried the scent of newly plowed earth, freshly mown hay, sweet-smelling silage, and redolent mountain laurel, the state flower. Natural springs fed clear, trout-filled Yellow Breeches, Conodoguinet, and Letort Creeks, flowing eastward to the Susquehanna River, and a sixteen-mile stretch of the Appalachian Trail coursed through the valley. The city of Carlisle, with a population that varied between twelve and sixteen thousand souls, served as the center of business, culture, and light industry, including the Masland and Sons carpet factory. Carlisle, like all small cities, had problems, to be sure, but they were minor compared to those of Pittsburgh, Philadelphia, Scranton, Johnstown, and other, larger cities. For Frank Masland, the valley possessed every amenity a person could want, and he referred to it lovingly as the "Blessed Valley."[11]

Masland spent nearly his entire adult life in the town and outskirts of Carlisle. Located about twenty miles southwest of Harrisburg, Carlisle was founded by Scots-Irish immigrants from northern Ireland in 1751. Named for its sister city in England, Carlisle became the county seat for Cumberland County. During the Revolutionary War period and well into the 1800s, it was recognized for its agricultural products, natural springs, and iron forges. Prominent residents included James Wilson, James Smith, and George Ross, signers of the Declaration of Independence, and the Revolutionary War folk heroine Molly Pitcher. In 1794, President George Washington and Treasury Secretary Alexander Hamilton met there with a show of force to put down the challenge to central authority known as the Whiskey Rebellion. A haven for runaway slaves, Carlisle supported the election of Abraham Lincoln in 1860 and was briefly occupied and shelled by Confederate forces shortly before the Battle of Gettysburg. The Carlisle Barracks, established in 1777, gained renown a century later as the Carlisle Indian Industrial School, where the great Olympian Jim Thorpe played football; today it serves as the US Army War College. Carlisle is also home to Dickinson College, Masland's alma mater.[12]

Dickinson College was established by Philadelphia physician Dr. Benjamin Rush in September 1783, just a few days after the official conclusion of the War of Independence. Rush named the college for John Dickinson, a fellow Revolutionary War patriot who at the time was president (governor) of Pennsylvania and Delaware. A decade later, the college burned down. Rush headed a rebuilding campaign. With contributions from President Thomas Jefferson, Secretary of State James Madison, Secretary of the Treasury Albert Gallatin, US Supreme Court Chief Justice John Marshall, and scores of other donors, the campaign raised enough money for architect Benjamin Latrobe to design a new building of fire-resistant gray limestone. Located on High Street, the new building, called "Old West," opened to students in the fall of 1805. Over the years, numerous distinguished alums walked through its doors, including President James Buchanan and US Supreme Court Justice Roger Taney.[13]

Frank Masland entered Dickinson in mid-September 1914. The incoming class of 110 students, the largest in history up to that time, included eighty-three men and twenty-seven women, most of them hailing from Pennsylvania. African American students were accepted, though few enrolled and none were permitted to participate in intercollegiate sports. There is no evidence that Masland associated with any minority classmates.[14]

Then affiliated with the Methodist Church, Dickinson prided itself on its tradition of providing students with a liberal arts education. Besides attending required weekly chapel, Masland took courses in algebra, oratory, English rhetoric and composition, German prose and poetry, and the political and constitutional history of England during his first year. Born to wealth and privilege and realizing that he could always earn a living by working in the family carpet business, Masland was more sociable than studious. He joined Alpha Rho Chi, a Christians-only fraternity that forbade dancing, and attended its social functions, including hay wagon outings to local nature sanctuaries such as Flat Rock and Doubling Gap. These outdoor ventures were far more interesting to him than classroom and chapel activities.[15]

Initially forgoing participation in sports, Masland had time to socialize and often did so with female classmates. On one occasion, with approval from the student senate, his fraternity good-naturedly hazed him publicly for spending time with too many women "promiscuously."[16]

Masland joined the football team as a sophomore, playing quarterback and halfback before breaking an ankle. His younger brother, Paul, a far better athlete, started at offensive and defensive guard. Their father, Frank Sr., helped the financially strapped team by providing money for leather helmets, footballs, and red and white sweaters and blankets embossed with a giant letter D. The contributions of the Maslands did little to boost the team's performance, as it suffered dreadful losing seasons. But the brothers Masland, like other young Caucasian men of the middle and upper classes, were encouraged to follow the example of Theodore Roosevelt by pursuing rugged physical activities to build character and upright citizenship.[17]

Masland was not a motivated student. There is no evidence that he involved himself with any of the serious campus topics of the day, such as downsizing campus prayer week, training citizen soldiers for possible involvement in the war in Europe, prohibiting the manufacture and sale of alcoholic beverages, and granting women the vote and equal rights by amending the US Constitution.

At that time, Masland had little passion for politics, but he did have a penchant for trouble. The college had no policy banning the possession of weapons, but Masland gained local press attention when he reported the theft of a loaded Ives-Johnson revolver and $44.00 from his fraternity room desk. Eventually, a maintenance worker was nabbed for the crime. Ironically, Masland explained that he kept the revolver handy to prevent burglaries.[18]

Masland was also a prankster. Periodically, he hid alarm clocks in the front of the chapel, their raucous clatter set to disrupt the solemnity of a meditation, prayer, speech, or sermon. When W. E. Robinson, a professor of oratory, parked his automobile outside the building where he taught an evening class, Masland and several other culprits removed its tires and some of its parts and physically carried it to Bosler Hall, where they "parked" it inside with a sign reading "A Ford Can Go Anywhere." "Better here than a thousand miles away," muttered the bewildered professor. In another caper, Masland and three accomplices pilfered the college chaplain's bicycle and somehow managed to dangle it from the tail of a copper mermaid perched atop "Old West" so that the mermaid appeared to be riding it. They affixed a sign that read "Better than a Ford." The press photographed the dangling bicycle, and the image also appeared on a postcard. The college never learned the identities of the perpetrators of either heist.[19]

As often happens with carefree, adventurous males, Masland matured after falling in love. In 1915 he met and was smitten with Virginia Sharp, the sister of his fraternity brother Reuben Sharp. The Sharps traced their paternal lineage to colonial New Jersey. The daughter of a physician, Virginia hailed from Mullica Hill, New Jersey, a small, upscale town about twenty-five miles southeast of Philadelphia. With plans to become a medical doctor like her father, brother, and several other family members, both male and female, Virginia attended Temple University and was dating a Dickinson student who was a friend of Reuben's. Masland was determined to win her over. Learning that his rival drove a prestigious Mercer convertible, Masland purchased an equally flashy Stutz convertible. Although the sporty car probably had little to do with it, Masland eventually won her hand. Not entirely over his high-spirited ways, he occasionally breezed around in his open Stutz with Virginia's pet pig seated between them on the front seat.[20]

Although he was not a gifted student, Masland displayed a talent for writing. In "An Evening on the Lake," an essay he submitted for a first-year class in rhetoric and composition, he wrote gracefully and movingly about his connection with nature. After an evening meal, the story began, he strolled from his tent to an unnamed lakeshore (probably Little Sebago Lake in Maine), where he spotted some canoes. "The invitation was irresistible—the setting sun, to be followed soon by a perfect moon, the calm lake barely ruffled by the soft breath of the evening wind, the numerous coves and islands with an air of mystery heightened by the semi-darkness of the afterglow, the canoes eager to have their hot sides cooled by the wash of the waves." He paddled out some distance and then lay on his back and drifted aimlessly, "mindful only of the sublime beauty of the departing day and approaching night." He heard the evening song of birds and "the soft splash of a fish jumping for a night moth."[21]

Then came the stars, "the eyes of the night," and the moon, "the monarch of the night," penetrating the darkness with a warm glow. Those twins of nature soon were followed by "the crowning glory of the night," the aurora borealis. For an hour, "that great mystery of the north, slowly stretching out a finger, now here, now there," illuminated the northern sky and filled him with wonder. When the northern lights dissipated, he paddled back to his tent "to sleep the sleep which comes to him whose body is tired with the joy of healthy exercise and whose soul has been stirred by the wonder of the Lord's creations." Though the writing is sometimes overblown, Masland's short essay shows a talent with words, a passion for nature, a belief that connecting with nature was akin to connecting with God, and a foreshadowing of his commitment to wilderness preservation. "An Evening on the Lake" is similar to a story by the naturalist and future Wilderness Society president Sigurd Olson as a young North Woods canoe guide.[22]

With a faint notion that he might want to become an attorney, Masland withdrew from the college in June 1916 to enter law school; it was not unusual in those days to pursue a law degree after two years of college. He entered the Dickinson School of Law in September. Though unaffiliated with Dickinson College, the law school's campus abutted that of the college and its students were eligible to play on the college's sports teams. Masland attempted to play football for the red and white in 1916 but injuries sidelined him for the season.

More interested in pursuing Virginia than in acquiring a law degree, Masland withdrew after one semester. Although his time at the law school was brief, he impressed people with his likeable personality and potential for success. Upon his departure, he received a warm letter from Agnes Trickett, whose husband, William, served as dean of the law school. "I am sorry to learn of your separation from the school," she wrote. "I hope you will see clear to the resumption of your studies sometime. I was hoping to get better acquainted with you, as the year advanced, but this satisfaction I must forego. It will be a pleasure to hear from you and about you, and to know of your happiness and success in whatever vocation you take up."[23]

Masland's decision to leave law school also was driven by his belief that the United States would be drawn into the Great War and that he would be required to enlist. Until that day arrived, he preferred to spend time with Virginia in Mullica Hill rather than in a Carlisle law school classroom. In the spring of 1917, the Sharps announced the couple's engagement.

As Masland predicted, the United States entered the Great War in early April. He was one of four million idealistic young men and women who served their country in the hope of making the world safe for democracy. There was something noble about "shedding blood freely to protect the peace, liberty, justice, and morality of the world against a menace that cannot be withstood in any other way," wrote the youthful editor of the *Dickinsonian*. "We believe in this war. It has been forced upon us by an insidious and depraved people, imperialistic and autocratic," he continued. "We fight for democracy against autocracy, for freedom of the seas against piracy, for liberty against murder and slavery."[24] Masland shared these sentiments, and he and his brother, Paul, joined the US Navy. Paul served on a coal carrier in the English Channel. Frank never left the Eastern Seaboard, manning patrol boats and commanding submarine chasers off the New Jersey and Virginia shores.

His first craft was the fifty-seven-foot family yacht, *Kuwana II*, lent to the US Navy Department by his father for one dollar per month. He spent most of 1917 at the Philadelphia Navy Yard and other East Coast ports. Aided by his father's lobbying efforts with the Navy Department, he was promoted to ensign in mid-November and given command of a submarine chaser M 426. Shortly after this promotion, he was granted a leave, which he used to marry Virginia in a ceremony at the Methodist Church in Mullica Hill in January 1918. After a brief honeymoon, he returned to duty, patrolling the waters off the mid-Atlantic Seaboard, seeing little action and recording no kills. Although he was frustrated that he saw no combat, he doubtless was relieved when the war's carnage ended with the armistice of November 11, 1918.[25]

Although the bloodletting had ended, Masland's commitment to the navy had not. No longer on the prowl for enemy submarines, he was transferred to a dispatch boat in Norfolk, Virginia. Meanwhile, Frank Sr. pressed the Navy Department for the early release of his sons, thus enabling them to return to college or go to work establishing the new carpet plant in Carlisle. The brothers were not discharged from the navy until 1921 but were released for college or civilian work in April 1919 while continuing to serve in the naval reserves.[26] Both took jobs with Masland and Sons. Frank headed the relocation to Carlisle and became plant manager, while Paul moved into the financial office. Both would serve the remainder of their working lives as company men. They would guide the company through the Great Depression and into robust growth during World War II. Their economic success gave Frank an opportunity to engage with pristine nature and to devote his remaining years to its protection.

CHAPTER 2

Carlisle

Masland never felt comfortable in Philadelphia or any other large city. But the small town of Carlisle gave him a sense of belonging. He had gone to college there and favored it as a site for a new factory. Before relocating there, he had worked at various tasks with the company in Philadelphia in the months after his discharge from active military service. His first job, he later recalled, was running a loom in the Philadelphia shop. Another responsibility was to drive his Stutz convertible, a .45 caliber automatic pistol on the passenger seat, to the Corn Exchange Bank at Second and Chestnut, pick up the payroll, and return it to the factory. In the summer of 1919, at the request of his father and his uncle Maurice, he agreed to oversee the relocation of the Masland mill to Carlisle. That community and its rural environs would remain his home for the rest of his life.[1]

A city of slightly fewer than 11,000 souls in 1919, Carlisle, like other communities throughout the Western world, was recovering from losing loved ones in the war and in the devastating flu pandemic of 1918–19. Worldwide, the pandemic may have killed as many as 40 million people, including 675,000 Americans. Philadelphia, a city of 1.7 million and the location of the US Naval Yard where Masland had been stationed, was hit particularly hard, suffering more than 12,000 deaths. In one week in mid-October, the virus claimed 4,597 Philadelphians. Corpses, like trash, rested on front porches or curbsides awaiting pickup by trucks. Health professionals, undertakers, politicians, and loved ones were all stressed and terrified by the threat of the deadly scourge.[2]

In Cumberland County, Pennsylvania, which comprised Carlisle, Mechanicsburg, Boiling Springs, and other small cities and towns, the virus claimed 275 lives, about 1 percent of the population. Because sailors and soldiers from the Philadelphia Navy Yard, Fort Dix, New Jersey, and Camp Meade, Maryland, passed through Carlisle for points west, the Carlisle Indian Industrial School was closed and refitted as the US Army Medical Center to treat flu victims. The acting state commissioner of health closed saloons, bowling alleys, and schools in October 1918. Stores were forced to curtail their business hours and funerals had to be private. All the Maslands were spared, and, fortunately, the great pandemic ended suddenly in early 1919.[3]

In addition to the devastating effects of a world war and influenza epidemic, Americans faced disruptive changes in the first two decades of the twentieth century, including the shift from an agrarian rural society to an industrial urban order; the direct election of US senators; the prohibition of the manufacture, sale, and transportation of alcohol; and the vote for women. The nation also suffered a postwar recession, race riots, a president incapacitated by a stroke, and turbulent labor strikes. It is little wonder that the residents of Carlisle welcomed the opening of a new factory.

In mid-March 1919, at approximately the same time that it was publishing worrisome stories about the "alarming" growth of the radical Industrial Workers of the World, the imprisonment and deportation of radicals, and the need to raise money for children orphaned by the flu pandemic, the *Carlisle Evening Sentinel* noted that a Philadelphia textile firm had scouted a property in town for a new rug factory. Two months later, it announced the sale of the twenty-six-acre Bixler Farm and Carlisle Agricultural Society fairgrounds to Masland and Sons for $33,000. At a town meeting, fifty business executives agreed to pledge a total of $7,000 toward the sale price. The meeting, chortled the *Evening Sentinel*, was "one of the biggest things in the history of the town."[4]

Over the next few months, contractors set to work erecting "a large, modern and up-to-date rug manufactory" on the land abutting the Pennsylvania and Reading rail line. At an estimated cost of $275,000, the one-story 210-by-478-foot brick building would accommodate two to three hundred workers. Frank and Paul Masland would manage the new facility and live in Carlisle, noted the *Evening Sentinel*. "They are loyal Methodists, and we know they will find a warm welcome here." The opening of the factory was the best news in years, it crowed. Carlisle's other newspaper, the *Herald*, also gushed about the new factory, noting progress on construction of the building, the arrival of looms, and the training of workers to run them. Masland and Sons also bought a lot on Spring Road adjoining the factory on which to build thirty "ready-cut" homes. Frank Masland also headed the real estate arm of the new enterprise.[5]

In early July 1919, he moved to what he would call the "blessed" Cumberland Valley. Descended from pioneer stock, its residents were self-reliant, hardworking, churchgoing people. The valley also was blessed with cool streams, abundant woodlands, and lush fields, offering opportunities for fishing, hunting, hiking, and birding. Until they could own their own house, Frank and Virginia (she had given up her medical career) lived in the Molly Pitcher Hotel. Frank worked at the factory for $33 per week, overseeing factory production, while Paul helped run the office.[6]

With financial help from Frank Sr., Frank and Virginia bought a home at 52 Conway Street in Carlisle, where they lived for a decade. They also started a family. Frank III, nicknamed Mike to avoid confusion, was born in 1921, and David followed two years later. Mike would eventually succeed his father as president and then CEO of the company, while David became a physician.

While the first mill building was being erected, Frank used existing structures to begin production. Once the home of clucking chickens, the former fairgrounds Exhibition Hall housed twenty looms, which made carpets that were then sent to the Philadelphia mill for printing. Masland used the fairgrounds gatehouse as his office. His first weavers were ten men who had formerly worked for the defunct Beetem Rag Carpet Mill in Carlisle. Periodically, Frank Sr. and Maurice Masland would drive to Carlisle from Philadelphia to offer advice and assess the production process.[7]

Uncle Maurice, more than Frank Sr., became a mentor to twenty-four-year-old Frank Jr. In the expectation that Frank would one day take over the business, Maurice trained him in an assortment of jobs, first in the Philadelphia mill and then as general manager of the Carlisle factory and the company-owned homes. He was "like a second father to me," Masland remembered. "Where he went I went. I had his complete confidence. He told me that he knew his son could not take his place and expected that someday I would—but neither of us suspected it would be so soon."[8]

In the 1920s, as general manager, Frank Jr. directed the day-to-day operation of the Carlisle facility, including hiring nonunion workers and overseeing the construction of mill buildings, company houses, and production. "One of the busiest men at the plant is Frank Masland Jr., but he is nevertheless uniformly courteous," wrote a reporter for the *Carlisle Evening Sentinel.* "It was fun, it was challenging," Frank remembered. "It was a great opportunity for a young fellow, a tremendous learning experience." From the start, he was adamant that there would be no union. He referred to workers as "associates" rather than employees, initiated a group insurance plan, an athletic association with baseball, softball, bowling, and basketball teams, and a monthly company magazine called the *Shuttle,* for which he wrote dozens of essays over the years. The company used money from cafeteria sales to fund sports uniforms, a clambake, Ladies Day, a Christmas party, and an annual picnic at Hershey Park, which was a paid holiday. Although freshly launched, the business made holidays of the first two days of November for the beginning of the Pennsylvania hunting season.[9]

After a brief slump early in the decade necessitated the closing and eventual sale of their Philadelphia mill, the economy limbered up and then boomed as the building and automobile industries produced a demand for carpets in homes, hotels, hospitals, schools, theaters, offices, and cars. Masland recalled taking a sample of automobile carpet to the Ford plant in Detroit, Michigan. While he was displaying it, Henry Ford arrived, took out a large screwdriver, and scraped its blade over the face of the carpet. Pleased by the result, he said, "That'll do," and went on his way. In addition to supplying auto manufacturers, Masland fed demand from other consumer and industrial markets by hiring more skilled workers, developing a new copper-jacketed machine that could crank out more than a thousand printed carpets per day, introducing new velvet and Oriental product lines that became bestsellers, and advertising in popular magazines like the *Saturday Evening Post* and the *Ladies' Home Journal.*[10]

As a young man and novice business executive in the 1920s, Masland was immersed in relocating and expanding the family carpet-making business and had little time for adventure or conservation-related activities. As president of the company during the Great Depression, he was preoccupied with the company's economic survival. A conservative Republican, he supported Calvin Coolidge and Herbert Hoover and abhorred the liberal federal policies instituted during Franklin D. Roosevelt's New Deal that promoted big government, massive national spending, a welfare state, and the growth of labor unions. Calvin Coolidge was his idea of a successful president, he later deadpanned, because "he did what you should do—nothing." Masland also admired the light federal-management touch of Herbert Hoover.[11]

Masland identified with many features of 1920s conservatism. In *White Protestant Nation,* the historian Allan J. Lichtman argues that the modern conservative movement was rooted in the 1920s rather than in New Deal liberalism. Recoiling from the wrenching changes brought on by urbanization, immigration, industrialism, and the Great War, conservatives feared losing their Anglo pioneer cultural and political heritage, which was based on free enterprise and Caucasian Protestant Christianity. The conservatism of the 1920s, Lichtman observes, was firmly against pluralism, cities, labor unions, science, communism, and big government—and decidedly pro-business. With the exception of science, Masland shared all of those views.

The Masland brothers, like most business executives, believed that good times would continue to roll, but of course they did not. "The year 1928 is going out with a well blazoned path of prosperity, contentment, political quietude and pleasant assurances of a continuance during the year 1929," read a story in the *Carlisle Evening Sentinel.*[12] But optimistic expectations and flush times ended in October 1929, when the stock market crash sent the economy into free fall. Frank Masland Sr. lost most of his fortune in the crash and had to return to working for the company.

Despite its diversified economy—dominated by farming, textiles, railway track components, and shoe manufacture—Carlisle suffered along with the rest of the nation. Its unemployment rate reached 30 percent by 1932. Cumberland County used its emergency fund to hire two hundred men to build sidewalks in the city. In 1932, President Herbert Hoover agreed to aid the distressed economy through the Reconstruction Finance Corporation (RFC), a federal agency empowered to extend up to $2 billion in loans to banks, mortgage companies, states, and cities. At the time, it was a bold move, but it did little to help. Banks continued to fail and people continued to look in vain for work and went hungry. In Carlisle, stores like Myers Furniture discounted their wares, including Masland rugs. Masland and Sons cut the price of its 9-by-12 Argonne rug to $18.50. "Everyone is acquainted with Carlisle's Great Factory," the *Carlisle Evening Sentinel* proclaimed. "You all know the value in this rug and of course recognize our loss in this removal sale." Elsewhere in the city, desperate men resorted to stealing food. In September, Judge Fred Reese sentenced two young African American men and their female accomplice to eighteen months in the state penitentiary for stealing chickens. "There is only one way to stamp out chicken stealing and that is to deal substantially with every case," admonished the no-nonsense judge.[13]

Pennsylvania governor Gifford Pinchot publicly bemoaned the RFC's "harsh and senseless delay" in extending aid. In a telegram to President Hoover, he stated that citizens "were rightfully indignant" because Pennsylvania had completed the necessary paperwork "and still the hungry are not fed." The RFC board, he continued, was "punishing the poor. Pennsylvania asks for bread and the Reconstruction Finance Corporation gives nothing but words." Masland was not yet the manic writer of letters to the editor that he would become, so there is no record of his stance on the RFC, but he regarded Hoover as a great president.[14]

Federal recovery and relief programs, nicknamed the New Deal, began in earnest in 1933 under the administration of the newly elected president, Franklin D. Roosevelt. Federal programs paid the jobless in Carlisle fifty cents an hour for a thirty-hour week, removing trolley tracks, repairing the military barracks, and constructing roads, sewer lines, and federal buildings. The National Recovery Administration benefited industrial workers by fostering collective bargaining, improved working conditions, and standard working hours. In addition, the state government provided the needy with seed and fertilizer for thrift gardens, including nearly twenty-one hundred in Carlisle.[15]

Not surprisingly, Masland and Sons struggled during the decade-long economic abyss. For the ten-month period from May 1929 to March 1930 alone, it announced a loss of nearly $133,000. To make matters worse, its president, Maurice H. Masland, died in April 1930, two years after moving to Carlisle. Upon his death, the stockholders asked Frank Jr., then thirty-six years old, to head the firm. With advice from his father and brother, he led the company through "a hand to mouth existence." He streamlined operations so that the factory operated at 30 percent capacity, laying off some workers and reducing the hours of others. The threadbare company paid no stock dividends until 1941 and dodged demands from banks for the repayment of loans. Continued sales to the auto industry and the introduction of a new, high-end Wilton carpet helped stanch the economic bleeding. In fact, Masland later wrote, the introduction of the Wilton line in 1936 "literally saved the company."[16]

Taking advantage of a buyer's market in the depressed economy, Frank and Virginia purchased a neglected three-hundred-acre farm on Old York Road outside Carlisle in 1934. It was skirted by Yellow Breeches Creek and Mountain Creek, fertile open fields, and dense forests full of hardwoods. The house was in disrepair. Its roof had caved into the basement, so Frank and Virginia named it Fallen Arches and slept in the barn with their two young boys while contractors restored the house into a grand estate that they called home for the remainder of their lives. Although they did not travel to Europe like many elite American families, they had the means to hire help, send their sons to upscale prep schools and colleges, sail, fish, hunt birds on the Chesapeake shore, and visit Florida.[17]

At Fallen Arches, the Maslands became friendly with the Craigheads, nature-loving neighbors down the road who had a summer estate called The Farm or Craighead Station. Frank Craighead Sr. was an insect specialist with the US Forest Service. His twin sons, Frank Jr. and John, and daughter Jean became companions with the Masland boys. Frank Masland considered the Craigheads practically family. And Frank Masland IV believes that the Craigheads were instrumental in his grandfather's interest in environmentalism. The children visited one another's homes, played, swam, and fished in Yellow Breeches Creek, and one summer the twins and David Masland spent ten weeks traveling cross country in a 1926 Chevy, camping their way to the Grand Tetons of Wyoming. The Craigheads possessed what Jean Craighead has described as a "naturalist gene." As teenagers, the twin boys gained national attention in *National Geographic* as falconers. The boys went on to become noted wildlife biologists and played a formative role in promoting and drafting legislation in the 1960s for the national Wild and Scenic Rivers program. Jean wrote popular young-adult nature books. The fathers, Frank Craighead Sr. and Frank Masland Jr., eventually worked together during the formative years of Everglades National Park at midcentury.[18]

Throughout the Depression decade, Masland, like most conservative Republican business leaders, bewailed Roosevelt's costly relief, recovery, and reform programs, among them the Public Works Administration, Works Progress Administration, Tennessee Valley Authority, and Social Security Administration, deeming them precursors of a socialist state. In contrast to Allan Lichtman, historian Kim Phillips-Fein sees the modern Right as grounded in the antipathy of American business executives toward the liberal state established by FDR during the 1930s. Leaders like Pierre, Irénée, and Lammot du Pont, J. Howard Pew of Sun Oil, and Alfred P. Sloan of General Motors were convinced that Roosevelt was a threat to private property, laissez-faire capitalism, and the US Constitution. The New Deal, said Irénée du Pont, was "nothing more or less than the Socialistic doctrine called by another name." The du Ponts and other prominent corporate and political leaders formed the bipartisan American Liberty League in 1934 to thwart what they regarded as FDR's effort to create a totalitarian state. Organizations like the National Association of Manufacturers opposed labor unions and the New Deal. Masland did not join the American Liberty League, but he shared their beliefs, and he later became an officer of the National Association of Manufacturers and shared its opposition to labor unions. Conservatives in the 1920s and '30s said little about nature and conservation. And neither did Masland until after World War II.[19]

FDR also promoted labor's right to organize. "For the first time in American history," write labor historians Foster Rhea Dulles and Melvyn Dubofsky, "a national administration was to make the welfare of industrial workers a direct concern of government and act on the principle that only organized labor could deal on equal terms with organized capital. Heretofore, labor unions had been tolerated; now they were to be encouraged."[20]

During the first hundred days of the New Deal, at FDR's request, Congress enacted the National Industrial Recovery Act. A new federal agency, the National Recovery Administration, authorized each major American industry to establish codes preventing overproduction, unfair competition, and unconstrained layoffs. Section 7(a) of the legislation declared that the codes of fair competition should recognize labor's right to organize and to choose representatives to bargain with management without being intimidated or threatened. The codes also required employers to comply with minimum wage and maximum hours requirements. A National Labor Board would settle disagreements between unions and management. Cooperating industries received blue eagle decals to place in their windows. President Roosevelt characterized the law as "the most important and far reaching legislation ever enacted by the American Congress." The US Supreme Court negated the law's long reach by declaring it unconstitutional. But the Wagner Act of 1935 and Fair Labor Standards Act of 1938 granted industrial workers the same major provisions, including the right to organize and a minimum wage and maximum number of hours.[21]

The code of fair competition for the carpet and rug industry covered thirty-five firms. Carpet sales in 1933 were estimated to be $60 million, with a workforce of sixteen thousand, compared to $167 million in 1928 from nearly thirty-three thousand employees. Three plants—Alexander Smith, Mohawk, and Masland and Sons—accounted for approximately 50 percent of sales. Hours for the industry were set at forty per week, with a thirty-five-cent-per-hour wage in the North and thirty cents in the South. Because sales were seasonal, workers could work forty-eight hours per week, but no more than ten hours per day for six weeks during peak production periods. The code also applied in every respect to section 7(a) of the National Industrial Recovery Act, which recognized labor's right to organize and bargain collectively. Masland, like many business executives, believed that unions would force wage increases, cause strikes, and be infiltrated by communists determined to overthrow capitalism. But Masland and Sons, in a spirit of economic nationalism, grudgingly agreed to abide by the provisions of the code.[22]

The company experienced few labor difficulties. And Masland worked, sometimes using preemptive, underhanded methods, to keep it that way. Anticipating efforts to organize the laborers at his mill, especially given FDR's encouragement of unionization, he used informants within his workforce and at the regional Textile Union Hall in Philadelphia to report on plans to unionize the Carlisle shop. In May 1934, the regional office of the National Labor Relations Board called him on the carpet, so to speak, for firing a worker who was trying to organize a union. But Masland convinced the NLRB that the worker had been fired for leaving his loom for too many smoke breaks. Despite intense and sometimes violent union activity nationwide in the late '30's, especially in the automobile and steel industries, Masland and Sons remained nonunion and tranquil.[23]

Despite his loathing for FDR, Masland had much in common with the president. Both were born to privilege and enjoyed the strenuous life and organizations, like the Boy Scouts, that promoted it. They liked sailing, saltwater fishing, and hunting. Both loved trees and lived on rural estates that they sought to make partially self-sustainable. Roosevelt sold some of his trees to lumber companies; Masland grew some of his own food, raised chickens, sold hay, and rented adjoining fields to farmers. But Masland seldom made allowances for people he regarded as socialists. With his business's (and capitalism's) survival uppermost in his mind, he gave scant attention to FDR's massive achievements in the field of conservation.

Roosevelt took a binary approach to conservation. During the New Deal, wise-use conservation policies included establishing the Soil Conservation Service to help prevent the erosion of landscapes and a massive federal jobs program to provide flood control and cheap electricity by building hydroelectric dams on the Tennessee River and on the Columbia River at Bonneville, Oregon, and Grand Coulee, Washington. During the Depression, as historian Clayton Koppes has written, "dams were extraordinarily powerful cultural icons. They were symbols of both human control of nature and the nation's triumphant combat with depression."[24] For Masland, they were evidence of a socialistic power grab.

The Civilian Conservation Corps was the most popular of FDR's economic relief programs. Nearly three thousand CCC camps were established in the 1930s, introducing more than three million young men to the vigorous and disciplined outdoor life by employing them to plant trees and build campgrounds, trails, stone walls, rustic cabins, roads, and parks. Perhaps thanks to Governor Pinchot's influence, more CCC camps were established in Pennsylvania, including one in Carlisle, than in any state except California. There is no evidence that Masland paid any attention to the program.[25]

The Roosevelt administration, led by the Republican interior secretary, Harold Ickes, gave added impetus to aesthetic conservation. It created wildlife sanctuaries and recreation areas and expanded the national park system by establishing new units, including Cedar Breaks, Great Smoky Mountain, Big Bend, Shenandoah, Olympic, Isle Royale, and numerous other national parks and monuments. National park acreage swelled from 14.5 million in 1933 to 20.3 million in 1946. During that same interval, the number of national monuments jumped from thirty-three to eighty-six. FDR also gave the National Park Service jurisdiction over all national battlefield sites and federal buildings in Washington, DC. In 1935 he signed the Historic Sites Act, transferring all federal historic sites to the NPS. This act also established the Advisory Board on National Parks, Historic Sites, Buildings, and Monuments to counsel the department and interior secretary on national park issues, including adding new units to the system. Ironically, given his animosity toward FDR, Masland would devote three decades of his life to the Advisory Board. During that time, he would advocate for a major conservation effort like Roosevelt's, minus FDR's commitment to the construction of hydroelectric dams on free-flowing rivers.[26]

Historian Neil Maher has persuasively argued that Roosevelt's conservation program, especially the Civilian Conservation Corps, was transformative in the evolution of the modern environmental movement. By providing jobs to enrollees and invigorating recreational opportunities for ordinary city folks, the extremely popular CCC brought added attention to wild nature, healthy outdoor recreation, and a wider acceptance of the welfare state. But not everyone was enthusiastic about the activities of the Corps. Advocates of wilderness protection bemoaned the construction of roads in pristine national forest areas. Organizations like the Audubon Society protested the draining of wetlands to combat mosquitoes and other insects. Other individuals railed against upsetting the balance of nature through predator control and the introduction of plants and animals into landscapes where they were nonindigenous. These concerns, Maher argues, spurred the causes of wilderness preservation and ecology, which evolved into a new environmental ethic. That new outlook, with strong grassroots support, focused less on the efficient use of resources and aesthetics and more on stewardship of the earth and the protection not only of wilderness but of human health and indeed entire ecosystems, emphasizing the interconnectedness of all life-forms. After the war, Masland adopted that viewpoint himself.[27]

In 1940, anticipating US involvement in World War II, Masland directed that some of his looms be converted to the manufacture of cotton duck. He provided samples of the heavy fabric to Quartermaster General Robert Stevens, who approved the quality for military use should the need arise. A few months later, Masland also repurposed a portion of the company machine shop for the manufacture of gun barrels and other military ordnance. Both decisions proved wise and profitable.[28]

Masland hoped that the United States could avoid entanglement in another European war, but he feared the country would be drawn in as it had been a generation earlier during the Great War. In the presidential election of 1940, he believed that the Republican nominee, Wendell Willkie, would be more inclined to avoid war than Franklin Roosevelt, running for his third term in office. In the company newsletter, he urged Masland and Sons employees to vote and gave several reasons why he and the entire board of directors backed Willkie. It is not known how the company employees voted, but Pennsylvanians gave the edge to the experienced FDR over Willkie, a corporate executive who had never run for political office.[29]

The United States entered the war when the Japanese bombed Pearl Harbor on December 7, 1941, the day before Masland's forty-sixth birthday. On that infamous day, Masland was duck hunting on the Chesapeake Bay. After learning of the bombing and FDR's declaration of war, he promptly converted all looms and the machine shop to the production of canvas and ordnance. Soon the plant was bursting at the seams, its workforce leaping from four hundred in 1941 to thirty-three hundred two years later. With the slogan "For God and Country," Masland employees worked in three eight-hour shifts, twenty-four hours per day, seven days a week. "We were all soldiers then," remembered one employee.[30]

The looms rolled out a variety of cotton duck products, including tarps, tents, bunk bottoms, bomber hangars, parkas, and trousers. The company also developed a process for water-resistant and fire-retardant canvas, treating both its own products and those of competitors. Masland and Sons bought vacant buildings in Carlisle, where it manufactured, treated, and stored canvas duck. By 1942 it had become the largest producer of duck in the world. "Approximately 80% of all the fabricated canvas goods produced for the armed forces during World War II were made in Carlisle," Masland stated. "At the peak of wartime activity, over 110 miles of duck a day were fabricated in the Masland mill." The machine shop produced gun barrels for naval destroyers and torpedo heads for submarines. For five consecutive years, the US Army and Navy awarded the mill an "E" for excellence.[31]

Not surprisingly, the firm benefited financially from the herculean growth of business, despite the existence of an excess profits tax. Masland initially protested the imposition of a $60,000 excess profits tax in 1943 until the firm's accounting department informed him that it would work the figure down to $14,000. In a private communication, Paul Masland noted that the plant's enormous earnings were dominating the industry. "Put this in your private files or burn it," he instructed. In 1943, after paying taxes and stock dividends, the company declared a profit of nearly $280,000. The next year it netted $402,000, and in 1945 it reported a profit of $1.4 million. The Maslands also benefited personally. In addition to being the major stockholders, Frank Sr. earned $12,000 as chairman of the board, and Frank Jr. and Paul made $25,000 each as president and treasurer, respectively. The average annual salary of a Masland employee in 1945 was about $3,000.[32]

With the Carlisle mill operating around the clock and the available pool of women and able-bodied men already tapped out, Masland and Sons was desperate for workers. "Back in those days," recalled former associate Annie Snyder, "somebody walked in for a job, you just made sure they had a pulse and that was it." At Frank Masland's request, in 1944 the War Department supplied the mill with three hundred German prisoners of war, some of whom had served in General Erwin Rommel's famed Afrika Korps. The Geneva Conventions prohibited the use of POWs for the making of war materiel, so Masland used them for grunt work, like carrying heavy rolls of canvas to women at sewing stations. They wore "PW" uniforms and were supervised by their own officers, who were not required to perform manual labor. Initially, the POWs were transported to the factory by bus from the New Cumberland Army Depot, twenty-four miles northeast of the factory. But in July they were relocated to a tent camp adjacent to the Masland plant, where they remained until October 1945.[33]

Masland did not forewarn his regular employees about the use of German prisoners until they arrived. To forestall resistance, he informed his associates that the German prisoners were helping to make products that would comfort their loved ones overseas and maybe shorten the war. Employees were instructed not to speak to the prisoners, but that directive was almost immediately ignored. Masland workers brought cigarettes, chocolate, sandwiches, and other treats to the POWs. And the prisoners sometimes placed small side bets on whose seamstress could produce the most piecework. The work, one POW recalled, was "hasty and hard," but his co-workers were usually kind. Indeed, after the war some of the mill employees and former prisoners corresponded and visited with one another.[34]

There were few acts of resistance by the POWs. On one occasion a prisoner escaped but was found a short distance away, sitting along a riverbank, because he wanted a look at some greenery. During the German counteroffensive against the Allies at the Battle of the Bulge in December 1944, a few POWs staged a work slowdown, but it ended quickly when Masland told them that they wouldn't eat if they didn't work. Masland had sympathy for the POWs and wanted them treated as he would want his son Mike to be treated if captured while serving in a tank unit in the European theater.[35]

Like most Americans, Masland was pleased when the atomic bomb attacks on Hiroshima and Nagasaki ended the war in the Pacific. Nor did he express misgivings about the potential danger of nuclear power to the environment or the survival of humankind.[36] With the war over, he focused on converting the plant to the production of domestic goods. Having amassed large profits during the war, the process of reconverting the looms proved seamless. He now had the opportunity to delegate responsibility for day-to-day business operations and to take time during the postwar years to travel, seek adventure, connect with the natural world, and engage in conservation activity. Little did he realize that he would dedicate the rest of his life to the preservation of nature.

CHAPTER 3

From Carpets to Conservation

The responsibility of running a business during the Great Depression and then World War II left little opportunity to engage with pristine nature. But with the end of those crises and his business thriving, Masland took time to connect with rough backcountry. During the postwar years, he evolved into an ardent and active preservationist.

At the war's conclusion in August 1945, Masland promptly focused on returning his company to the manufacture of wool and cotton carpets, correctly expecting that the pent-up demand from hotels, motels, offices, hospitals, churches, automobile companies, ships, trains, and households would yield handsome profits. With the slogan "Home Means More with Carpet on the Floor," he stirred demand by advertising in popular magazines, radio, and in the new medium of television. He also expanded the company's product line by creating a sportswear and outdoor equipment department. To meet demand, he expanded the factory floor space, increased the salesforce, and opened regional showrooms in most major American cities.[1]

Determined to prevent unions, he kept his thirteen hundred associates satisfied with decent wages and fringe benefits, including resuming publication of the *Shuttle*; reinstituting company-sponsored sports teams, a glee club, and the annual picnic at Hershey Park, with bus transportation; recognizing longtime service with a gold watch and dinner; closing the plant on the opening day of deer-hunting season; and introducing a profit-sharing plan, partially subsidized health and hospital benefits, a suggestion box, and an annual $20,000 college scholarship fund for the children of employees. Like many industrialists, he portrayed himself as a popular and beneficent employer. And in many ways, he was. "I had played baseball and bowled and gone to mill picnics and they knew me. Every week I was in the mill. I stopped and talked to the women burlers and beamers and to the men weavers. I knew them all by name and they knew me. Union efforts didn't have a chance."[2]

Besides personal contact and bulletin board postings, he communicated with associates through the *Shuttle*. His column at the beginning of each monthly issue constituted an editorial page and a chance to express his views in writing, which he enjoyed doing. Topics ranged from explaining the employee profit-sharing plan, warning of the threat of postwar communist expansion, extolling the virtues of capitalism over socialism, condemning President Truman's socialistic flirtation with a national health insurance plan, expressing his belief that only the teachings of Christ could bring lasting peace to a jittery world, and stressing the importance of savoring the beauties of nature.[3]

In "To a Tree," an early piece of allegorical nature writing, he declared that "of all God's creations, to me, nothing exceeds the mystery and majesty of a tree." A mighty tree in the fullness of life might be toppled by a small insect or a microscopic organism, but in death it "gives of itself that life may be born again. It is eternal." John Muir once wrote that natural landscapes were "the terrestrial manifestations of God" and that nature was "a window opening into heaven, a mirror reflecting the Creator." Experiencing a universal force or God through nature was one of Masland's lifelong themes, as it was for other preservationists like Muir, Sigurd Olson, and Aldo Leopold. That view set Masland apart from most conservatives, who rarely rhapsodized about the wonders of nature and the necessity of federal authority to protect them. There is no evidence that Masland read or corresponded with conservative intellectuals like Joshua Crane, Friedrich von Hayek, or Russell Kirk, although later in life he read the articles and columns of William F. Buckley and George Will. By and large, conservative writers, academics, and politicians did not make conservation a priority in their ideological agendas. But sometimes Masland was conflicted. He believed that conservation should be a bipartisan effort. At times, however, his fear of socialism got in the way, causing him to disparage the efforts of dedicated environmentalists like Supreme Court Justice William O. Douglas or Congressman Phillip Burton, whom he regarded as left-wingers. He also scolded conservatives like Will and Buckley who downplayed the importance of conservation.[4]

In addition to his personal experiences, Masland's views on conservation were shaped by reading outdoor magazines like *Field and Stream* and the *Sierra Club Bulletin*, *Audubon*, and other publications of conservation organizations. He also was moved by the wilderness and pro-land messages of Leopold, Olson, and, later, Wallace Stegner. Masland shared Leopold's view that committing to a land ethic "changes the role of *Homo sapiens* from conqueror of the land community to plain member and citizen of it."[5]

With the Depression and World War II behind him, Masland experienced nature firsthand in the American Southwest and in Carlisle at Fallen Arches and at a newly acquired company retreat called Kings Gap. Built in the early 1900s as a summer home by James Cameron, grandson of Simon Cameron, Abraham Lincoln's secretary of war, Masland and Sons purchased the posh twelve-hundred-acre Kings Gap estate in 1951. Located ten miles from Carlisle, the twenty-four-room, eight-bath brownstone mansion was reached by an unpaved four-mile private road that wove its way through hardwood trees to the top of South Mountain. The estate served as a swanky, woodsy venue for special family gatherings, company meetings, and visiting corporate and political dignitaries. Befitting a lord of the manor (or a nineteenth-century industrial titan), Masland fitted out the grounds with a caretaker, an Irish wolfhound named King, walking paths, and flower beds. In addition to comfortable accommodations, Kings Gap offered Frank and Virginia solitude, breathtaking views of the Cumberland Valley, hiking opportunities, and abundant wildlife. Although not open to employees, each spring Masland invited local townsfolk to Kings Gap for an Easter sunrise religious service and breakfast.[6]

Fallen Arches, the three-hundred-acre Carlisle family estate acquired in the early 1930s, served as the epicenter for most family get-togethers. With spacious fields, woods, a barn, stables, horses, farm animals, swimming pool, and guesthouse, it was an ideal playground for grownups and children. In many ways, the estate resembled Frank's boyhood home in Bustleton. His young sons could ride horses, hunt, fish, camp, and trap animals for their pelts. And Masland could tend a small garden, plant tree seedlings and flowers, and commune with nature.[7]

While Frank spent his days at the factory office, Virginia raised the children, who from infancy referred to their parents by their first names. Virginia ran Fallen Arches as a subsistence farm, hiring neighborhood women to help shell, chop, and can vegetables and Charles Forney to tend to the cows, the planting, and the butchering of ducks, chickens, and livestock. "Uncle Forney," as he was known to the grandchildren, had lost his nearby farm to foreclosure in the early 1930s and worked for the Maslands for nearly three decades. Virginia's brother, Bill Sharp, also came to work the farm.[8]

Virginia Masland doted on the children and six grandchildren—Ellen Colcord ("Collie"), David, Frank IV ("Landy"), Janet, Jonathan, and Kim. She was "a grandmother's grandmother," recalled Frank Masland IV. She was an "absolute teetotaler" but liked to eat and became stout in middle age. Convinced that she and Frank were going to become poverty-stricken at any moment, she economized by wearing plastic jewelry and modestly priced clothing, and she stocked her basement with home-canned goods. Her grandson remembers her churning butter and wringing a chicken's neck before dunking it in scalding water before plucking.[9]

Unlike Frank, Virginia was not fond of roughing it outdoors, and she refrained from speaking out on political, social, and conservation issues. Like many women in the 1940s and '50s, she was content to be a homebody, helpmate, and doting mother and grandmother. Nonetheless, she was the "driving force" at Fallen Arches, recalled grandson David Masland Jr., and a steadying influence on Frank's life. "She set him free to roam the world, while she ran Fallen Arches," as Frank IV put it.[10]

Frank was less reticent and frugal than Virginia, voicing his opinions readily and lavishly spending money on clothing, automobiles, photography and motion picture equipment, fishing and hunting gear, home improvements, and travel. In many ways he was a bon vivant, like his father. He had given up pipe smoking and had a modest appetite for food, but he enjoyed fine dining, wine, Jim Beam bourbon, luxury hotels, and exclusive social clubs. But he could just as readily sleep on the ground and eat beans from a can by a campfire. He maintained a lanky frame throughout most of his life, and his most distinctive facial features were his piercing blue eyes and bushy brown eyebrows.

His hobbies included travel, photography, reading, and writing observations and editorials for the *Shuttle*, an occasional essay in national magazines, and numerous letters to editors, politicians, and close friends. His personal papers are heavily weighted toward his activities after World War II. He did not keep a diary or journal but was a self-described "compulsive letter writer," dictating correspondence that his longtime secretary, Lula Diehl, transcribed and typed up. He authored so many letters to local newspapers that the editors imposed a limit of one letter per person per month. His son Mike once quipped that he was going to place a dictating machine in his father's coffin. Masland joined the local country club but rarely played golf and seldom watched television until late in life. He developed no attachment to spectator sports. He relished the natural world, wildlife, flowers, and especially trees. The grounds were sprinkled with scrawny, scraggly trees, noted his grandson, but he refused to harvest them and could not resist planting new ones even in his nineties.[11]

A pious Methodist, he attended Allison Church regularly in Carlisle, honored the Ten Commandments, supported missionary efforts to minister to the physical and religious needs of refugees abroad, donated money to the local YMCA, and considered it shameful for businesses to operate on the Sabbath in peacetime. He disapproved of divorce, homosexuality, abortion, immoral behavior, bawdiness, crude jokes, and sexual liberation. He once hired a private detective "at considerable expense" to investigate alleged sexual improprieties at Cumberland County Fair "girly shows." The detective reported nudity and offers of sexual conduct that "exceed anything found in smutty literature and pornography." Masland brought the detective's findings to the attention of the local authorities and was miffed when they took no action. And during the sexually liberated 1960s and '70s, he was appalled by song titles like "Love the One You're With," television shows like *All in the Family*, and risqué theater productions like *Garden of Eden*, a play performed at a Florida University in which Eve wore only a fig leaf and Adam a banana.[12]

The Maslands enjoyed leisurely, comfortable sojourns together, but Frank also sought more physically challenging encounters with primitive nature, much as Theodore Roosevelt and Gifford Pinchot, two wealthy Republicans of an earlier generation, had done. Roosevelt nearly killed himself rafting Brazil's wild River of Doubt in 1912. Masland, four decades later, put himself at risk traipsing through Panama's harsh Darien jungle. Pinchot, who had served as TR's chief of the US Forest Service, sailed to the remote Galapagos Islands of Ecuador, where he spent days collecting wildlife specimens and relishing the sublime wildness of the flora and fauna. Masland made the same trip two decades later and, like his fellow Pennsylvanian, wanted the pristine area preserved for posterity. From the Galapagos, he followed Pinchot's course to Panama's San Blas Islands and admired the simplicity of the Indigenous people. Whether it was the Americas or (later) Africa, Masland was impressed with Indigenous people who seemed to live in harmony with all creation. With an unquenchable adventurous spirit and the money to partially satisfy it, he joined the Explorers Club, an elitist organization formed in 1904 to promote scientific exploration of the earth, oceans, and space. He carried the Explorers' flag to the American Southwest and several other remote landscapes, including Antarctica.[13]

His adventures enthralled the grandchildren. "He could be acerbic and loving, but he was only rarely, if ever, dull," recalled grandson Frank IV. "His third-floor study was a virtual museum dedicated to his life and adventures, with artifacts and mementos from every corner of the globe. . . . [A] stuffed golden eagle sat perched on his desk, and on the walls hung the shell of a Galapagos tortoise and a six-foot rattlesnake." Adorned with Native American artifacts from the Southwest, the study was large enough to comfortably seat several people for motion pictures and slides of his adventures. "As a young boy, I spent countless hours in that study, fascinated by everything that I saw," Landy recalled. Grandson David recalled that the spacious room was also adorned with Navajo rugs, a gun cabinet, a massive movie screen, a fly swatter made from a wildebeest tail, and chairs with sealskin-covered seats.[14]

Masland's roaming began in 1948. Not content to look through a window or windshield, he sought to experience nature on foot or by pack animal, primitive watercraft, or backcountry Jeep. He was especially drawn to the natural splendor of the largely unvisited and harsh canyon country of the American Southwest. Returning from a business trip to California in 1939, he stopped to visit the South Rim of the Grand Canyon. He recalled peering through a telescope at the Colorado River some five thousand feet below and being struck by an urge to experience it from the bottom up, on a boat. He was further enticed by a 1946 *Saturday Evening Post* article about river runner Norm Nevills, who piloted passengers through the canyon's fast water. "It's the experience of a lifetime," Nevills responded to one of Masland's inquiries. "Wait till you see a sunset from the bottom of the canyon!" Jouncing through roiling water, he continued, "is the sport of Kings! There is no thrill in the world like that of sliding out into the brink of a rapid, and then being suddenly gathered up and almost hurled down into the roaring fast water below!" Barely able to contain his enthusiasm, Masland committed to the 277-mile run of the river from Lees Ferry to Hoover Dam for three weeks in July 1948 at the whopping cost of $1,100.[15]

Since 1938, Nevills, who worked for the US Geological Survey, had guided passengers down the San Juan River in southeastern Utah and the Colorado River in northern Arizona, quickly gaining legendary status. His fleet consisted of four hefty cataract boats that together accommodated ten to twelve passengers. With a wide stern and tapered bow, the plywood craft resembled a rowboat. One passenger sat atop the foredeck and another one or two perched atop the aft deck, while the pilot, equipped with ash oars, sat between them on a small bench. Provisions were stored in water-resistant containers beneath the fore and aft decks.[16]

At age fifty-two Masland stood an inch shy of six feet, weighed 180 pounds, and was physically fit. Although experienced at canoeing and roughing it from his teenage camp days in Maine, he wondered whether he would be able to withstand the desert heat for three weeks on a churning river in a desolate canyon. Fifty, he thought, was "the truly dangerous age," because "at that age [a man] may possess the means and thus do those things which by that time he should have sense enough not to do." Disregarding his own internal warnings, he eagerly plunged ahead.[17]

The group met at Art Greene's Marble Canyon Lodge hard by the Vermilion Cliffs, about seven miles from the launch point at Lees Ferry, Arizona. Nevills and his wife, Doris, arrived at the lodge airstrip in their private plane. Shortly thereafter, Nevills demonstrated his skill as an aircraft pilot to the group that had assembled atop Navajo Bridge, which spanned the river to the Navajo Nation. In swashbuckling style, he looped his small plane back and forth under the bridge, seemingly almost skimming the river's surface. His derring-do might have reminded some of his passengers of the adage "there are old pilots and bold pilots, but there are no old, bold pilots"—but not Masland. "After watching that exhibition of skillful flying," he later wrote, "I had a much better idea of the nature of the man with whom I was to travel." Sadly, however, the adage about daring pilots proved true for Nevills.[18]

On July 12, 1948, the day after the flying stunt show, the four-boat fleet launched from Lees Ferry, piloted by Nevills, Otis ("Dock") Marston, Nevills's son, Garth, and Frank Wright. Masland was the only inexperienced river runner among the six-person party of four men and two women. As a novice, he developed an unusual technique for meeting a rapid. Boats usually engaged the rapids bow first, but the Nevills fleet went stern first. Masland lay belly down on the stern, hitting the rapid with his neck extended. Garth Nevills called it a "fish-eye" approach, and Masland was thereafter nicknamed "Fish Eyes."[19]

After a week, the party reached Bright Angel Creek at the base of the five-thousand-foot-deep canyon, where a National Park Service concessionaire offered meals, hot water, and lodging at Phantom Ranch. During a three-day layover, one couple departed and four new experienced river runners arrived.[20]

For the next two weeks they bounced, bobbed, and glided through the canyon until they reached Lake Mead at Hoover Dam. Nevills made the trip fun, recalled one voyager. The group sang silly songs, engaged in water fights, and ate beef tongue sandwiches with mustard for lunch. The rugged excursion with enjoyable companions left an indelible imprint on Masland. "I like your desert country and I like your rivers," he told Nevills. "I like the thrill of the rapids, the isolation of the Canyon, the association with a congenial group around a campfire in the evenings and the beauty and peace of starlit nights. I hope to see a lot more of the desert, your rivers and the Norman Nevills." The ninety-seventh person to traverse the entire 277-mile stretch of the river from Lees Ferry to Hoover Dam, Masland took pride in joining the River Rat Society and designed a ten-carat gold pin for its members. Upon his return to the East, he wrote a privately published account of his adventure and delivered talks accompanied by slides and films of the trip to an assortment of groups. "Fish Eyes has really gone into this River Rat Society whole hog hasn't he?" one passenger commented to Nevills. "Well, you can chalk up another person you have given the disease to."[21]

Identifying his "disease" as "river rabies," Masland conceded that he had contracted a severe case. "Unless my mind is thoroughly tangled up with something else it immediately reverts to the river, the friends with whom I made the trip and to the beauties of the Canyon and the peace of the starlit nights." Virginia said that Frank "dreams Grand Canyon and talks little else to anyone who will lend a listening ear." On his return from the river, he toured Yellowstone National Park but found it overcrowded, filled with "screwballs," and unable to measure up to the vastness, rawness, and solitude of the canyon country.[22]

Masland cherished the Grand Canyon but, like many elitists, feared that visitors loved it and many other units in the park system too much. He tried to have it both ways when it came to the dual purposes of the National Park Act of 1916. In theory, he paid lip service to the parks as pleasure grounds, because democratic access and enjoyment resonated with the public and brought more congressional appropriations and additional units to the system. In practice, however, as his reference to Yellowstone "screwballs" attests, he understood that democratic access meant more tourist accommodations, crowds, vehicles, noise, unsavory characters, rowdy behavior, and overall disruption of the landscape. Greater public use of automobiles, as historians Paul Sutter and David

Louter have shown, fed demands for roads into the backcountry and gently used parts of the parks. That threat, which Masland also feared, helped propel the move to safeguard the wilderness areas of the national parks and forests through congressional legislation. Though conflicted, Masland was at heart an elitist who preferred a more physically demanding, off-the-beaten-path, nonmotorized experience, like his trip down the Colorado River. "I have never enthused over the slogan 'Parks are for People,'" he once wrote Paul Pritchard, executive director of the National Parks Conservation Association. "National Parks are for the preservation of national biomes—and that comes first and people second." This viewpoint did not resonate with most conservatives or westerners.[23]

Masland's Colorado River rafting adventure was transformative in four important ways. First, he equated it with a quasi-religious conversion experience that changed the direction of his life. Second, he became an opponent of plans to construct more federal dams on the Colorado River. Third, he became a supporter of the budding wilderness movement. Fourth, he formed several new and lasting friendships.

To describe Masland's Colorado River engagement as an epiphany or spiritual journey would not overstate its significance for him. It was similar in some ways to Aldo Leopold's "spiritual revelation" after shooting a predator animal in a New Mexico national forest. As a hunter, Leopold believed that he was saving the local deer herd. But after seeing the "fierce green fire" in the wolf's eyes flame out and die, he realized that he was wrong and became an opponent of killing predators and a champion of wild nature.[24]

Masland was likewise transfixed and transformed by "shooting" the Colorado River. "I love every drop of its muddy waters . . . because within its canyons I was reborn," he once wrote. "There are those who seemingly run the river completely unaffected by the supremity of God's handiwork, seemingly utterly unaware of any contact with eternity," he wrote fellow voyager Rosalind Johnson. "For me, there is nothing I have ever done that is spiritually as refreshing and stimulating."[25]

Masland was one of many active conservationists raised in devoutly religious households who equated connecting with nature with a spiritual experience. In *Faith in Nature,* historian Thomas Dunlap has shown that Ralph Waldo Emerson, John Muir, and Sigurd Olson all viewed the wilderness experience as a religious quest. "People go to the wilderness," Olson once wrote, "for the good of their souls."[26]

Unfortunately for Masland and other river runners, the wild river was also good for damming and stimulated interest among dam builders. Besides nourishing his soul, Masland's western river experience instilled in him an aversion to plans by the Interior Department's Bureau of Reclamation to build massive hydroelectric dams on western rivers, especially if they intruded upon a national park or monument. Most conservatives who opposed the federal construction of hydroelectric dams did so for three reasons: they were frightfully expensive; they competed with private power generation; and they embodied overreach by a government bureau crazed with dam building. Masland shared those general sentiments, but he cared more about preserving the Colorado River than about safeguarding the public purse or promoting the economic interests of private utility companies.

Already plugged by Hoover Dam at its lower end, the Colorado River's sheer canyon walls upstream made ideal locations for more dams. In the late 1940s, the Arizona congressional delegation proposed legislation to siphon water from the Colorado River to Arizona's water-depleted central valley. The Central Arizona Project called for the Bureau of Reclamation to undertake the project at a cost to taxpayers of nearly $800 million. Water from Lake Havasu at the existing Parker Dam on the Colorado would flow in an open concrete aqueduct to the Phoenix area, some 240 miles away. Power to pump millions of gallons daily uphill to the aqueduct and money to pay for construction costs would come mainly from electricity produced by a massive new hydroelectric dam upriver at Bridge Canyon. Fiscal conservatives decried its expense and Californians opposed the scheme because they believed that Arizona was pirating Colorado River water that rightfully belonged to them.

When Masland learned of the project, shortly after completing his second expedition down the river, he became an early critic, arguing that the proposed Bridge Canyon dam would gag a free-flowing majestic river and back water into the existing Grand Canyon National Monument. "The dam builders don't conquer or master anything. They simply ruin it," he fumed to Otis Marston. "For me every turn of the river, every inch of every high walled side canyon, each boulder and crevice holds its secret that the voice of the river is either whispering confidentially or roaring into my ears."[27]

Masland felt that the entire 277-mile Grand Canyon, not just the portion preserved in the national park system, should be off-limits to further commercial development. The canyon, he insisted, "provides an escape from the sordid and the ugly. . . . If a person has a soul, the canyon fills it with everlasting beauty. If his fibers feel an urge to relax, the canyon brings home to him that it is a very natural urge. If his muscles tingle for physical combat, the opportunity is ever present." Only a few Americans understood that the canyon was grand outside as well as inside the national park. "I think if people as a whole knew that there is no other river like it that the Bureau of Reclamation, which is one of the most sadly misnamed of all government agencies, wouldn't be permitted to continue with its wrecking operations," he groused to a friend.[28]

His position anticipated an argument that would come later from the Sierra Club and other conservation groups, but in 1950 his was not a common voice. Fellow river runner Nancy Streator, a young college student in 1948, remembered Masland as "a wonderful person" who "was very interested in conservation before it was popular." As it turned out, Congress delayed consideration of the Bridge Canyon dam project until the US Supreme Court settled the squabble between Arizona and California over their respective shares of the river's annual flow of water. The Court eventually decided the issue in Arizona's favor in 1963, but the bitter political controversy over the proposed dam lingered for another half decade.[29]

Masland's lengthy ride between desolate canyon walls, and his later exploration of the rugged, remote southwestern canyon country by foot and pack animal, helped convert him to the escalating wilderness movement. In the mid-1930s, Bob Marshall and other founders of the Wilderness Society sought to set aside primitive areas of mainly national forests as "wilderness forever," to borrow a phrase from Howard Zahniser executive secretary of The Wilderness Society. By the mid-1950s, Masland had set himself apart from wise-use conservationists and most conservatives by becoming a supporter of the Wilderness Act, which was eventually passed in 1964.

Along with zeal for river running and the canyon country, Masland developed strong friendships with his fellow whitewater rafters. In 1948 he corresponded frequently with Nevills and gifted him with books, copies of the *Shuttle,* and a water-resistant parka, tent, totes, duffle bags, and tarps. In return, Nevills lent him films and agreed to give him retired river-running items such as oars and a cataract boat. He also lured him into another trip by offering to let him pilot a boat through a river rapid.[30]

Masland also developed a lifelong friendship and voluminous correspondence with Otis Marston. A retired stock analyst and fellow conservative Republican from Berkeley, California, "Dock" (or "Doc") Marston was environmentally minded well before his first river trip at age forty-eight in

1942. In his twenties he was an active skier before the use of tow bars, and he befriended Francis Farquhar and other members of the Sierra Club and became entranced by the Grand Canyon during his 1925 honeymoon there. Although he did not experience an epiphany, as Masland had, he did become obsessed with the history of Grand Canyon river runners and became the foremost authority on the subject.

Marston spent decades gathering diaries, pamphlets, letters, logs, and other historical accounts for a book on the subject that he never published. Considering others equal and perhaps superior, he questioned Nevills's reputation as the river's foremost river pilot, attributing it mainly to self-promotion. Barely disguising his resentment publicly, he unloaded in letters to Masland, portraying Nevills as an eccentric and overrated boat pilot, mentally unbalanced, reckless bordering on suicidal, and as an unfaithful husband who allegedly had a sexual fling with a young female passenger on one of his trips. Masland dismissed the character failings Marston attributed to Nevills and defended his ability as a river publicist and boater. "He's a boatman, Doc. In my book he's tops."[31]

Years after Nevills's death, Masland recommended to the US Board on Geographic Names that it name one of the Colorado's rapids for him. Requesting Marston's blessing, he downplayed Nevills's character flaws, saying they only made him more interesting and that everyone had failings: "My conscience isn't clean. I don't want someone writing a book on the things I should have done and didn't." Masland credited Nevills with making him a preservationist. He "opened up a whole new world to me. He remodeled my life," he wrote. "All my activities in the field of conservation, all the honors that have come to me in that field I owe to my first run down the river with Norm Nevills." Unmoved, Marston wrote a letter to the board opposing the honor and accusing Masland of "romanticizing" Nevills's accomplishments. The board sided with Masland, naming Mile 75.5 of the Colorado River Nevills Rapid. Despite their disagreement over Nevills, Marston and Masland remained friends and shared many outdoor adventures together over the years.[32]

In July 1949, Masland returned to the Colorado for another river trip with Nevills. Rafting in higher water, he found this trip more thrilling than the first one. And, as promised, Nevills permitted him to take a boat through Badger Creek Rapid. Masland also formed another lasting friendship with passenger Dr. Josiah (Joe) Eisaman of Pittsburgh. Masland experienced a health issue along the river, enduring days of severe pain from a dust particle that lodged in his eye. "I had to make the trip with a hat, a pair of dark glasses and with a handkerchief tied around my right eye," he informed Marston. "I couldn't stand light in it at all," he said, and got no relief until his return home, where he got treatment. His eye laceration did not sour him on the experience. Running the entire river for a second time "has simply made me more insatiable," he informed Marston. "I love it, every inch of it, especially those parts I fear. . . . It was a swell ride from end to end. The kind that makes a chap want to do it all over again." Despite his zeal, he promised Virginia that he would forgo the river the following year.[33]

On the same excursion, Masland met fellow voyager Mary Abbott, an artist from Concord, Massachusetts. A descendant of Presidents John and John Quincy Adams, she had run Utah's San Juan River with Nevills in 1948. She and Masland hit it off. Besides being a skilled painter, wood carver, and sculptor, Abbott was a river runner, horsewoman, angler, hunter, and adventurer. She was a "very remarkable person who has been all over the world and had a multitude of experiences that range from an extended period on the Powell [Arizona] Plateau breaking wild horses to hunting big game with native guides in Tibet," he informed Marston. "She loved the Canyon this year, stating that in form and color there is no place in the world that could compare with it . . . and she has seen a lot." Abbott and Masland became lifelong friends and made additional river and backcountry journeys together; Masland confided in her as he did with no other correspondent. There is no evidence that the two became lovers, but there is little question, says Frank Masland IV, that Masland was "smitten" with Abbott.[34]

In mid-October 1949, Norm and Doris Nevills, both barely forty years old, died near their home in Mexican Hat, Utah, when their Piper J-3 Cub *Cherry II* crashed into a cliff shortly after takeoff. Fortunately, their two young daughters were not with them. Named with a Utah bank as executor of the Nevills estate, Masland had to deal with financial and property issues and with finding someone to raise the two young daughters, Sandra and Joan. He offered to raise them himself, but the girls were raised separately by aunts in California and Colorado.[35]

The Nevills tragedy shocked the River Rat community—all but Dock Marston. "Such an end to him has been forecast many times," he told Masland. "If ever a death was forecast in the stars, that one was." In his log, Marston stated that Nevills was reckless, careless regarding airplane maintenance, and perhaps suicidal. Other river runners, devastated by the loss, suggested placing a plaque on a canyon wall to commemorate Nevills's sterling reputation as a river pilot.[36]

Marston considered any commemoration foolish. "The tragedy of Norm was not in his death but in his life," he wrote Masland. Nevills, he said, was a self-promoter who downplayed the skill of other river guides and exaggerated his own. "He wasn't who people thought he was," he complained to the superintendent of Grand Canyon National Park. "He wasn't the greatest boatman on the river or the world's number one fast water man whatever that may mean."[37]

Masland disagreed and worked to offset Marston's campaign against commemorating Nevills. "Most people would regard me as a hard-boiled, elitist business titan," he told Marston. "Actually, I belong to that great mass of common people who are romanticists and sentimentalists." True, he admitted, a plaque may be "silly, but what of it. A great many of the sweetest things in life are silly as hell if we think cold-bloodedly about it." It was also true that Nevills had faults and made mistakes. But who did not?[38]

With the clear majority of canyoneers in agreement, including, finally, the reluctant Marston, Masland proceeded with plans for the commemoration. He persuaded Abbott to design a commemorative bronze plaque, which he paid for when other river runners, "reluctant bozos," he called them, were slow to contribute. In addition to paying for the plaque, he picked up the tab for the invitations and programs. When Colorado canyoneer Preston Walker bowed out as committee chair, Abbott took over, and she and Masland organized a riverside memorial service for Nevills with little help from other canyoneers.[39]

The death of Nevills, a respected mutual acquaintance, drew Masland and Abbott closer as friends. In late May 1950 Masland attended her art show in New York City and purchased several of her black-and-white drawings of the Grand Canyon. He also hired her to carve a locust wood mace, or staff, for use in all official ceremonial functions at Dickinson College and to craft a wooden wildlife scene for placement above the fireplace mantel at the company retreat at Kings Gap. When Abbott completed a raft trip of the upper Colorado River with Frank Wright, who had taken over Nevills's business, Masland rewarded her with a River Rat pin symbolizing the "most exclusive of organizations." When Masland held a meeting of the Eastern River Rat Society at his company's retreat at Kings Gap, Abbott and Marston attended. Abbott also joined Frank, Virginia, and others for a sunrise Easter service in 1952.[40]

Tentatively, at first, they exchanged views on political issues. When Abbott, a Republican, expressed horror at Senator Joseph McCarthy's anticommunist witch hunts, Masland refused to comment because he agreed with the Wisconsin senator's charges that the federal government, labor unions, movie industry, and school systems were riddled with traitors. When Abbott suspected Masland of being a Harry Truman supporter, he set her straight. Truman and Secretary of State Dean Acheson, he said, were responsible for the Korean War because they virtually invited the Soviet-directed North Korean attack on its neighbor by failing to make clear that the United States would defend South Korea from outside aggression. As for Truman, he told Abbott, "there are no members of the animal kingdom who would associate with him other than homo sapiens." Truman, Adlai Stevenson, and other notable Democrats, he charged, "would sell their souls to the C.I.O." He expressed disdain, too, for the newly elected US senator John F. Kennedy but hoped he would be more of an anticommunist than his defeated rival, Henry Cabot Lodge. Though he preferred the conservative Ohio US senator Robert Taft, he eventually supported the Republican nominee, Dwight D. Eisenhower, over Adlai Stevenson in the presidential elections of 1952 and 1956. But Eisenhower eventually displeased him because he accepted far too much of the liberal state instituted by FDR and Truman.[41]

Although he promised Virginia that he would not return to the Colorado River in 1950, he did raft the tamer San Juan River in southern Utah with fellow Pennsylvanian Joe Eisaman. Their adventure was full of hardships and mishaps. From Pennsylvania they drove to Colorado's Mesa Verde National Park but did not see much of the Indian ruins owing to several days of hard rain. From Mesa Verde they motored to their launch point at Mexican Hat, Utah, on the San Juan River. At Mexican Hat Lodge, Masland came down with indigestion and diarrhea and took a large gulp of a pink liquid that he had packed for such emergencies. Unfortunately, he gulped it down before noticing that the pink substance was marked "calamine lotion." Worried, he asked Eisaman if it would poison or maybe kill him. "How would I know," responded Eisaman, "I'm an obstetrician." Having recovered from the intestinal ailment and calamine "poisoning," he and Eisaman took a small plane to nearby Monument Valley, spending several days with a Navajo guide, exploring by foot and pack animals the majestic arches, spires, and Indian ruins of the harsh Navajo backcountry.[42]

Upon their return to Mexican Hat, they accompanied river guide Frank Wright on an expedition down the San Juan River for 113 miles to the junction of the Colorado and then another 78 miles to Lees Ferry. Twelve other passengers traveled in four cataract boats; Masland and Eisaman tagged along in Masland's recently purchased Folbot kayak, or "foolboat," as he came to call it. A lightweight two-person folding kayak with a nylon skin, the Folbot proved difficult to maneuver and easy to puncture. With much of the San Juan shallow or dry, the voyagers were forced to wade or walk, hauling the boats behind them. One evening, Masland suffered painful burns when he walked barefoot over an abandoned campfire that had not been entirely snuffed out. The water was higher once they reached the Colorado, but the weather was worse, with thunder, lightning, wind, and torrential rain. Drenched and bedraggled, the passengers were relieved when they finally reached Lees Ferry. Despite the hardships, Masland regarded the raw experience worthwhile because he had traveled with "good comrades who had been tested and proven in every respect, true sportsmen who could take it and come through physically, mentally, and spiritually." And, he concluded optimistically, there were plenty more rivers to run.[43]

After nearly two years of preparation, the Nevills dedication took Masland again to the American Southwest in the summer of 1952. With Phoenix council member and soon to be US senator Barry Goldwater serving as master of ceremonies, the dedication took place on July 11, under the nearly nine-hundred-foot Navajo Bridge spanning the Colorado River at Marble Canyon. Guests included Nevills's mother and daughters, Masland, Abbott, Marston, and several other canyoneers. The bronze plaque featuring an empty cataract boat was bolted to a large riverside boulder. Dedicated to Norm and Doris Nevills, the inscription read: "They run the rivers of eternity." (The plaque is now housed at the Navajo Bridge Visitor Center overlooking Marble Canyon.) Masland was pleased with the event, especially the artistically handsome plaque.[44]

To further honor the memory of Nevills, the following morning Masland, Eisaman, and Abbott embarked on a lengthy "dedication" raft expedition down the Colorado River. Upon its completion, Abbott returned to Massachusetts, while Eisaman and Masland motored thirty-five miles on a dirt road to the Havasupai Reservation, where an Indian guide took them by packhorse "on the darnedest ride" he ever took: to Havasu Falls, fifteen hundred feet below. After clambering back to the rim, they continued to Grand Canyon National

Park, dined uneventfully with Barry Goldwater, and then spent five days with a Navajo guide exploring the "back beyond" of Monument Valley. "You certainly have developed a taste for this western country," wrote Harold Bryant, superintendent of Grand Canyon National Park.[45]

Masland's love for the remote American Southwest and its rambunctious rivers prompted him to join the growing conservation movement to protect and preserve them. Another massive dam project surfaced in the early 1950s when the Bureau of Reclamation proposed a series of ten dams on the Colorado River and its tributaries to provide flood control, water storage, irrigation, hydroelectricity, and recreation for residents of the Upper Colorado River Basin states of Colorado, Utah, Wyoming, and New Mexico. Echo Park in Dinosaur National Monument on the Utah-Colorado border would be flooded by a dam in the Colorado River Storage Project (CRSP). Conservationists condemned the proposed Echo Park dam as a threat to the principle of national park inviolability. Masland agreed and joined the campaign to block it. The controversy over the CRSP, according to historian Mark Harvey, "was the first major clash between preservationists and the dam builders in the postwar American West."[46] By the mid-1950s, Masland had evolved into an avid seeker of raw nature, a fervent preservationist, and a defender of the national park system and the remote canyon country of the American Southwest. The carpet king had become a conservation crusader.

CHAPTER 4

Nature in the Raw

Whether it was the desolation of the Galapagos Islands, the jungle of Panama, the backwaters of the Everglades, or the starkness of the American southwestern canyon lands, Masland savored what he called "nature in the raw no matter where I find it." He also relished associating with Indigenous people who lived simply. He was especially moved by the desert country of the American Southwest and the Navajo and other Indigenous people who lived there. The canyon lands and desert country, unlike the Colorado River, were isolated and untrammeled. And he was at the forefront of safeguarding it from commercial development as a national park or preserve.[1]

As early as 1953, he complained that the Colorado River had become another "Coney Island chute-de-chute" that was being overrun by rafters and littered with refuse. He was also agitated by the proposed Echo Park dam's threat to the national park system and the impact the dam would have on the raw backcountry of Dinosaur National Monument. Politically, Masland was a hard-line conservative who defended what historian Arthur Schlesinger Jr. has called the "old order" that prevailed before the onset of FDR's New Deal. Masland voiced unfiltered opinions, both privately and publicly, about the loss of traditional family and church values, the influx of immigrants, America's drift toward socialism, and the possibility of the US government's being overtaken by communist infiltration or Soviet aggression. He identified closely with Senator Barry Goldwater and *National Review* editor William F. Buckley, two conservatives whose views were considered extreme by liberal Democrats and many moderate Republicans.[2]

Seemingly determined to make up for lost opportunities and perhaps as a distraction to the conflict in Korea that he believed President Truman was badly mishandling, Masland went on a nature engagement binge in the early 1950s. In addition to his river trips, he yachted to the Galapagos Islands, trudged through a jungle in Panama, and wandered through the swamps and waterways of the Florida Everglades.

He disliked the flatness, humidity, and commercialism of Florida but developed a lifelong attachment to the Everglades that rivaled his love for Pennsylvania's Cumberland Valley and the southwestern canyon country. Located on the southern tip of Florida, the Everglades, larger than the state of Delaware, consists of more than seven thousand square miles of waterways, swamps, grasses, mangrove trees, and wild habitat for a variety of birds, reptiles, and mammals. In 1934 it was set aside as a wilderness reserve under the jurisdiction of the Fish and Wildlife Department of the Department of the Interior and was eventually designated a national park in August 1947.

Daniel B. Beard became the new park's first superintendent. The son of Daniel Carter Beard, founder of the Sons of Daniel Boone and Boy Scouts of America, Beard Jr. was a graduate of Syracuse University who went to work as a wildlife biologist in CCC camps for the Park Service. The Park Service asked him to conduct a study of the flora and fauna in the Everglades; his 1938 study, recommending that the area be preserved as wilderness forever, helped prepare the path to park designation.[3]

It is unclear when Beard and Masland became acquainted, but by 1950 they had developed a warm friendship that lasted until Beard's death in 1977. Sometime after World War II, Masland helped Beard map out the boundaries of the proposed park, and in 1950 he and Frank Craighead Sr. joined Beard in further studies of the vast, largely unknown interior of the fledgling park. Craighead focused on the flora and fauna, while Masland busied himself mapping canoe routes, hiking trails, and suitable wilderness campsites. "The Glades are primeval wilderness," he wrote Dock Marston. "They have not been effected [*sic*] by civilization's march. There is virtually no solid ground. Birds were everywhere."[4]

When comfortable lodging became available, Frank and Virginia spent nearly every winter at a motel in Flamingo within the park's boundaries. John Doerr, a chief naturalist with the Park Service who had befriended Masland on a Nevills rafting trip, advised Everglades Park personnel to be sure the Maslands were welcomed and comfortably accommodated during their 1953 and subsequent visits. Frank Masland, he stated, was "TOPS," and so was

Mrs. Masland. They loved the national parks, he continued, and were "genuinely hospitable people. Everything they do reflects their genuineness." For the next four decades, during those mainly leisurely winters, Frank served as another set of eyes and ears for the Park Service on conditions and activities at the Everglades. And, characteristically, he let his opinions be known, including the elitist point that vacationers and anglers in camping trailers were ruining the natural setting.[5]

In his defense of pristine wilderness, the park system, and untamed rivers, Masland shared the view of Pennsylvania Republican representative John Saylor. Raised in a religious household in Johnstown, Pennsylvania, Saylor attended Methodist-affiliated Franklin and Marshall College and then obtained a law degree from the Dickinson School of Law in Carlisle. When the United States joined the war in 1941, he enlisted, serving on a US naval destroyer in the Pacific. After the war he was elected to the US House of Representatives, serving Johnstown and several other Appalachian communities in southwestern Pennsylvania from 1949 through 1973.

A hulking, blustering, gruff, and sometimes profane conservative Republican, Saylor, like Masland, was a virulent anticommunist who warned that the Republic was threatened internally by subversion and externally by Soviet aggression. He believed in limited federal authority, restrained fiscal spending, private property, states' rights, judicial restraint, and a strong military. The representative of a bituminous coal–mining district, he was, however, a fervent protector of labor unions. As a member of the influential House Committee on Interior and Insular Affairs, which held sway over most legislation relating to conservation, "Uncle John," as he was known by Sierra Club leaders, was also a passionate advocate of strong federal authority when it came to protecting the national parks, wilderness, forestland, and wildlife. He also insisted that once a national park or monument had been established, it remained inviolate. Moreover, he became the first member of the House to sponsor a wilderness bill (in 1955) and the Wild and Scenic Rivers Act a decade later.[6]

Except on the subject of labor unions, Masland and Saylor were conservative allies. Perhaps because Masland was a generation older, the two were not close, but they were friendly, communicated mainly by telephone, and respected each other as kindred conservative Republicans who held the sanctity of the national parks, Indigenous people, and wilderness in high regard. Like Saylor, Masland became an environmentalist long before that outlook and term became fashionable. To Masland, wild places were sacred and required federal protection in the same way that the national government protected individual rights, domestic order, and national security. With respect to public lands and wildlife, Masland's anti-statism, like Saylor's, was usually suspended in favor of federal activism.

Masland's zeal for the American Southwest seemed insatiable. When a planned raft trip through Dinosaur National Monument on Colorado's Yampa River failed to materialize because of low water levels, he joined Marston in running the Colorado River by motorboat in 1954. The wind was high, the water low, and the rocks and sheared propeller pins abundant. Overall, the lengthy motorized trip did not measure up to previous ones in a cataract boat and soured Masland on motorized rafting, though not quite enough that he completely abandoned it.[7]

Upon seeing the tiny remote town of Moab, Utah, overrun by prospectors during the uranium boom, Masland wanted to revisit the pristine canyon lands of the Southwest before they, too, fell prey to commercial development. During a 1952 visit to the Navajo backcountry with Joe Eisaman, Masland had spotted what he believed to be a massive sandstone arch several miles in the distance, and he was determined to visit and photograph it. Since no one in the area had heard of it, his friends began to refer to it as the "phantom arch."

He persuaded Marston, along with Bill Belknap and Jorgen Visback of Boulder City, Nevada, to join him in his "Arch Safari" in late September 1954. The party met at Kayenta, Arizona, and drove by Jeep to the Navajo trading post operated by Ralph and Madelene Cameron. There, they rented ten horses and hired wranglers Tom and Nancy Daly and Indian guides Buck White-hat Chathaigal and Bahe Ketchum. While awaiting Buck White-hat's return from a dance, the party spent two days climbing Navajo Mountain, the 10,387-foot sacred Native American peak straddling the Utah-Arizona border. When White-hat returned from the dance, he said he knew of a large arch twenty miles southwest of Navajo Mountain near Cummings Mesa, but it was in rough slickrock country. Undeterred, Masland asked him to lead the way. "We were deep in Navajo Canyon, about as far from civilization as you can get in the United States," wrote Belknap. After a four-day ride, Masland spotted the arch through binoculars near a distant butte. Steep, slick terrain necessitated a roundabout route. "At last we rounded a corner," wrote Visback. "Out in front like a gigantic horseshoe magnet—there stood the arch. Its size exceeded all expectations. Frank turned around, his grin a foot wide."

The arch measured 230 feet wide and 177 feet high. Theretofore unmapped and unnamed, they called it Arch in the Sky.[8]

Masland described the expedition as "the fulfillment of a lifetime dream. My being was constantly filled with the lonesome, magnificent beauty of the depths of the canyons and the heights of the buttes." If he was not the first white man to "discover" the arch, he didn't care, he informed Marston. "My memories would be no less pleasant." Shortly after his return to Pennsylvania, Masland received a ditty from Visback recognizing his discovery:

There was a young man from Carlisle
Whose rugs made a helluva pile
On a four-day march
He found a new arch
And returned to Carlisle with a smile!

Decades later, the US Board on Geographic Names designated the structure southwest of Navajo Mountain on the Navajo reservation Arch in the Sky to honor Masland. And his friend Marston began referring to him as "Arch Eyes" rather than "Fish Eyes."[9]

Enthralled by the harsh landscape, Masland made yet another pack trip to the Utah and Navajo backcountry in the fall of 1955. The party included Marston and five other male adventurers, a horse wrangler, and the same two Indian guides. Masland wanted to invite Mary Abbott, but Marston resisted, prompting Masland to write Abbott, "I think of you many times on those trips Mary. I know you would enjoy them. It seems unfair that trips such as this should be exclusively the privilege of the male sex." He also thought of her when he was in Pennsylvania. "Never do I visit Kings Gap but what I think of you. Nothing gives me more gratification than to just sit and look at your marvelous wood carving."[10]

Although he complained that the Colorado River was overrun with people, flies, and refuse, Masland found it difficult to resist and took another voyage with Marston and Eisaman by motorboat in the summer of 1956. Taking on a major rapid in a small boat was "a contest all the way," he told the *Philadelphia Inquirer*. "There is the element of the unknown. Once you head into a rapid, you and your companions are on your own. You can't call time out.... The thrill is incomparable." Moreover, the lack of creature comforts forced one to connect with nature. "You go to bed with the sun and get up with the sun. You sleep on the ground, cook your own food and drink river water. It's a wonderful existence." Of course, by writing and lecturing about the thrill of confronting the rapids, he contributed to the allure of the sport and the consequent problem of overuse that he often complained about.[11]

It was not such a wonderful existence for fellow boater Willie Taylor. On the second day of the trip, he suffered chest pains. With oxygen unavailable, Eisaman administered morphine. After a restless night sleeping on the ground, Taylor died the next morning of apparent heart failure. His companions, aware of his deep love for the canyon, laid him in a shallow grave high above the river at Mile 45, chiseled his name and date of death on the face of a rock, said a brief prayer, and motored away, completing their sojourn ten days later. Masland took the ghastly experience in stride. "The cold drinks at the head of Lake Mead," he reported matter-of-factly, "never tasted better." Though deaths and severe injuries were rare, Masland again promised Virginia that he would not run the river in 1957.[12]

Forgoing more river running, Masland continued to spend considerable time, effort, and money in the 1950s and early '60s exploring portions of reservation land that were known to several Navajos but not to Anglos. Created by treaty in 1868, with parcels added by executive order over the years, the Navajo reservation covered twenty-seven thousand square miles (more than seventeen million acres) in northeastern Arizona, southeastern Utah, and northwestern New Mexico. In total, it was larger than ten US states. Its seat of government, the Tribal Council, was in Window Rock, Arizona. The Diné, as the Navajos on this reservation referred to themselves (Diné means "the people"), earned their livelihood mainly by raising horses, goats, and sheep and by bartering their wool, rugs, jewelry, and other crafts at one of several licensed trading posts on the reservation, including those run by J. L. Hubbard, Harry Goulding, and Ralph and Madelene Cameron. Many Navajos distrusted these white traders and sought to remove them from the reservation, but Masland liked the Camerons and believed they dealt fairly with the Diné.[13]

In fits and starts, policymakers had sought for two centuries to end the special legal and financially burdensome relationship between Native American tribes and the federal government by dissolving the tribes and assimilating Indigenous people into mainstream society. That policy goal was called "termination" in the 1950s, when Republicans gained political ascendance. A few tribes were terminated in that decade, but the Diné had adapted to a subsistence economy and insisted on self-determination rather than termination.[14]

Like many reform-minded whites who professed concern for the overall welfare of Indigenous people, Masland sympathized with the goal of assimilation. He adopted the same kind of paternalistic approach toward Indigenous people that he did toward his workers at the carpet company. Throughout his life, he defended the work of the Carlisle Indian School. Established by Civil War veteran Lieutenant Colonel (later General) Richard Henry Pratt in 1879, the United States Indian Industrial School, or Carlisle Indian Industrial School, took young boys and girls away from 140 tribes and transported them to Carlisle, where they were taught English, Christianity, and rudimentary reading and arithmetic. The goal was to strip them of their customs, culture, and heritage—their Indianness—and assimilate them into white mainstream society. Before closing in 1918, more than ten thousand students, including the famous Olympian and sports icon Jim Thorpe and Hall of Fame Major League Baseball pitcher Charles Albert "Chief" Bender, attended, but fewer than two hundred graduated. Although the Carlisle School traumatized Indian youth, denigrated their traditions, and mainly failed as an experiment in assimilation, Masland lauded it.[15]

He took a similarly paternalistic position on the Navajo people. He believed that the Diné possessed an inner peace that whites should emulate. However, on matters of health care, economic development, and the management of pristine landscapes, they should rely on experts outside the tribe.[16]

In addition to contributing financially to various religious missions, Masland used his influence to help Navajos suffering from tuberculosis. In the mid-1950s, TB sanatoriums were located off the reservation and were not open to Native Americans even if beds were available. Two Seventh-day Adventist missionaries, Pastor Marvin Walter and his wife, Gwen, a nurse, took Masland by Jeep to a hogan to visit an afflicted man. Furious that the man could not receive care in a sanatorium, Masland took the issue to the Interior Department and the policy of Navajo exclusion soon ended, although not in time to save that man. Frank Masland, Gwen Walter recalled, was "very much interested in doing things to benefit the people and the country. He's really the man who helped us get the Indians into the TB hospital."[17]

Masland showed a special affinity for his Navajo guides White-hat, Bahe, Sid Whiskers Doughi, and Toby Owl. He corresponded with them semiregularly and gave them presents of new rifles, blankets, wool-lined leather coats, saddlebags, sweaters, Swiss army knives, and a fiberglass boat. They in turn dictated replies to Madelene Cameron, who forwarded them to Masland. They addressed him as "Friend" or "Brother," prompting him to write atop one of the salutations: "The highest honor a Navajo can bestow—treasured by me beyond words." Occasionally, they replied to Masland in handwritten letters displaying humor and concern. "It was grate to know that you had a pleasure trip to a cross the ocean," wrote Bahe Ketchum. "You must be tired to ride a horse all the was [way]." Learning that Masland might visit Japan, guide Toby Owl asked, "Who would be my friend if they killed you?" Beyond their thanks for his generosity, they suggested other remote backcountry to explore and apprised him of developments in Navajo country, including near-famine conditions due to water shortages and dwindling numbers of sheep. They reduced their consumption, they said, "but even a fly prefers meat."[18]

Masland respected the culture of the Navajo people but believed they could improve their standard of living through education on the reservation and by adding industry to their subsistence economy. Rather than remove Navajos from their homeland to learn industrial skills, he advocated bringing industry to the reservation. But by the mid-1950s the Navajos were already diversifying their economy by leasing some of their land to oil and mining companies. The royalties were modest, however, and Navajos who worked in the unventilated uranium mines contracted lethal diseases from radiation poisoning.[19]

Navajos were rightly skeptical of well-meaning efforts to alter their traditional ways and were inclined to look the federal gift horse in the mouth. Offers of help from do-gooder reformers and federal authorities frightened them. Federally directed self-help programs usually resulted in the loss of land, dignity, traditions, homes, and self-determination. Addressing the issue of soil erosion on the reservation in the 1930s, New Deal specialists, led by John Collier, head of the Bureau of Indian Affairs, launched a livestock-reduction program to prevent overgrazing. Thousands of sheep, goats, and cattle were killed to protect vegetation. New Deal officials downplayed drought as a possible cause of erosion, ignored the importance of sheep to Diné culture, and shunned the input of Navajo women, who controlled most of the livestock and grazing range. By 1955 the sheep population on the reservation had been reduced to one-third of its early 1930s level, with no change to the vegetation. The outcome, writes historian Marsha Weisiger, "has been a collective memory of trauma, a long-lasting rejection of range conservation policies, and a chronic wasteland."[20]

What the Navajos needed in the 1950s, they informed Masland, was a steady supply of water to maintain their subsistence economy and protection from thoughtless tourists who defaced their land, prehistoric homes, and ancestral artifacts. Filmed in the enchanted Monument Valley, popular Western movies like *Stagecoach*, *My Darling Clementine*, *Fort Apache*, and *She Wore a Yellow Ribbon* stimulated tourism and, with it, mistreatment of the land and Native artifacts. Navajo concerns prompted Masland to intercede on their behalf with Glenn L. Emmons, commissioner of the Bureau of Indian Affairs, and Secretary of the Interior Douglas McKay. In short, he advocated federal action, including the construction of a dam, to help the people for whom he had a special fondness.[21]

Prior to 1964, private citizens had little influence over the administration of public lands and protection of the ecosystem. But the Wilderness Act of 1964 authorized all Americans to petition Congress on the issue of wilderness designation, and the 1970 National Environmental Policy Act enabled public input on the federal environmental-impact process. Though there were few opportunities for citizen activism during the early postwar decades, Masland had an insider's track to the Interior Department.[22]

In various letters and a 1955 memorandum titled "Some Thoughts Concerning the Navajo Problem," Masland made three recommendations. First, to protect the landscape and prehistoric Navajo ruins from further disfigurement, the primeval Monument Valley area should be designated a national monument or national recreation area and be patrolled by Park Service personnel or Navajo rangers trained by the Park Service. Second, the Bureau of Reclamation should dam the San Juan River in New Mexico to provide the Diné with water for irrigation. Third, a hydroelectric dam should be built to supply the power to develop industry on the reservation. A cheap source of electricity might lure industrialists, in cooperation with the tribe, to build factories that would employ thirty thousand Indigenous people at a "starry eyed dream" site he dubbed Navajo City.[23]

Masland's remedy for the so-called Navajo problem reflects in microcosm his approach to all Indigenous people. Layered with paternalism and Anglo superiority, it was akin to President Lyndon Johnson's attempt to end the Vietnam conflict by converting the Mekong River into another Tennessee Valley Authority project. A series of US-funded hydroelectric dams on the river, LBJ believed, would promote agriculture, industry, prosperity, American goodwill, and an independent, noncommunist government.

Similarly, Masland hoped to make the Navajos successful capitalists and less reliant on federal largess. He did not want to dispossess or relocate them, the fate of other tribes in the past in the name of assimilation. Nor did he want to move them to make national scenic preserves more pristine, unpolluted by human presence. "The Navajo is in many ways a superior person. He is intelligent and a capable administrator. He is a successful agriculturalist and stock raiser," he informed McKay. With the completion of a San Juan dam, the "result might be the development of a Navajo economy based on agriculture, stock raising and industry. If the Navajo could continue his pastoral pursuits, vastly increase his agricultural activities and be provided with the additional opportunity to apply his demonstrated administrative skills to the development, operation and management of industry, conceivably he would become a capitalist, a productive and converted member of our free enterprise system."[24]

Navajo culture, in Masland's view, should not remain frozen. The San Juan dam, located outside a national park or monument, would allow for a blending of traditional and new ways and a path "from the dole to economic independence." Additionally, it would benefit the overall economy of the Southwest and the nation, "be one of the truly great experiments of a humanitarian nature," and "provide a valuable opportunity for the study of the potentials of semi-primitive people."[25] Likely to help benefit an economically beleaguered Indigenous people and simultaneously promote capitalism, the San Juan was one of the few federally financed multipurpose dams that Masland supported. But he soon changed his mind.

The Bureau of Reclamation did in fact have plans for a dam on the San Juan River, but they fell well short of Masland's lofty aspirations. Located in northwestern New Mexico and renamed Navajo Dam, the facility originally provided no hydroelectric power and no irrigation for the Navajo Nation. It served mainly the irrigation and municipal water needs of the city of Farmington and its environs. (In 1962, Congress finally enacted legislation bringing irrigation from the impoundment to more than a hundred thousand acres of Navajo land.) But without hydropower, the dam could not stimulate industry or create Masland's Navajo City of thousands of budding capitalists. Although Masland abandoned his dream of bringing industry to the Diné, he clung to the fantasy that much of the pristine Navajo country could be protected as a national park.[26]

By 1956 his focus had temporarily shifted from helping the Navajos to helping uphold the integrity of the national park system. Navajo Dam was included as a key unit in the massive Colorado River Storage Project Act. Another proposed unit in that contentious legislative package, Echo Park dam, would have intruded upon Dinosaur National Monument, triggering intense opposition from conservationists, including Masland.

Masland's love for raw country, which began with that first raft trip down the Colorado River, turned into national park advocacy during the fight against the proposed Echo Park dam. The Korean War had delayed action on the proposal for three years, giving Masland hope that the new Eisenhower administration would oppose it. Eisenhower's appointment of Douglas McKay as secretary of the interior pleased him. McKay had been a fellow member of the business-friendly, anti-union, conservative-leaning National Association of Manufacturers, and Masland regarded him as "a real man" and "straight shooter." At Masland's request, McKay agreed to receive an honorary degree and speak at Dickinson College in 1953. During McKay's brief stay at Kings Gap, Masland raved about the thrill of rafting wild rivers, showed films of his trip, and urged McKay to oppose damming the Yampa River at Echo Park. McKay remained noncommittal, but Masland was encouraged nonetheless. "He is a grand chap, honest, fearless, capable, and very likeable," he told Abbott.[27]

His personal appeal to McKay proved unsuccessful. McKay, like James Watt three decades later, was receptive to opening federal reserves to commercial development, thus earning the nickname "Giveaway McKay." "We cannot continue to grow as a nation and as a prosperous people if we adopt the narrow view of conservation as requiring the locking up of our resources," said McKay, speaking for many westerners who believed that eastern elitists were attempting to treat public land in the West as an outdoor museum.[28]

The Eisenhower administration gave its support and Congress initiated hearings on the Colorado River Storage Project (CRSP) bill in 1954. The trouble, Masland complained to Marston, "is that somebody has convinced McKay and all interested members of the Eisenhower family that the dams in that section of the world are necessary. The whole thing is built on that fallacy. Since McKay hails from a power area in the northwest [Oregon], it isn't too difficult to sell him on the power idea." Masland apparently believed that the economically distressed Navajos were more deserving of a federal multipurpose dam than less distressed nonindigenous westerners.[29]

Three distinct lobbying groups—the Trustees for Conservation, the Citizens Council on Natural Resources, and the Council of Conservationists—embarked upon a massive publicity campaign against the bill, arguing that short of a war or some other national crisis, the national parks were inviolate. A dam at Echo Park would set a precedent, they argued, for the construction of a dam in any national park or monument. If a dam, why not a hotel, restaurant, or some other commercial establishment? By joining the Trustees for Conservation and serving on the executive board of the Council of Conservationists, Masland allied himself with that position.

He also allied himself with Fred Smith, who headed the Council of Conservationists. A wealthy conservative Republican, Smith was a successful public relations specialist, the vice president of the Prudential Insurance Company, and a major consultant to multimillionaire Laurance Rockefeller. Smith gained notoriety during the Echo Park controversy by purchasing a full-page advertisement in the *Denver Post* opposing the proposed dam as a menace to the sanctity of the national park system. He and Masland became friends, longtime correspondents, and fellow conservative preservationists.[30]

As a director and soon-to-be vice president of the business-friendly National Association of Manufacturers, Masland blocked a move by some members of that organization to endorse the CRSP. He also continued to lobby against the Echo Park dam with McKay and members of Congress, including the Pennsylvania delegation, minus Saylor, who staunchly opposed the project owing to its vast expense and intrusion upon a national monument. Republicans, Masland argued, should distance themselves from the proposed dam because it would backfire politically on the party. The project would not be popular with easterners, especially conservative Republicans, he argued, who lambasted it as a costly federal boondoggle, a boon to irrigation that would produce more farm products in an already saturated market, and an unfair federal subsidy that would produce public power more cheaply than privately generated energy. The Reclamation Bureau's appetite for damming western rivers was insatiable, he believed, and, like other conservatives, especially in the East, he regarded the bureau as a prime example of federal power gone mad. Publicly, he denounced the proposed dam as a threat to the national park system, as did Marston, who penned an essay in the influential anti–Echo Park dam book *This Is Dinosaur: Echo Park Country and Its Magic Rivers,* edited by the prominent writer and historian Wallace Stegner.[31]

Small in numbers in the mid-1950s, conservation groups organized a massive public relations attack in books, speeches, and opinion pieces in the mainstream and western press. Owing to negative publicity, damning testimony from conservation leaders and Saylor during congressional hearings, and overwhelming opposition from conservationists and eastern legislators who held the balance of power, Congress removed the Echo Park dam from the CRSP bill in favor of a taller dam at Glen Canyon. Ironically, the loftier dam at Glen Canyon gagged a little-known wild river canyon and caused reservoir water to seep into Rainbow Bridge National Monument. Masland and most other conservationists did not see that threat to Rainbow at the time. And only a few of them were aware that a beautiful wild canyon would be lost. "I am delighted to hear that your efforts in the matter of the dam have been rewarded. Good for you and the other conservationists—and the Democratic senator from Mass!" Abbott noted playfully. Ignoring the reference to John Kennedy, Masland worried that the proposed Echo Park dam would resurface because western dam proponents were persistent.[32]

For the next decade, Masland continued to explore the southwestern canyon country and to advocate the federal protection of raw nature on the Navajo reservation and the immediate surrounding slickrock region. He also continued to defend the sanctity of the national parks and to promote congressional legislation promoting the parks and the preservation of wilderness. At the same time, he advanced his hard-line and often contentious conservative political views at the local, state, and national levels.

CHAPTER 5

Politics in the Raw

As a business executive, private citizen, and Dickinson College trustee, Frank Masland seldom refrained from advancing his conservative views. At times, especially in private correspondence and at Dickinson College, these views created controversy and smacked of extremism. On the subject of conservation, however, he remained steadfastly nonpartisan and often paddled upstream against the main current of conservative thought, insisting that the federal government had an obligation to protect and preserve nature's wild and scenic treasures.

Like his friend and frequent correspondent Senator Barry Goldwater, Masland was a conservative Republican who loved the natural world but feared federal power. Both men believed that some of the scariest words in the English language were "I'm from the government and I'm here to help"—except when that adage applied to preserving public lands.

In *Loving Nature, Fearing the State,* historian Brian Drake intriguingly observes that the modern American environmental movement was not driven solely by liberals and moderates at ease with federal authority. A few nature-loving anti-statists—like Goldwater, iconoclastic nature writer Edward Abbey, and others—also served the environmental movement. Although he was not included in Drake's study, Masland fits the same mold. Like other nature-loving conservatives, he was sometimes conflicted about specific environmental issues, and he derided environmentalists whom he considered soft on communism, even quasi-socialist, but he did not desert the cause during the backlash against environmentalism during Ronald Reagan's presidency.[1]

Raised in different parts of the country and a generation apart, Masland and the younger Goldwater were kindred spirits. Despite their opposition to intrusive federal power, both believed that conservatives should conserve and that federal authority was necessary to shield natural resources from commercial despoliation, to safeguard scenic and historic treasures, and to protect the environment. Both came from privileged families. Goldwater inherited from his grandfather and father a swanky department store in Phoenix, Arizona; Masland took over from his paternal forebears a plush carpet business in Carlisle, Pennsylvania. As young men, both developed a love for the outdoors and possessed the wealth to finance their adventures. Both respected the Indigenous people of the Southwest and shared a passion for photography and the desert and canyon country of that region. In middle age, each man took a raft trip with boatman Norman Nevills and were smitten by the Colorado River. Both privately published accounts of their expeditions. And, in maturity, they both worked in the federal government whose powers they sought to restrain.[2]

As hard-line conservatives, Masland and Goldwater supported free-enterprise capitalism, individual initiative, federal fiscal discipline, states' rights, and traditional family values while opposing an activist government, labor unions, and the internal and external threat of communism. In the early 1950s, they supported Senator Joseph McCarthy's reckless campaign to expose communists in virtually all walks of American life. They sympathized, too, with the extreme anticommunist aims and claims of the John Birch Society. (For a short time Masland even joined the obsessive organization.) And both men advocated a strong military and an assertive foreign policy to thwart the advance of communism, including the war in Vietnam.[3]

But Masland and Goldwater differed in the particulars of their environmental perspectives. Goldwater was a wise-use conservationist in the tradition of Gifford Pinchot and came to environmentalism as it crested in the late 1960s and early '70s. Masland admired the preservationist outlook of John Muir and was at the forefront of the midcentury preservationist movement. Goldwater supported the construction of multipurpose dams on the Colorado and other western rivers for the economic benefits they would bring to the region. Masland opposed dams on those rivers, especially if they intruded upon a national park or monument. Goldwater opposed the Wilderness Act;

Masland favored it. Goldwater supported a private effort to build a cathedral on the South Rim of Grand Canyon National Park. Masland opposed it as an unnecessary intrusion, asserting that God could be experienced within the walls of the canyon instead of inside the walls of a church.[4]

Both conservatives tried to serve two masters: nature and their constituencies. Goldwater's constituents were the residents of Arizona. Masland's were the associates and stockholders of Masland and Sons. As an elected official representing water-starved Arizona, Goldwater had a responsibility to support popular causes like multipurpose dams and democratic access to national parks, monuments, and forests. Masland believed he had a responsibility to company stakeholders to oppose what he regarded as the drift toward a federally managed economy and overly stringent federal regulation of automobile emissions and sales. Drake points out that after the significant conservation achievements of the Nixon administration, Goldwater's conflicted "commitment to federally centered environmentalism would often founder on the rocks of his conservatism."[5] Masland, too, was conflicted about many aspects of environmentalism, especially regulations relating to industrial pollution, but he steered a steadier course toward the preservation of public lands and nature. Goldwater, for example, approved of Interior Secretary James Watt's efforts in the early 1980s to open more public lands in the West to development, while Masland condemned Watt's assault on the public lands and national parks.

Politically, Masland was further to the right than Goldwater, especially when it came to social issues and the threat of communism, whether internal or external. Masland, for example, joined the paranoid John Birch Society, as noted above, while Goldwater did not, though he sympathized with their policies. The senator also was more tolerant of conspicuous consumption, alcohol abuse, divorce, homosexuality, and sexual liberation than Masland was. Indeed, Masland's far right views have damaged his reputation as a conservationist.

At the local level, Masland used his influence as a business executive and official with the Pennsylvania Manufacturers' Association to support conservative political candidates. In the early 1950s, Pennsylvania's traditionally dominant Republican Party was wracked by division between moderates and conservatives. Heavily influenced by Sun Oil, the Pennsylvania Railroad Company, and the Pennsylvania Manufacturers' Association, the conservative wing of the party carried great political weight, including the governorship. In

Cumberland County, middle-of-the road Republicans were led by Cumberland County commissioner Oliver Dickey and conservatives by the so-called Wade-Masland faction (George Wade was a state senator). In addition to county elective offices like commissioner, treasurer, district attorney, sheriff, and coroner, patronage jobs were at stake. Masland downplayed the rift in the party as inconsequential until George Leader captured the governorship, the first time a Democrat had occupied that office since 1934. That sobering result caused Republicans, including Masland, to put aside their differences. Having gained a foothold, however, Democrats became a competitive party in the state in the following decades.[6]

As a Dickinson College trustee, Masland played conservative politics to the hilt. Taking seriously his duty to promote the best interests of the college, he formed a close relationship with President William Edel and became increasingly involved in campus policies. Masland recommended Edel, a former classmate and fraternity brother, for the college presidency, a role in which he served from 1946 until 1959. Masland was appointed vice president of the board of trustees in 1954. "During the Edel years," he wrote, "I spent a goodly portion of my time in the president's office. We were in frequent consultation. I gave of my time and, to the extent that I could, of my finances." He helped bring notable guest speakers to the college, among them Interior Secretary Douglas McKay and US Attorney General Herbert Brownell Jr.; instituted an annual award for a prominent scientist to honor Joseph Priestley, the discoverer of oxygen, and an Edel award for a major artist; and spearheaded a campaign to establish a monument in memory of Noah Pinkney, a "former slave and Christian gentleman who for more than forty years sold pretzels and gave lavishly of friendship at East Gate," as Masland put it. When the Allison Methodist Church burned down, Masland persuaded the board of trustees to authorize a loan of $200,000 for the rebuilding project. Less charitably, and impelled by his obsession with combatting communism, he also engineered a campaign to dismiss a faculty member.[7]

The story of Laurent R. LaVallee is a shameful chapter in Masland's life story. Born in Worcester, Massachusetts, LaVallee received an undergraduate degree from the University of Colorado and a PhD from Syracuse University. In 1953 he was hired as an assistant professor of economics at Dickinson College. In 1955, former Communist Party member Herbert Fuchs, in testimony before Joe McCarthy's House Un-American Activities Committee (HUAC), identified LaVallee as a fellow member of a party cell while they worked for the National War Labor Board from 1942 to 1944. HUAC subsequently subpoenaed LaVallee to testify. When he learned of the subpoena, President Edel asked LaVallee if he had been a Communist Party member; LaVallee said no. He also stated that he would invoke his Fifth Amendment right against self-incrimination before HUAC because he did not wish to be an informant. Edel was opposed to that approach and told LaVallee that if he cooperated with HUAC he would keep his job. When LaVallee refused, Edel informed fellow Pennsylvanian Francis Walter, the chair of HUAC. As planned, LaVallee pled the Fifth more than fifty times in his testimony before HUAC on March 1, 1956.[8]

Upon returning to Carlisle, Edel, after conferring with Masland, informed LaVallee that he had enough grounds to suspend him from teaching if he failed to respond to questions relating to communism. When LaVallee refused to provide satisfactory answers, Edel suspended him with pay, pending approval by the board of trustees. LaVallee's "answers to my questions on the aims of Communism," Edel later explained, "raised in my mind grave doubts whether any man with so unrealistic an understanding of the present international situation should be teaching on any college faculty." With Masland, in effect, manipulating the trustees, LaVallee's suspension was assured.[9]

Students and faculty, the American Civil Liberties Union, and the American Association of University Professors protested the arbitrary action. Insisting that LaVallee be reinstated, students displayed signs reading, "If Dickinson teaches democracy, why doesn't it practice democracy?" and "If 'no person shall be forced to testify against himself,' what did LaVallee do wrong?" In less than twenty-four hours, students presented a petition with 370 signatures protesting the unfairness of LaVallee's suspension. And the student senate approved a resolution reading, "The Student Senate feels that Dr. LaVallee should be reinstated until proved incompetent, for his absence is detrimental to the academic good of the economics department and the students thus affected."[10]

At a special meeting, the faculty took similar action, pointing out that LaVallee should be suspended solely for a lack of teaching competence and only by the board of trustees, not the college president. It called for a separate faculty session to evaluate LaVallee's teaching ability and demanded to be represented at the trustees' executive committee hearing.[11]

Edel provided the faculty with several reasons for suspending LaVallee. First, in refusing to answer HUAC's questions, he had challenged the integrity of a congressional committee. Second, he had failed to acknowledge knowing Fuchs. Third, he refused to identify documents presented to him by HUAC. Fourth, he would not sign a pledge declaring that he was not a communist. Finally, he refused to acknowledge the Communist Party as a conspiracy. LaVallee informed his colleagues that he was not a communist but had briefly known Fuchs during World War II. He did not sign an anticommunist oath on the advice of counsel and refused the committee's request to identify certain papers because he assumed they were communist documents. He had declined to answer the question of whether communism was a conspiracy because it was a "when did you stop beating your wife" inquiry that had no correct reply. And he conceded that he lacked respect for HUAC because he considered it "oppressive and dangerous to public welfare." Given the lack of evidence regarding his performance as a teacher, the faculty requested LaVallee's reinstatement.[12]

Headed by Masland, the executive committee of the board of trustees met in Harrisburg in mid-April. In a private letter, Masland left little doubt about the outcome. He informed Marston that LaVallee had been identified as a communist and that he was defended by a New York attorney and had the backing of the American Association of University Professors and Dickinson faculty members. "This trial is a matter of vital importance, not only to Dickinson College but to all educational institutions. It involves fundamental principles," he told Marston. Unfortunately, those principles did not include teaching competence or fairness. As for LaVallee's refusal to testify, Masland said, "I don't believe anyone should run out of any situation that involves the most serious threat with which we are faced—Communism."[13]

The behind-closed-doors meeting was attended by lawyers representing the college and LaVallee and a representative of the students and one of the faculty. Given his friendship with Edel and his disdain for communism, unions, and liberal views, Masland should have recused himself as chair of the executive committee; instead, the committee served as LaVallee's jury and its chair, Masland, as the judge. The Faculty Committee on Academic Freedom and Tenure said LaVallee's teaching competency had never been questioned and recommended his reinstatement. And HUAC had refused to bring any charges against him. But the outcome was never in doubt. The executive committee voted not only to sustain LaVallee's suspension but to terminate his contract at the end of June.[14]

LaVallee appealed the committee's decision to the full board of trustees. Chaired by Masland and attended by more than thirty trustees, the meeting took place at Kings Gap in early June. The Faculty Committee on Academic Freedom and Tenure again recommended that LaVallee be reinstated and that his contract be renewed for another year. The administration, it stated, had failed to demonstrate that LaVallee was an incompetent teacher. Furthermore, there was no evidence that he tried to indoctrinate students with communist views. The full board nonetheless voted unanimously to endorse a resolution prepared and introduced by Masland terminating LaVallee's contract as of June 30, 1956. "Our world today is sharply divided in a war between those who defend human freedom and those who would extinguish it," it began. More than a quarter century of history has shown, it continued, that it was the relentless goal of monolithic communism to topple the governments of the free world. Indoctrinated communists used freedom against itself by entering the laboratory or classroom to subvert the education system. Consequently, the trustees of Dickinson College "record their unswerving opposition to the employment or retention in any position of trust, of Communists or Communist sympathizers." LaVallee ripped the decision publicly, pointing out that the trustees had turned aside a faculty recommendation that he be rehired and had terminated him for invoking his right under the Fifth Amendment of the US Constitution.[15]

It is probable that LaVallee was a member of a Communist Party cell during the mid-1940s, as were scores of other idealistic Americans during a time when the Soviet Union was an American wartime ally. The alliance came apart after the war, and much of the nation was swept up in the anticommunist sentiment known as McCarthyism during the Cold War. In fairness, it should be acknowledged that concerns about Soviet espionage and theft of technology during the war and its aftermath had some rational basis.

Masland was not alone in his attempts to liberate college classrooms from suspected communist teachers. Young conservative Yale graduate William F. Buckley Jr. published *God and Man at Yale* in 1951, arguing that the college's many atheistic, communist faculty members should be fired. He followed that volume three years later with a ringing defense of McCarthy in *McCarthy and His Enemies*. Although the intensity of McCarthyism was subsiding by mid-decade, conservatives like Buckley, Goldwater, and Masland continued to defend Joseph McCarthy and to lash out against the indoctrination of youth by leftist faculty members. Buckley once stated that he would rather leave the fate of the Republic in the hands of the first few hundred people listed in the Boston telephone directory than with the Harvard faculty.[16] Masland and Edel, using an unfair administrative process and an uncritical public press, orchestrated LaVallee's ouster and ruined his teaching career, consequently earning the long-lasting disdain of the Dickinson faculty. While neighboring Lycoming College in 1957 and Lebanon Valley College in 1959 presented Masland with honorary doctoral degrees, Dickinson College never did. In his obsession with anticommunism, Masland's disservice to LaVallee and to the principle of fairness was simply unjustifiable.

Masland expressed no misgivings concerning his Rasputin-like role in removing someone he considered a former and perhaps contemporary communist tool at his alma mater. Indeed, after firing LaVallee, Masland suggested to Edel that the political science department was overloaded with liberal Democrats and needed an infusion of conservatives. He also believed that the national government would soon be controlled by socialists if Republicans failed to win the White House in the 1956 presidential election. "The AF of L–CIO has got this country organized, precinct by precinct, from one end to the other," he groused to Marston. Unless the Republican Party became better organized, the United States would have a "Labor government" run by Walter Reuther, "who is a left-wing Socialist."[17]

Masland's preoccupation with the threat of communism led to another controversial episode in his career: his membership in the John Birch Society. Named for a US Army special forces operative and Baptist missionary who was captured and killed by Chinese Communists shortly after World War II, the society was founded in Indianapolis in December 1958. The founders included Robert W. Welch Jr., a sixty-year-old multimillionaire candy maker from Belmont, Massachusetts; oil-refining tycoon Fred Koch of Wichita, Kansas; Robert Stoddard, president of Wyman-Gordon Industries of Worcester, Massachusetts; and other wealthy white men. Masland became a charter member.[18]

Impressed by Welch—a fellow National Association of Manufacturers member—and his anticommunist message, Masland invited him to speak at Dickinson in 1957, a year after he had enraged the faculty for spearheading the drive to fire LaVallee. Welch provided the names of conservative economists who could replace the purged LaVallee. Later the same year, at Welch's request, Masland joined the John Birch Society's council as an adviser and annual $500 contributor.[19]

Welch directed policy, using the council mainly to show the public that men of substance and standing shared his anticommunist outlook. He published the core beliefs of the John Birch Society in the organization's *Blue Book* and reported on achievements, goals, and policies in the monthly magazine *American Opinion*. Organized nationwide in small chapters, Americanists, as members called themselves, paid dues and received literature published by Welch. They also wrote articles and editorials and made speeches reflecting the society's anticommunist and ultranationalistic viewpoints. Membership lists were secret, but their numbers were estimated to total between sixty and a hundred thousand in 1960.

Because he believed that communists had made major strides in the suppression of religion and freedom, Welch contended that Americanists were the last line of defense in the protection of liberty. The society's positions became increasingly extreme. It considered the fluoridation of water for the purpose of preventing tooth decay as government overreach that could be used by evildoers to poison or mentally derange unsuspecting citizens. It urged US withdrawal from the United Nations, which it saw as a communist front organization determined to establish a socialistic, one-world order. It advocated the impeachment of Chief Justice Earl Warren for his ultraliberal US Supreme Court decisions. The communist conspiracy, Welch maintained, included state and national government officials, labor and teachers' unions, supporters of welfare, and civil rights activists. Eventually, he even claimed that the conspiracy included former president Dwight Eisenhower, his brother, Milton, Secretary of State John Foster Dulles, and CIA director Allen Dulles. As much as Masland shared Welch's rabid anticommunism, the latter's characterization of Eisenhower as a closet communist was a bridge too far, and he regretted the public ridicule that followed.[20]

The mainstream media, and even other conservative organizations, began to portray the so-called Americanists as crackpots and lunatics. In 1961 folk singer Pete Seeger mocked the organization with a song he titled "The Jack Ash Society." Welch characterized himself as an ordinary guy "with one wife, two sons, a Golden Retriever dog and 14 golf clubs." He did not understand any of them, he said, but loved them all. In a speech to Alpha Chi Rho, his former fraternity at Dickinson College, Masland downplayed the extremism of the organization and touted Welch's ability and devotion to the cause of individual liberty, describing him to Mary Abbott as "one of the most honest, dedicated, courageous, unselfish persons I know. Also, one of the most brilliant."[21]

Masland was only slightly less extreme than Welch in his views. He never accused anyone of being a communist, he told Marston, unless they had been identified by FBI director J. Edgar Hoover. Of course, Hoover had an exceedingly loose definition of communism. Regarding charges that the Society was antisemitic Masland offered a non-denial denial, pointing out that textile importer Alfred Kohlberg was a founder and council member and journalist Willie Schlamm was a principal editorial writer for the organization's publications. Like nativists in the mid-nineteenth and early twentieth centuries, Welch and Masland had a fear of European immigrants and New York City lawyers. But Masland's xenophobia bordered on virulence. "Long ago I concluded that nothing good ever comes to America out of European's mass migrations. Whenever the spillway opens the scum flows through. I do not know of any of their refugees since World War Two who lived up to their obligations, who gave evidence of any real sense of responsibility or of appreciation," Masland fumed to Abbott. "Sooner or later, they gather together in a group, working, saving, joining a union, embracing a racket and ultimately voting for a Stevenson or a Kennedy."[22]

While never directly expressing anti-Semitic sentiments, Masland, like many white Anglo-Saxon Protestants of his generation, rarely associated with Jews and seemed indifferent toward them as an oppressed minority. Despite his rabid anticommunist views, Masland did not see Israel as an ally deserving of American protection from Soviet aggression. He resented the pro-union, liberal political views of most Jews, was upset when his college fraternity began admitting non-Christians, and wondered why virtually all doctors offering advice on national television were Jewish.[23]

Uncomfortable being associated any longer with the notorious right-wing fringe group, largely because it would undermine his credibility as a nature preservationist and endanger his membership in exclusive social groups like the Cosmos Club, Masland resigned from the John Birch Society in May 1962. The pressure of other responsibilities, especially in the field of conservation, prompted his resignation, he told Welch. His antigovernment and anticommunist views were not in question, he said, but the preservation of natural wonders was in many ways "as important as the battle against Communism or Socialism for unless we preserve our God-given resources we are without anything worth defending, either militarily or in the cold war."[24] He would spend the next two decades working in a federal bureaucracy that had been established to protect the most majestic of those God-given resources.

CHAPTER 6

The National Park Service

Masland's passion for unspoiled backcountry, wild rivers, and the national parks led to an unpaid job with the National Park Service. In August 1956, a few months before stepping down as interior secretary to run for the US Senate, Douglas McKay appointed him to the Advisory Board of the National Park Service. It was the only federal agency, Masland once wrote, with which he wished to be associated, and he regarded his term on the board as "the best six years of my life."[1]

Composed mainly of acclaimed scientists, historians, literary figures, and naturalists, the unpaid eleven-member Advisory Board on National Parks, Historic Sites, Buildings, and Monuments was established in 1935 to monitor conditions in existing national parks, evaluate potential additions, and counsel the secretary of the interior on all matters relating to units in the system. Its workload and significance depended upon the interior secretary's use of it.

In 1950 Congress increased members' term of service from four to six years. Every other year, two new appointees replaced two outgoing ones. Appointed by the interior secretary and instrumental in its influence on the National Park Service, the board met twice yearly, usually once at a national park and once in or near Washington, DC. Prior to the Nixon presidency, members were politically nonpartisan. One of only two members from industry when he was appointed in 1956, Masland served as chair of the Advisory Board from July 1959 through June 1962. When his six-year term expired, he was named to the newly created National Park Service Advisory Council, a select group of ex-Advisory Board members who participated in meetings, made reconnaissance trips to the parks, and counseled the Park Service director and interior secretary on a variety of issues. In all, he served more than thirty years on the board and the council. Under a sympathetic interior secretary and in the years before legislation solicited input on environmental issues from citizen activists, the two groups had an outsized influence on decisions regarding the national parks.[2]

Since they would be working closely with the Park Service, board appointees were usually cleared with the director. Assistant Secretary of the Interior Wesley D'Ewart informed Director Conrad Wirth that McKay wanted Masland appointed to the board. Additionally, the Park Service's chief naturalist, John Doerr, who had accompanied Masland on a Nevills rafting trip, wrote a glowing letter of recommendation. Masland, Doerr wrote, was a successful and amiable business executive with a keen interest in the national parks, the welfare of southwestern Indigenous people, and the protection of chunks of primeval desert country in the American Southwest and other "out-of-the-way places." In mid-May 1956 the Interior Department announced Masland's appointment.[3]

In the late 1950s and '60s, the Advisory Board provided an elite pathway by which problems relating to existing parks and monuments, and potential scenic and wilderness additions to the system, could be brought to the attention of the NPS and Interior Department. Masland capitalized on his insider's opportunity but understood that the effectiveness of the Advisory Board depended on the receptiveness of the Park Service director and secretary of the interior. As historian Samuel Hays has observed, the board's recommendations were listened to in conservation-friendly administrations but ignored in unsympathetic ones. Secretary of the Interior Fred Seaton, McKay's successor (1956–60), held the board at arm's length, while Stewart Udall (1961–69) embraced it.[4]

Occasionally, members of Congress influenced selections to the Advisory Board. In 1958, Senator Barry Goldwater gave his blessing to the appointment of Arizonan Ned Danson. And Senator Arthur Watkins pushed hard for the selection of a member from the intermountain states. Furious over the removal of the Echo Park dam from the Colorado River Storage Project, Watkins believed the Advisory Board was composed of national park and wilderness purists who sought to "fence off" the arid West. Why not appoint a "desert rat" who favored both scenery and irrigable water? It appeared, he scowled, "that the views of us arid Westerners who contribute the bulk of the vast domain ruled by the Interior, do not count very much when it comes to the advisory counsel [*sic*]." They were, in fact, "crown colonies which must be content with absentee landlordism." He attached to his letter a scathing *Salt Lake Tribune* editorial titled "Why No Westerner?" and signed off sarcastically as "one of your subjects, who can claim sovereign right to only 30 percent of our State's land surface." Shortly after receiving this rebuke, Secretary Seaton named Harold Fabian to the Advisory Board. Head of the Utah State Parks system, Fabian proved to be less amenable to public resource development than Watkins anticipated, and Utahans and other westerners would anguish over the fencing off of public land and resources for the next sixty years.[5]

In 1956 Masland and Fred Smith, an insurance executive and trusted adviser to multimillionaire conservationist Laurance Rockefeller, joined the Advisory Board, replacing noted publisher Alfred A. Knopf and Charles Woodbury, a horticulturist and member of the Wilderness Society executive council. Other members of the board included John Oakes, head of the *New York Times* editorial page; Ulysses S. Grant III, an officer with the US Corps of Engineers who opposed the Echo Park dam; and Horace Albright, former director of the NPS. The addition of Masland and Smith indicated that business executives and their perspective mattered. Fabian would join the board two years later in 1958.[6]

A spirit of comradeship, trust, and political nonpartisanship prevailed among board members and the Park Service. Over the years, Masland gained the trust and respect of NPS directors Conrad Wirth, George Hartzog, and Russell Dickenson. And he developed warm relationships with fellow board members Fred Smith, Horace Albright, historical cartographer Carl Wheat, archaeologists Edward Danson, J. O. Brew, and Emil Haury, noted nature writer Sigurd Olson, and Marian Sulzberger Heiskell. Heiskell, the daughter of *New York Times* publisher Arthur Hays Sulzberger and wife of Andrew Heiskell, chair of Time Inc., became the first female board member. A Jewish Democrat and a director of the New York Times Company, she and Masland shared a love of nature and became friends and frequent correspondents. He offered her suggestions for conservation-related features in the *New York Times*, and she occasionally followed through. Although Masland despised most liberal publications, he abided the *New York Times* because its preservationist stance usually mirrored his own.[7]

In *America's National Parks and Their Keepers,* historian Ronald Foresta downplays the role of the Advisory Board, characterizing its members as prestigious frontmen who pandered to the will of the Park Service. It occasionally differed with the NPS on park issues, he concedes, but "was more often a source of support than advice for the agency." In the 1950s, as Foresta notes, the board acted mainly in a supportive role, but in the following decade, during Stewart Udall's stint as interior secretary, it functioned as a key source of advice. Udall, Park Service directors, and Congress all sought and valued the counsel of the board. In their memoirs, Park Service directors Conrad Wirth, George Hartzog, and Gary Everhardt all claimed that the board's recommendations were invaluable. Composed of private citizens eminent in fields related to the parks, the board, Everhart wrote, "is perhaps the most important link in providing the public with an opportunity to contribute to the formation of national policy . . . and serves as a kind of board of directors, advising the Secretary of the Interior on all matters affecting the parks." True, the board was supportive of the secretary's policies, but only after its voice had been heard through internal, private discourse.[8]

Board members also possessed intangible influence with policymakers and the public. Knopf headed one of the most prestigious publishing houses in America and printed books favorable to conservation causes. Oakes served the cause as editor of the *New York Times,* as did Melville Grosvenor, president of the National Geographic Society and editor of its magazine, and prizewinning authors Bernard DeVoto and Wallace Stegner. Additionally, board member Fred Smith had the ear of Laurance Rockefeller, who used his wealth and influence to benefit a variety of national park endeavors.

Moreover, board members were in periodic contact with the leaders of congressional committees and subcommittees with jurisdiction over the parks. Wayne Aspinall, the powerful Democratic chair of the House Interior and Insular Affairs Committee, valued the opinions of the Advisory Board. According to Hartzog, Aspinall would not act on park legislation until he received the recommendations of the board. Masland's correspondence with fellow members reveals a board that took its responsibility seriously, engaged in thorough and sometimes heated internal discussions, refrained from partisan political discourse, and possessed the credentials to be taken seriously by Aspinall and other members of Congress.[9]

A wise-use conservationist from western Colorado, Aspinall became chair of the Interior Committee in 1959 and was the nemesis of preservationists because he opposed locking up natural resources and supported the federal construction of hydroelectric dams on western rivers. He was a diminutive man in physical stature and often small-minded in terms of the seniority system and congressional prerogatives. He ran his committee with an iron fist; preservationists had to deal with him gingerly because he was touchy, and his committee held life-or-death control over legislation relating to the national parks and wilderness. Without his cooperation, environmental legislation invariably suffered a slow death. Fortunately, environmentalists had an ally in John Saylor, the equally autocratic, blustering minority leader of the House Interior Committee, who had strong ties to the Sierra Club and Wilderness Society. Aspinall respected Saylor and the input from experts on the Advisory Board, which generally resulted in bipartisan compromise legislation.[10]

Masland first met his associates during an Advisory Board excursion to Virgin Islands National Park in December 1956. Established on the island of St. John the previous August, the new park consisted of eleven thousand pristine acres of stunning Caribbean beauty donated to the American public by philanthropist Laurance Rockefeller. "The Board consists of diverse, interesting and friendly personalities, all of whom possess unusual capacity and all of whom are genuinely interested in Park and Conservation projects," Masland reported to Park Service director Wirth. He also was impressed with the commitment of the Park Service staff. "There is no group with which I am acquainted in government services as dedicated as those in the National Park Service," he added. Before leaving the Caribbean, the board toured the islands of St. Croix, St. Thomas, and Puerto Rico, where Masland could not resist an invitation to ramble through a jungle.[11]

At its business meeting, the board officially opposed a proposal to build a spacious nondenominational church on the South Rim of the Grand Canyon. Funded by contributions from private citizens, the so-called Shrine of the Ages Chapel project was endorsed by Wirth. The Advisory Board, however, bashed the proposed structure as "Hollywoodish" and passed a resolution, co-written by Masland, opposing it as an artificial and unnecessary intrusion into the park. Objections from the board and preservationists nationwide prompted Wirth and other supporters to change course, eventually building a less ornate chapel in Grand Canyon Village outside park boundaries.[12]

In addition to the Shrine of the Ages Chapel, Wirth authorized, but did not endorse, a student-initiated program to provide nondenominational summer religious services to park visitors. Established in 1953, a group called A Christian Ministry in the National Parks recruited seminary students from various faiths to provide sermons, Bible study, and other religious services. Student ministers were paid by working for park concessionaires during the week as clerks, bellhops, cooks, and in other menial jobs. In a decade of religious awakening, especially among Protestants, the program rather casually won support from the Park Service and from conservationists like Horace Albright, David Brower, Howard Zahniser, and Frank Masland.[13]

The Shrine of the Ages Chapel and A Christian Ministry were tangential to Wirth's more ambitious plan to improve the experience of park visitors. Articles in popular magazines like *Harper's* and *Reader's Digest* berated Congress and the Park Service for permitting roads, campgrounds, and visitor centers to fall into disrepair. A year before Masland joined, the Advisory Board received a grant from the Paul Mellon Foundation and hired a research firm to survey park visitors. The survey showed that visitors were chiefly professional, business, and management workers who possessed little knowledge of the parks. The solution, the board concluded, was to make the parks more attractive to blue-collar wage earners through publicity and improved amenities.[14]

In response to public criticism, Wirth proposed a massive facelift for the parks, endorsed by the Advisory Board. "Mission 66" called for generous annual congressional appropriations for infrastructure improvements in time for the Park Service's fiftieth anniversary in 1966. With park visitation surging from 20.9 million in 1946 to 48.8 million in 1955, the proposal had widespread public appeal, prompting Congress over the next decade to lavish money on the NPS for roads, parking areas, scenic pullouts, trails, camping and picnic areas, visitor centers, comfort stations, power and sewer installations, staff housing units, and maintenance buildings. In addition, concessionaires upgraded their lodges, restaurants, and other facilities. Wirth pegged the cost of the ten-year program at $787 million, but an accommodating Congress appropriated slightly more than $1 billion. "Congress," the program's historian has written, "had rediscovered the national parks."[15]

Wirth was pleased with the public reception of the program, but many preservationists had reservations. Mission 66 stated as one of its goals the preservation of park biota and wilderness by concentrating tourists and facilities within specific park enclaves. But some park purists, among them Devereux Butcher, Olaus Murie, David Brower, Joseph Wood Krutch, and Ansel Adams, ripped the program for being overly accommodating to tourists, promising too many roads, comforts, and conveniences. Masland sympathized with that view but supported Mission 66 because it brought public support, congressional funding, and new energy to the Park Service. He also understood the inherent tension between the twin NPS goals of providing public enjoyment and protecting natural habitat. He preferred that the national parks serve as nature museums rather than adult playlands. But pragmatism carried the day.

Masland, however, was troubled by the growing divisiveness within the conservation community. Conservation organizations had united to block the construction of the Echo Park dam, but cracks were appearing in that coalition. As a member of the Advisory Board and the Council of Conservationists, he believed that preservationists had an opportunity to make significant additions and improvements to the national park system, including a potential Navajo National Park, if they worked together. The failure of conservation groups to unify behind causes and their pursuit, instead of their specialized agendas, was a lifelong Masland grievance.

He was especially upset when Fred Smith, the director of the Council of Conservationists, a key lobbying group, removed Joe Penfold, Zahniser, and Brower, three ardent park purists, from the executive board. Smith characterized Brower as a "crackpot" who would "sell his grandmother down the river if he thought it would advance his position"—and the only issue Zahniser really cared about was the proposed wilderness bill. But Masland was impressed with Brower, who had been named the Sierra Club's first full-time executive director in 1953. "Dave Brower is a young, intelligent, energetic, consecrated, likeable chap who in the years ahead can do much for the cause of conservation if he will learn the value of moderation and cooperation," he informed Dock Marston. But if Brower and other conservation leaders failed to work in harmony with one another and with the Advisory Board, "the forces of exploitation will win the battle." Fed up with Brower's aggressiveness and budget-breaking leadership, the Sierra Club's executive board eventually replaced him as executive director in the late 1960s. Masland also turned against Brower in the 1970s, accusing him of being a radical environmentalist.[16]

The rift among conservationists in the late 1950s foreshadowed wider divisions in the decades to come. Some activists emphasized the wise use of and equitable access to national resources; others stressed the preservation of wild and scenic public lands; still others, particularly in the decades to come, championed federal regulations to protect the biosphere. At various times in the twentieth century, one viewpoint prevailed over the others.

Virtually all conservationists paid lip service to each of these positions but invariably preferred one over another. At heart, Masland was a preservationist and made his mark as one.

Despite Masland's desire for harmony, criticism of Mission 66 persisted. In a front-page editorial in the *National Wildlands News*, Devereux Butcher slammed the Advisory Board for not being "fully alert" to "the resort development trend of Mission 66. . . . Over the last decade, the Park Service, to an alarming degree, has evolved into an organization to provide public amusement. Surely the Board knows the very purpose of the national parks is being defeated because of this." To soften the criticism, Butcher credited the board with advocating the establishment of a fifteen-thousand-acre Chesapeake and Ohio National Park astride the Potomac River, an Ozark Rivers National Monument, and a barrier dam for Rainbow Bridge. He also conceded that the board was not "a rubber stamp" for the Park Service and that its members were dedicated to the principle of park integrity. Though he pulled his punches, Butcher's criticism hurt. Masland alerted Conrad Wirth to the piece, but Wirth considered Butcher overly zealous in defense of park purity. "He is just about impossible," he told Masland. "As a matter of fact, Frank, I don't even read his paper so he can't get my blood pressure up too much." Masland would eventually conclude that the emphasis on catering to visitors had ruined the Grand Canyon, the Everglades, and several other parks. But in the 1950s he supported most of the Mission 66 program.[17]

As support for wilderness preservation grew, so did criticism of the road-building activity of Mission 66. Modern roads were constructed to Flamingo Bay in Everglades National Park and to the quarry site at Dinosaur National Monument. Over the heated objections of Brower, Adams, and other Sierra Club members, the Park Service widened and modernized the narrow dirt section of the Tioga Road to Lake Tenaya in Yosemite National Park. Roads also were planned for the Navajo reservation. In all, the Park Service constructed or modernized twenty-seven hundred miles of roads under the Mission 66 program, dramatically increasing public access to wilderness backcountry. "The unexpected impact of greater access to park backcountry provided additional ammunition for critics of Mission 66," writes Richard West Sellars in *Preserving Nature in the National Parks*. Roads to the Navajo Nation proved a double-edged sword. They increased access for tourists, but they also made it easier for the Diné to sell their wares to buyers off the reservation.[18]

While the Mission 66 program drew the ire of many wilderness preservationists, Masland, Wirth, Albright, and Olson understood that political trade-offs were necessary as part of the double mandate to promote access and preserve park integrity. Sellars notes that prior to the Wilderness Act of 1964, "preservation efforts that were not accompanied by development for public use were vulnerable and likely to fail." The accommodation of tourists, Sellars observes, "provided utilitarian grounds for preservation. It served as a defense against massive intrusions such as dams and reservoirs and as a means for keeping visitors in designated areas, thereby protecting undeveloped country. National Park development was locked with preservation in a state of perpetual tension—both supportive and antagonistic."[19] Park preservationists like Masland understood the need for such a political trade-off to gain congressional appropriations for more acquisitions to the national park system. At the same time, however, he believed that roadbuilding could be overdone and that if the natural landscape, flora, and fauna were not protected, the parks would not be worth visiting.

The iconic and iconoclastic nature writer Edward Abbey was not inclined to compromise on roads in the national parks or any other subject. An independent, quirky contrarian, Abbey promoted wilderness preservation in his eloquent books and essays rather than work with mainstream conservation organizations prone to compromise. In *Desert Solitaire,* his classic account of serving as a ranger at Arches National Park in the late 1950s, he tore into the Mission 66 road-building program. Dirt roads and hiking trails were sufficient for most park visitors, he argued in a chapter titled "Polemic: Industrial Tourism and the National Parks." But at Arches, paved roads brought hordes of motorized visitors, comfort stations with electric lights and flush toilets, and herds of aluminum-sided campers and house trailers.[20]

Abbey noted that the Park Service's dual mission produced conflict between developers who emphasized public enjoyment and preservationists who stressed leaving the parks unimpaired. The key issue, he understood, was accessibility. The developers catered to the "indolent millions born on wheels and suckled on gasoline" and the avaricious tourist industry—filling stations; oil companies; automobile, camper, and motorboat dealerships; road-building and heavy equipment suppliers; motels; restaurants; and roadside stands. "The Developers insist that the parks must be fully accessible not only to people but also to their machines, that is, automobiles, motorboats, etc. The Preservers argue, in principle at least, that wilderness and motors are incompatible and that the former can best be experienced, understood, and enjoyed when the machines are left behind."[21] Abbey left no doubt that he sided with the preservationists. And so did Masland, at least privately.

Outwardly, Abbey and Masland appeared to have little in common. Abbey was raised by struggling working-class parents in a nonreligious household; his father was a socialist. He was not an atheist, he said, but rather an "earthiest." Nor did Masland and Abbey share a similar personality or code of moral behavior. Abbey's persona was outsized, spontaneous; Masland's was reserved, measured. Masland's conduct was straitlaced and dignified, Abbey's bohemian and free-spirited—he was an irreverent, hard-drinking womanizer who used crude language, had been married five times, and was often an absent parent. Like Masland, Abbey drove a Cadillac, but he referred to his flashy '75 convertible as a "Pimpmobile," a description Masland would not have appreciated. Both men were veterans, but Abbey disliked the military and opposed American involvement in the Vietnam War. Masland supported the development of a nuclear arsenal as a deterrent to Soviet power. Abbey opposed the development of nuclear weapons because, he quipped, "they take all the fun out of war."[22]

But in other ways the Pennsylvania-born men were kindred spirits. Both called Appalachia home—Abbey was from the Allegheny Hills of Indiana County in western Pennsylvania. Both men drew inspiration from Appalachia's green hills, dense woods, meandering streams, fertile farms, and weather-battered barns and silos. Both loved to plant trees and lamented the rapid disappearance of small farms. Each preferred village to urban life. They were both adventurous and comfortable in raw nature, and both were ardent anti-statists. Abbey disdained socialism, liberalism, capitalism, and unrestrained industrial growth. "Growth for the sake of growth," he once wrote, "is the ideology of the cancer cell." Abbey described himself variously as an agrarian anarchist, a nonviolent anarchist, and a libertarian, advocating decentralized power, maximum individual freedom, and pure democracy. He decried the unchecked growth of the American Southwest, especially Arizona, and so did Masland. Both men were against more dams on the Colorado River and disparaged the Bureau of Reclamation as a demonic federal bureaucracy obsessed with building dams. Neither was a misogynist, but neither supported women's liberation. Both Abbey and Masland were strident defenders of gun rights, fearing, as Abbey put it, that "if the government outlawed guns, only the government would have guns. . . . Only the government and a few outlaws"—like himself. Masland and Abbey were also avid opponents of immigration, especially of undocumented workers from Mexico and other Hispanic countries. They insisted that the influx of immigrants contributed to the growing problem of overpopulation and the dilution of America's western European cultural and political heritage. Perhaps facetiously, Abbey advocated using the US military to halt illegal immigrants at the border, supplying them with weapons, and sending them back to their homeland to fight their oppressors.[23]

Despite being fervently antigovernment, both men believed that federal authority was necessary to preserve wilderness and national scenic treasures. Masland shared Abbey's "basic assumption that wilderness is a necessary part of civilization and that it is the primary responsibility of the National Park Service to preserve *intact and undiminished what little still remains*." Wilderness was also vital, Abbey wrote, because humans were wild animals. "Every man needs a place where he can go crazy in peace." Both admired the Navajo people. Both worked for the federal bureaucracy they criticized. Abbey served as a ranger at Arches, Everglades, Canyonlands, and numerous other national parks and monuments. Masland dedicated half his life to the Park Service. Both were nature lovers and held national park personnel in high regard. Both had a reverence for the desert and canyon country of the American Southwest. Like Masland, Abbey had taken a two-week river trip on the Colorado River through Glen Canyon in 1959; his biographer James M. Cahalan characterized it as "one of the most formative experiences of his life."[24]

Masland admired Abbey as a nature writer even after his promotion of ecoterrorism in the 1975 novel *The Monkey Wrench Gang*. Responding to a fan letter from Masland via postcard, Abbey wrote, "Much thanks for the great letter! You were so lucky to see so much of the SW before the developers and goddamn dam builders overran it. Tell me more about that arch on Cummings Mesa. And I'm glad you like my books."[25] The two nature lovers doubtless would have made compatible and mutually fascinating river-running companions.

Masland also recommended curbing recreational activities in national parks, including "tote-goats" (ATVs) and motorboats. Although he had twice roared through the Grand Canyon on a motorboat himself, and his friends Dock Marston and Bill Belknap continued to do so, his suggested ban on motorboating and ATVs demonstrates both hypocrisy and a growing antipathy toward equitable access to the parks. Although his numerous suggestions met with limited success, he plugged away at his duties with the Advisory Board, visiting various national parks, monuments, and historic sites, evaluating potential additions to the park system, and attending meetings. "I have never enjoyed any work more than I do with this association with the Advisory Board and the Park staff," he told Marston.[26]

Masland found his work with the Advisory Board rewarding, but he yearned to return to the canyon country of the American Southwest. "I have nothing to look forward to except I hope, the trip into the Navajo country in the fall," he grumbled to Marston in March 1957. "I have to get out West somehow before the year is over. If I can't run the river, at least I've got to see the country and do that which I like next best, seeing it from the back of a horse." In 1957 he persuaded Marston to permit Mary Abbott to accompany them. "What a remarkable person she is," he said.[27] That same summer, a month before his September safari, as he called it, his brother, Paul, died from a malignant tumor. The trip would help him deal with the grief over the loss.

The trip combined informal park inspections with pleasure. From Carlisle, Masland motored west in his Cadillac. Accompanied by Virginia, Mary Abbott, and John Doerr of the Park Service, they visited Rocky Mountain National Park, Great Sand Dunes and Colorado National Monuments, and Mesa Verde National Park before arriving in Kayenta, Arizona. While Virginia and Margaret Marston stayed in a motel, Masland, Marston, Doerr, and Abbott, accompanied by Navajo guide Buck White-hat and wrangler Tom Daly, spent five days on horseback exploring the backcountry. On the second day, along a narrow slickrock trail, Mary's horse rammed her into a cliff outcropping, chipping a bone in her ankle. In extreme pain, she impressed her companions by nonetheless finishing the trip. "She is a great girl with plenty of courage," stated the admiring Masland.[28] Marston was so impressed with her grit that he invited her to join them the following year on a river expedition.

Masland's zeal for river running had waned. He would turn sixty-two in 1958, and oar-powered cataract boats were being replaced by motorized craft and rubberized rafts, as river traffic became steadily heavier. But he maintained his zest for exploring the little-known Navajo country and its sandstone buttes, canyons, cliffs, arches, and sweeping vistas. As an admirer of the desolate, rugged sandstone landscapes, he fretted that they would someday be subjected to commercial development, especially for their mineral resources. He had climbed five-thousand-foot Navajo Mountain, and as he rested in the shade of a tree he wondered whether, as a member of the Advisory Board, he could initiate action to preserve the mountain, sacred to the Navajos, and the adjacent untrammeled countryside for the American public. He would soon be deeply involved in that quest, which appeared more attainable after he was elected chair of the Advisory Board.[29]

Beguiled by the natural grandeur of the slickrock adjoining Monument Valley in northern Arizona and southern Utah, Masland pushed for its national protection, first as a board member and then as chair. In October 1956, he and Carl Wheat had raised the possibility of a new park with the Advisory Board and with Park Service director Wirth, who agreed to consider it. Meanwhile, Wheat approached Norman Littell, an attorney in Washington, DC, who served as general counsel for the Navajo people, about the possibility of the Diné requesting national park status for their remote and commercially unviable backcountry. Few Navajo people lived in the proposed park area, he stated, and those who did would not be dispossessed of their homes, the fate of other tribes in the past. Masland and Wheat also contacted Alden Stevens, secretary of the New York–based Association of American Indian Affairs, about cooperating with an effort to bring industry to the Navajo Nation. Both Wheat and Masland admired Navajo culture and wanted to preserve it. If the Tribal Council wished to create "a great National Memorial to their race and its past," Wheat and Masland would use their new positions on the Advisory Board to champion the idea with the Park Service. "No other Tribe in this country ever had a similar opportunity," wrote Wheat, "and most of the great and powerful tribes are now largely forgotten or little considered in their aboriginal homelands."[30]

Masland supported the idea of a Navajo National Park but was less optimistic than Wheat about Navajo cooperation. He shared with Wheat a love for the sandstone country and the Indigenous people who lived in harmony with it. "It is my belief the Navajo is capable of recognizing sincerity," said Masland. "He views all white men with a jaundiced eye. He is . . . a good judge of people[,] an instinctive judge. Since you and I are sincere in our sympathy and in our liking, I think that if we had the opportunity we might convince the Navajo that these things we advocate are for their own good." Unfortunately, though, he felt that they might never have a chance to lobby the Navajos on the subject. If the opportunity presented itself, "it would have to be handled with kid gloves and if at all possible in such a way that the Navajo will think they thought of it first."[31]

As Masland feared, the Navajos resolutely spurned the idea. Like other Indigenous people, they understood that in the past, as historians Mark David Spence and Karl Jacoby have shown, Native Americans had been pushed off their traditional lands and denied long-standing hunting, fishing, and foraging practices so as to make those rugged areas appear more uninhabitable and thus more suitable for national park status. Moreover, the Navajo people had been hurt more than helped by past federal initiatives like the livestock reduction program.[32]

The tribe's attorney Norman Littell, a white man and a former Rhodes Scholar, was an advocate of greater, not less, self-determination and proved to be a fierce champion of the interests of the Diné. He informed Masland and Wheat, "The Navajos know very definitely what they want to do with their lands, and also what they do not want to do and I can tell you that the policy is against extending any park service jurisdiction." When Masland questioned whether Littell spoke for the tribe, he learned that he did, and that Paul Jones, chair of the Tribal Council, had decided to preempt any federal initiative by establishing a Navajo Park Commission to deal with how to protect the landscape and its antiquities for posterity. Wheat and Masland next attempted to insert themselves as volunteer consultants for this newly established Navajo Park Commission but again were politely put off. By June 1957, the Navajo Nation had decided to establish a Navajo Park under the Tribal Council's jurisdiction.[33]

Despite the setback, Masland considered the tribal decision subject to change and continued to work for the next three years on a national park program that would be acceptable to both the Navajos and the Park Service. The Sierra Club's David Brower provided a sense of urgency by informing him that southeastern Utah was being encroached upon by roads, bridges, and commercial developers prospecting for uranium and oil. It would not be long, Brower warned, until the entire Utah-Arizona corridor would be ripe for commercial or tourist development.[34]

Masland tried to work around the Tribal Council's objections to federal protection of their land. In collaboration with Park Service and Advisory Board members, he pushed for a massive new national park and recreation area. Monument Valley would become a tourist mecca, so it should be designated a national recreation area, he argued. But he wanted what he called the "Navajo Mountain Quadrangle Area" preserved as a wilderness national park. Located in northeastern Arizona east of the Colorado River, it would include Navajo Mountain, Navajo (now Antelope) and Tsegi Canyons, and the ancient cliff dwellings—Inscription House, Betatakin, and Keet Seel—established in 1909 as Navajo National Monument. Northward, the desired parkland stretched into the slickrock canyon complex in southeastern Utah up to the San Juan River, taking in Rainbow Bridge National Monument, Paiute Canyon, and a rock formation known as Hoskinnini Monument. From a mountaintop, he had also viewed in the distance some additional reservation canyon country in southern Utah that his Navajo guides said had never been explored by whites. Masland planned to explore it with Navajo guides, but this so-called archaeological reconnaissance expedition did not come together until the fall of 1959.[35]

Meanwhile, on behalf of Wirth and the Advisory Board, Masland embarked upon a reconnaissance excursion to the Mojave Desert region on the Nevada-California border. In March 1959, he and Virginia motored from Pennsylvania through the southern states to Death Valley National Monument, where they spent ten days at the Furnace Creek Inn. By Jeep and by foot he toured the desolate, sizzling, sunbaked salt flats, dunes, and desert. In its raw beauty, Masland likened Death Valley to the canyon country and wished he could stay longer. He also suggested to the board and Park Service that Death Valley be elevated from monument to national park status, but this was not achieved until 1994. On the return home, they visited Padre Island, Texas, a pristine seashore that Masland recommended the Park Service designate for federal protection.[36]

Later that spring, at an Advisory Board meeting in Virginia, the board elected Masland to a three-year term as chair. He could not understand, he told Abbott with characteristic false modesty, "why they picked a mundane, pedestrian carpet manufacturer. It is an honor of which I am keenly aware and deeply appreciate," he said. "In a sense," he added, "it is the highest honor, I suppose, that could come my way in the avocations that interest me so greatly." It was a conspicuous honor, said Abbott, and "it is consoling to find that some people have discrimination." Masland proved to be a dedicated and highly respected chair, only the iconic Horace Albright matching his three-year stint as chair. Influential board members during Masland's term as chair included John Oakes, Ned Danson, Harold Fabian, Fred Smith, Stanley Cain, and Sigurd Olson.[37]

As chair, Masland pushed for additions to the park system, including Padre Island, Cape Cod, the Dry Tortugas Islands off the ocean side of southern

Florida, and the lake and alpine wonders of the northern Cascade Mountains of Washington. Those recommendations all eventually came to fruition.[38]

Masland used his organizational skills to make board meetings more businesslike, with set agendas, detailed minutes, frequent memoranda to members, and special committees to deal with specific park issues such as directing more attention and funds to park biosphere research and promoting conservation in the public schools. The actions of the board consisted primarily of memoranda and resolutions. Resolutions related to issues that the board believed required action by the interior secretary. Memoranda related to issues of which the secretary should be aware. As with his factory in Carlisle, Masland often visited the assets under his supervision. Unlike most board members and previous chairs, he had the wealth and the time to make periodic visits to the parks and to meet with park superintendents.[39]

Masland also had an excellent relationship with Park Service director Wirth, and the two men corresponded often by mail and telephone. Masland had little contact or communication with Secretary of the Interior Fred Seaton, who made little use of the Advisory Board, but that would change during the Kennedy administration. Masland also insisted that at least one of the two annual meetings of the board be held away from Washington so that members and the Park Service director would not be disturbed by phone calls and other distractions. In 1960, for example, the board met at Michigan's remote Isle Royale National Park, an island on Lake Superior with little telephone service and accessible only by boat or seaplane.

During his six years on the board, Masland's views corresponded closely with those of his colleague Sigurd Olson, who probably had the greatest influence on Masland's preservationist perspective. The two men were steady correspondents and shared campfires together on a hundred-mile canoe trip on the Suwannee River in Florida. Masland also read Olson's eloquent works on wilderness.

Raised in Minnesota, Olson was the son of a Baptist minister and for a time wanted to become a missionary. Instead, as a gifted writer and as president of the National Parks Association and then of the Wilderness Society, he became a missionary for the preservation of the wild. Shortly after stepping down as head of the National Parks Association, he was appointed to the Advisory Board. Though a lapsed Baptist, he developed a "wilderness theology" that Masland shared. In *A Wilderness Within*, Olson's biographer David Backes writes, "In wilderness humans could rediscover the timeless, creative force of the universe, regain a sense of being part of that force, and, in so doing, find salvation. Such an experience would make it impossible to maintain a purely anthropocentric worldview."[40] For both men, preserving nature was a psychological and moral imperative.

Determining what qualified as wilderness was not an easy task. The Forest Service took the view that primitive forest areas should be pristine. Other wilderness advocates insisted that gently used, grown over, or naturally restored lands should qualify. Historian James Turner points out that the Sierra Club and Wilderness Society suspected that the Forest Service demanded purity so that fewer areas would be designated as wild, thus leaving more primitive forests open for timbering.[41]

As members of the Advisory Board, both Olson and Masland believed that additions to the national park system and wilderness need not be pristine. Precious landscapes were falling prey to development and, they felt, must be preserved before they were bulldozed. "I, like you," Olson wrote Masland, "have no patience with people who are afraid the system is going down the drain with dilutions of areas which may not measure up at the moment to the highest standards. You and I think so much alike on this that we don't have to explain it to each other." Some purists, he continued, "act as though this was still a virgin continent with a century to put our house in order."[42]

While he was not a purist, Masland was an elitist, and he did not want the parks and public lands overrun with recreationists. But he was not entirely consistent in his views, as we have seen. He had used motorboats to run upstream on the Colorado River but later condemned their use on the Colorado and Yellowstone Lake. He often toured pristine landscapes by Jeep but opposed the use of ATVs in the backcountry of national parks and monuments. Once ATV use is permitted, he wrote, they multiply like "hamsters" and contaminate the landscape with their "spoor." He promoted conservation education in the schools, which stimulated greater interest in and pressure on the lands he wished to preserve. Even today, equal access remains a touchy issue, especially on public lands in the American West, with disagreement between preservationists and wise-use conservationists.[43]

Like most people, Masland yearned for recognition. He shared the wilderness viewpoints of Wallace Stegner, Aldo Leopold, Sigurd Olson, and Edward Abbey, connecting physically and emotionally with nature as they did. But he could not write with their elegance, nor did he receive their public accolades—and it stung. He compensated by working doggedly as an unpaid bureaucrat to familiarize himself with every national park and to expand and preserve the national park system and wilderness areas.

Masland supported the goal of establishing more national parks near population centers, especially in the eastern states, but he was not consistent about this either. He pushed hard for national park status for the Dry Tortugas Islands, sixty miles off the coast of Florida, Cumberland Island off the coast of Georgia, Congaree Swamp in South Carolina, and portions of the seashores on Cape Cod, Massachusetts, and Padre Island, Texas, but opposed park designation for the Gateway Arch in St. Louis and Cuyahoga National Park, the narrow ribbon of land along the Cuyahoga River, near Cleveland, Ohio, as too unimposing. Those easily accessible, urban-proximate areas did not measure up to his idea of natural temples. Masland showed far more interest in preserving less accessible rural landscapes than urban ones.

Masland gave priority to preserving the raw canyon terrain of the Southwest. Having missed out on a visit to canyon country with Carl Wheat in 1958, he scheduled a safari for the following fall. Under the auspices of the Museum of Northern Arizona but financed by Masland, the scientific reconnaissance party included Masland, Marston, Bill Belknap, Joe Eisaman, museum anthropologist Christy Turner, archaeologist Noel Morss of Harvard University's Peabody Museum, wranglers Tom Daly and Buster Ordiway, three Indian guides, and seventeen pack and riding animals. It was officially termed a scientific expedition with the goal of preserving Indigenous antiquities, but for Masland it was an attempt to draw national attention and federal protection to an indigenous landscape and wilderness wonderland.

Masland's party explored a largely unknown Colorado River tributary gulch called Mystery Canyon in southern Utah's San Juan County. The expedition to the robust backcountry north of Navajo Mountain provided more archaeological and geographical knowledge of the region, a scientific paper for Turner, and names, provided by Masland and recognized by the US Board on Geographic Names, for three theretofore unmapped areas: Anasazi, Moepitz, and Lehi Canyons. At night, he savored the rugged, untrammeled area: "I lay there looking at the stars, the gray sky, the moon on the cliffs, and I knew I was back home again." "It was a great trip," he told Marston enthusiastically, "the best of all, not only because it represented an achievement . . . but rather because this was in genuinely unknown country." He would later write that he was more familiar with Arizona and Utah than he was with western Pennsylvania. Among whites, his familiarity with canyon country was unsurpassed, and he would soon be recognized as the main advocate of federal protection of Utah's canyon lands, in much the same way that John Muir, years earlier, had been for the Sierra Nevada's Yosemite Valley, Enos Mills had been for what became Rocky Mountain National Park, and George Bird Grinnell had been for Glacier National Park.[44]

Upon his return from the expedition, Masland journeyed to the South Rim of the Grand Canyon for his first meeting as chair of the Advisory Board. Not surprisingly, he had placed on the agenda the future jurisdiction of the slickrock wilderness country on the Navajo reservation. By October he had reluctantly accepted that the Tribal Council would establish its own Navajo Park. But he hoped to collaborate with the Navajo Nation to limit the area open to commercial development. He had two other concerns. First, would Navajo rangers be competent stewards? And second, would the Navajos—with their goal of self-determination—seek jurisdiction over Rainbow Bridge and other national monuments on their land? Navajos regarded National Park Service monuments on their land with the same disdain in which the Park Service held private holdings in national parks. En route to the Grand Canyon board meeting, Masland met in Window Rock with John McPhee, administrative assistant to the Tribal Council. Masland suggested that at least two Navajo rangers be trained by the NPS and that before finalizing details on a Navajo Park, members of the Tribal Council consult with members of the Advisory Board. McPhee and Conrad Wirth were amenable to both suggestions, but they never advanced.[45]

Masland, Wheat, Danson, and other members of the Advisory Board were not alone in their concerns about the commercialization of wilderness on Indian reservations. Owing to Native American assertions of self-determination, supporters of the wilderness bill removed tribal lands from the proposed legislation. George Marshall, an executive of the Wilderness Society and brother of Robert, one of its founders, floated to David Brower the idea of offering federal subsidies to tribes who would agree not to develop wilderness, in the same way that farmers were paid not to grow crops.[46]

Brower forwarded Marshall's letter to Masland for his input. The idea that taxpayers would subsidize the preservation of wilderness on Indian lands stood no chance of success, in Masland's view. Moreover, Indian tribes were more inclined to commercial development than to preserving their scenic landscapes. "In a sense," he told Brower, "our Indian nations are like other 'newly liberated' peoples around the world. . . . They visualize commercial potentials much more clearly than they do corollary results. They have lived with their 'wilderness' through time without beginning. In many cases their 'wilderness' represents land the federal government did not want and with which the Indian has had to wage eternal combat in order to exist. Suddenly, the Indian is confronted with potentials lying under the earth and the white man's interest in recreation. He thinks of both as highly lucrative commercial ventures. This is natural."[47]

The wisest course of action regarding Indian wilderness, Masland believed, was for conservation groups to unify and to join the Park Service's Advisory Board to broker a compromise, persuading Indian nations to develop some of their land commercially and make other areas available to nonmotoring tourists as wilderness. Some of the wild nature that Masland hoped to protect on the Navajo reservation, including portions of what he called the quadrangle, would be covered by the Glen Canyon Dam, a project, he noted, that the Sierra Club should have fought harder to oppose. The dam, he observed, would give Navajos an opportunity to obtain hydroelectric power for homes and industry. Masland hoped that the tribe would zone the eastern part of their reservation—from Mexican Hat, Utah, south to Tuba City, Arizona—as commercial. The remaining expanse to the west, homeland to the Diné, who lived in hogans and clung to traditional ways, should be preserved as wilderness.[48]

In 1959, Masland had other pressing issues on his agenda as well. As chair of the Advisory Board, he and other conservationists faced the nettlesome issue of protecting Rainbow Bridge National Monument from being encroached upon by the Glen Canyon reservoir. In the Colorado River Storage Project (CRSP) compromise of 1956, Congress had dropped the proposed Echo Park dam, thus protecting Dinosaur National Monument from being flooded. At the same time, it authorized the construction of a higher-than-planned dam at Glen Canyon that would potentially spill water onto the mighty sandstone legs of Rainbow Bridge National Monument. To prevent that from happening and to preserve the principle of national park inviolability, Congress agreed to construct a barrier wall to protect the monument. As of 1959, however, Congress had not appropriated money for the construction of this wall. It was "one of the most disturbing problems with which I am engaged," he grumbled to Dock Marston. Flooding was "a possibility that established a precedent possessing infinitely dangerous potentials." He believed that the conservation organizations had "made the mistake of their lives when they gave up the Upper Colorado battle." "They considered that when they defeated Echo, they had won such an important engagement they could afford to default all others. They temporarily won a minor engagement and lost a war. . . . We might have stopped Glen Canyon," he said ruefully. The Sierra Club's Brower belatedly reached the same conclusion. So did Barry Goldwater. "The beauty of the canyons which are now covered by Lake Powell," Goldwater said in 1982, "are etched forever in my memory and it saddens me to think that my grandchildren will never see those magnificent creations of God. If I had to do it over, I would not support the construction of Glen Canyon Dam." This sentimental regret lost sight of the crux of the issue: that Glen Canyon, unlike Dinosaur, was not inside a park or monument.[49]

Masland set himself apart from most conservationists by opposing any additional dams on the Colorado River. Politics is sometimes called the art of the possible, and in 1956 there was no possible chance that conservation groups and dreamers like Masland had enough political clout to stop both of the proposed dams at Echo Park and Glen Canyon. Proponents of the Upper Colorado River Basin states were determined to obtain multiple federally constructed hydroelectric dams to provide power and reservoir water for their region. Stopping the Glen Canyon Dam would have required a political miracle.

But conservationists had won in the CRSP legislation a congressional commitment to prevent the possible swamping of Rainbow Bridge National Monument. As Advisory Board chair, Masland believed he had a duty to hold Congress and the Park Service to that commitment. He implored Conrad Wirth, the Sierra Club, the Wilderness Society, the National Parks Association, and other conservation organizations to alert the American public to the "very real" threat to Rainbow Bridge. "All of us on the Advisory Board," he wrote, "are keenly aware that if Rainbow National Monument is to be invaded by a hostile influence (there is no influence more hostile than the waters of a commercial dam) that the precedent established, not only reopens the Dinosaur threat, but opens all parks to potential commercial invasion." He also wanted the Interior Department to contain the expansive and expensive dam-building program of the Bureau of Reclamation. But Congress was more interested in building dams for recreation than in protecting hunks of arched sandstone. With the 1960 elections approaching, it delayed acting on the issue.[50]

Masland also despaired over the rapid loss of raw country. His beloved Colorado River was overrun with rafters. "The King [Norm Nevills] is dead and the old river is a thing of the past," he lamented in a letter to Abbott. "It is a new river, what there is left of it, and a new generation, the tin can and Kleenex generation."[51] With the river lost to motorized and rubberized boats and crowds of passengers, the desolate southwestern canyon country took on more importance to Masland.

Masland also fretted over the deterioration of another of his favorite nature retreats: Everglades National Park. The park, he complained to Wirth, was threatened by urban encroachment and poachers who were wantonly slaughtering alligators and spoonbill birds. Much of the urbanization at Everglades was spurred by the Mission 66 program, which had paved a forty-mile dirt road to Flamingo Bay, where Masland stayed. It also built a new marina and hotel. And park superintendent Warren Hamilton was either oblivious or indifferent to poaching. Hamilton had lost the respect of his staff and was "just plain dumb," in the opinion of park biologist Frank Craighead Sr. "If its indigenous fauna is not protected," Masland thundered, "there is little excuse for its existence and certainly it would cease to be of interest to the public. Poaching is a serious threat." The Everglades needed "a tough Superintendent and tough rangers. . . . Without them it is at the mercy of commercial interests and outlaws."[52] Wirth replaced Hamilton, but not until 1963.

Masland financed yet another "sand safari" to the southwestern quadrangle, bordered on the south by Navajo Mountain and on the north by the San Juan River, in September 1960. "For me," he wrote Marston, "as long as I have a four-legged animal, the canyon country, moonlight on the walls, the Arizona blue sky, and no telephones (or radios) I am happy." Led once again by Native American guides Buck White-hat, Toby Owl, and Dan Lehi, Masland, Christy Turner, Otis Marston, J. Ballard Atherton, and Tom Daly spent two weeks on foot and on horseback exploring and recording details of prehistoric sites and savoring the raw pinkish-orange sandstone canyons. Masland, as was customary, provided names for unmapped sites, like Nasja Canyon, that proved acceptable to the Board on Geographic Names.[53]

Not surprisingly, he made yet another pitch to Wirth for the protection of this area in collaboration with the Navajo people. "All of this land is primitive beyond words," he gushed. "I am certain that nowhere within the borders of the United States can there be an area more primitive, more unspoiled, more unique, more worthwhile saving." Time was wasting, he cautioned. "Three years have passed since I first pointed out this potential. It is awfully late but not too late, soon it will be too late."[54]

In addition to saving the national parks and wild nature from poachers, tourists, and dams, Masland was equally concerned about safeguarding the American citizenry from what he considered to be an intrusive federal government and ravenous Soviet-directed communist infiltration. The presidential candidacy of John F. Kennedy threw him into a funk. If elected, Kennedy would embrace the trend toward socialism initiated by FDR, Masland cautioned Abbott. Moreover, Kennedy appeared to be intent on building more multipurpose dams on western rivers. The United States, Masland dourly predicted, was about to enter a dark age like the one following the fall of the Roman Empire.[55]

Masland's views reflected the positions of most conservative Republicans, who despised the Roosevelt and Truman administrations for their support of labor unions and their lack of faith in the free market economy. They blamed Democrats for the political loss of China and North Korea by not being tough enough on the Soviet Union and Mao Zedong's Communist insurgents after World War II. Masland was in favor of reducing foreign aid and building up the American nuclear weapon arsenal for possible massive retaliation, should the need arise. Still a member of the John Birch Society in 1960, he shared that group's dogma on the importance of exposing and removing alleged American communist sympathizers from positions of influence. Politically, he was in step with conservatives like Sun Oil executive J. Howard Pew, writer William F. Buckley, and Congressman Barry Goldwater, but not with the mainstream electorate.[56]

On issues relating to conservation, however, this archconservative opponent of big government was at the forefront of a movement that became environmentalism. And as Advisory Board chair, Masland could influence policy, especially concerning matters relating to existing national parks and potential new ones. He could also affect public opinion on national parks as the recently elected vice president of the influential National Parks Conservation Association, a private organization of thirty thousand members dedicated to the preservation of the national park system.

To provide more time for excursions and for his duties with the Advisory Board and the National Parks Conservation Association, he turned over the day-to-day operation of Masland and Sons to his son Mike, while staying on as CEO. As we have seen, his opposition to government intrusion was selective, melting away when it served his purposes, and he was "delighted beyond words" when Interior Secretary Fred Seaton announced in December 1960 that the executive branch had set aside nine million acres in the new state of Alaska as the Arctic National Wildlife Refuge. Located in the upper northeastern corner of the state, the refuge, four times larger than Yellowstone National Park, was established to protect polar bears, caribou, and other wild creatures. (It has since been expanded to include more than nineteen million acres.) "Fred Seaton is going out in a blaze of glory," Masland chortled to Advisory Board member Carl Wheat.[57]

No matter who won the presidential election of 1960, Masland considered it essential that Conrad Wirth be kept on as director of the Park Service because he was experienced and politically savvy enough to resist threats of encroachment into the parks. "I think you know you have my respect, my admiration and my affection," he wrote Wirth. "In some fifty years of business and extracurricular activities I do not believe I have met anyone who gives so unsparingly of himself, who possesses greater dedication or whose integrity is less questionable than that of the Director of the Park Service, a man I am honored to call friend."[58]

As much as Masland loved his work on the Advisory Board, he periodically lapsed into dark moods, especially around presidential election time. He feared that America was doomed to become a socialist state, whether through internal indifference or by outside attack. Masland despaired over John F. Kennedy's election on November 8. Kennedy, he griped in a brooding letter to Abbott, had surrounded himself with socialist-leaning advisers, including labor leader Walter Reuther of the United Auto Workers union. Kennedy himself, Masland complained, "is arrogant. He has all the instincts, all the qualifications, all the obvious earmarks of an autocrat." The Russian Revolution of 1917 and FDR's recognition of the Soviet Union in 1933 did not frighten him as much as the Kennedy administration did, he said in a dark letter to former NPS director Horace Albright. "Washington is full of Fabian Socialists, residents of ivory towers, crackpot economists[,] elevated politicians, professional appeasers and dedicated opponents of the Free Enterprise System." JFK also concerned him because during the presidential campaign he pushed for the full development of western resources, especially hydroelectric dams, and might not be friendly to the national parks and Advisory Board. Kennedy, Fred Smith wrote Masland, was a reclamation man, and if a reclamation man witnessed someone pissing, he would try to capture the urine.[59]

Expressing the same frustration that half a century later would carry a billionaire real estate titan into the White House, Masland rued the decline of the white middle class, white Anglo Saxon Protestant heritage, national prestige, and rural America. Kennedy, he sneered, "was elected by our metropolitan cess pools, by a coalition of the individual blocs of which our metropolitan districts are made up. These blocs are no more the voice of America than the countries from which they hail." They possessed no more awareness of the values that built America—individual freedom, self-sufficiency, free-enterprise capitalism, and Christianity—than "their brothers and sisters still living in their native lands." What the nation needed, he concluded, was a leader who could unite nonmetropolitan voters and return America to a position of economic and military prominence. But he suspected that the election of 1960 was "the point of no return."[60] Little did he realize that one of President-elect Kennedy's advisers, perhaps the most liberal of the bunch, would become a staunch conservation ally and someone Masland would admire as the most influential interior secretary in the nation's history.

CHAPTER 7

Strange Bedfellows

Despite his disdain for liberals and dam builders who sought to clot the Colorado River, Masland worked closely over the next decade with the new secretary of the interior, Stewart L. Udall, a liberal Democrat from water-starved Arizona. They formed a friendly relationship, exploring the southwestern canyon country together and battling to preserve a large expanse of its harsh, sculpted terrain as Canyonlands National Park.

Masland deserves credit for being chiefly responsible for the establishment of the new park, which he called "a cathedral in the wilderness." Apart from Masland, only a few Native American guides, and perhaps Bates Wilson, superintendent of Arches National Monument, knew the area as well. Masland promoted the sandstone canyon and slickrock country of southern Utah and northern Arizona with the same gusto and passion that John Muir brought to the alpine grandeur of California's Sierra Nevada mountain range.

Since Masland would be working closely with the Interior Department, he was keenly interested in who might be named as its head. When rumors circulated that it would be the Arizona congressman, Masland was wary. Both he and fellow Advisory Board member Fred Smith initially regarded Udall as a "lightweight." They knew of Udall's support for multipurpose federal dams on western rivers, with their provision of cheap electrical power and reclamation of arid lands through irrigation. Udall's long-standing support for the Central Arizona Project, with its proposed dam at Bridge Canyon on the Colorado River, was especially worrisome. But Masland also understood that

Udall held the national park system, conservation, free-flowing rivers, and primeval landscapes in high esteem. "While Udall is by long odds the best of those who seem to be possibilities for Interior he is, unfortunately, first a Reclamation man," he maintained. He preferred an easterner for the post. "A Westerner," he continued, "is subject to entirely too many resource development pressures. Unless he gives way, he jeopardizes his political career." That assessment was on the mark.[1]

JFK appointed the Arizonan, and Masland's peak period of involvement and influence in national conservation issues came during Udall's tenure as interior secretary from 1961 to 1969. Though separated by a quarter century in age, and a Grand Canyon–sized gap in political philosophy, the two men shared a love of the natural world and a desire to protect it. "I am a 'conservationist' and a conservationist is one who conserves whether he is a Liberal or Conservative," Masland once said.[2] For the same reason, and in a time of political bipartisanship, Arizona's Republican senator, Barry Goldwater, also strongly supported Udall's nomination.

Masland wondered whether Udall would make use of the Advisory Board. If he did not use it more than Secretary Seaton had, it might as well be abolished, Masland told a fellow board member. Its fate was in "direct ratio to the value" the secretary gave it. Udall made the board relevant and instrumental in the expansion of the national park system.[3]

As a congressman, Udall had participated in an inspection tour of Navajo country in southern Utah and northern Arizona in the summer of 1960. By foot and helicopter, he and a gaggle of state and federal officials toured the primitive area to determine the best location for a small barrier dam that would protect the majestic Rainbow Bridge National Monument from the lapping waters of the soon-to be-completed Glen Canyon Reservoir. In a 1956 legislative compromise, Congress had approved the small diversion dam at Rainbow Bridge in order to achieve passage of the Colorado River Storage Project, with its high dam at Glen Canyon. Unlike the other inspectors, Udall hiked six grueling miles from the Colorado River to Rainbow National Monument. Like Masland, who had made several excursions to the area by foot, pack animal, boat, and Jeep, Udall was smitten with the stark beauty of the sandstone canyon country and did not support a small protective dam. It would be better, he stated in his report to the House Committee on Interior and Insular Affairs, to permit reservoir water to lap the sturdy legs of the massive Rainbow Bridge arch than to erect an unsightly barrier dam. He recommended that Congress, in cooperation with the Navajo Nation, establish a massive new national park on the Utah-Arizona border by expanding the boundaries of Rainbow Bridge National Monument. Masland had made the same proposal to Park Service director Conrad Wirth in November 1960, but he still also favored a barrier dam for Rainbow Bridge.[4]

On becoming secretary of the interior in January 1961, Udall's numerous Interior Department responsibilities included jurisdiction over the NPS and the federal dam-building Bureau of Reclamation. Though Masland had supported Republican nominee Richard Nixon for president, he reserved judgment on the jut-jawed, crewcut-sporting, forty-one-year-old Udall. Masland soon learned that the pro-dam Arizona Mormon was intelligent, determined, likeable, unpretentious, and hardworking. "He is a conservationist who is also a realist and recognizes that he has reclamation on his hands as well as conservation. I think, if anything, he tends to lean toward the purest side of conservation, but the showdown, of course, will come when reclamation and conservation collide head on and he has to make up his mind." When the showdown arrived, Masland expressed the "cockeyed notion" that Udall, Houdini-like, would somehow find an acceptable outcome.[5]

In a welcoming letter, Masland praised Udall for being ideally qualified "by knowledge, experience and by sympathy" for a cabinet position for which Masland had the highest respect. Though the post might attract less publicity than others, he said, "its ramifications are infinite and its effect on the lives of all citizens, though subtle, is great and lasting. As much, if not more than any other office, it is the protector of our national heritage." The Advisory Board, he told Udall, would offer its "service to you to the fullest extent of our capacity." Udall would take full advantage of that offer. Masland used his Cadillac to commute the hundred miles between Carlisle and Washington, DC, for meetings on park issues. He also communicated with the Interior Department by telephone.[6]

His first meeting with Udall took place in Washington on February 2, 1961. After exchanging pleasantries, they expressed their mutual enthusiasm for the potential establishment of a spacious new national park in canyon country, and Masland offered his initial thoughts on its possible boundaries. Tentatively called Navajo National Park, it would encompass traditional tribal lands such as Monument Valley and Rainbow Bridge National Monument, thereby possibly blunting conservationists' demand for a diversion dam. Soon after the meeting, Masland dictated an exuberant letter to Udall.

"I was most impressed by your determination and vision," it began. "There is so much to be done. The opportunity is so great, the requirements of future generations so important. It was a heartwarming and encouraging experience to find someone in a position of authority possessing concern at least equal to mine." He attached a map outlining the boundaries of the proposed Navajo National Park. His proposed domain excluded the holy Navajo Mountain but included Rainbow Bridge, cliff-dwelling Navajo national monuments, and additional territory to the north. He concluded by suggesting a visit to the potential park area.[7]

Udall invited him on two reconnaissance tours, one in the spring to Rainbow Bridge and another that summer to the proposed expanded canyon lands park area. "I certainly hope that you can find time to participate in the selection of lands for the new national park as I am confident that no one in the country has your insight into the scenic beauties of this particular area." Masland was delighted to accept.[8]

Masland could barely disguise his enthusiasm after his first few meetings with Udall and his team. "I may be a Republican," Masland wrote Advisory Board secretary Ned Danson of the Museum of Northern Arizona, "but I have a hunch it's going to be much more fun working with them than it has been recently." "Eager youth is on the move and at this stage of the game unwilling to admit for one moment that any desirable objective can't be accomplished," Masland informed Sig Olson after Udall's first weeks in office. "I don't think I have ever known anyone to move so far in so many directions in such a short period of time, as the secretary."[9]

Masland believed that Udall's zeal and determination boded well for the Advisory Board. The days of departmental drift and inertia were over, he informed the board. "He is young, energetic, determined, friendly and beyond doubt capable. There was a hustle and bustle that I had not previously experienced in Washington. . . . I suspect there will be few dull moments in the next few years. . . . I even entertain a suspicion the new Secretary may go so far as to put the Advisory Board to work."[10]

Although Udall was familiar with Masland's reputation as an avid conservationist, canyon lands explorer, and supporter of the national parks, he knew less about other members of the Advisory Board. Before putting it to use, he asked special adviser Wallace Stegner to report on the abilities of the members. The board was solid, Stegner assured Udall; the strongest members were Masland, "a good chairman and very well informed," Sigurd Olson, Stanley

Cain, and John Oakes. Thus assured, Udall made good use of the board over the next seven years.[11]

Masland's excitement over the impending trip to the Southwest in May 1961 dimmed somewhat when he learned that the reconnaissance party would be large and would include members of Congress and the press. Udall, he grumbled to Sig Olson, wanted to get a feel for the political as well as the physical landscape. "The chap is a political pro. There is no question about that."[12]

Udall undoubtedly had publicity in mind when he invited sixty people to join the expedition to the Rainbow Bridge area, among them four members of Congress, Park Service director Conrad Wirth, Bureau of Reclamation director Floyd Dominy, Dave Brower of the Sierra Club, Tony Smith of the National Parks Conservation Association, several Park Service officials, an assortment of reporters, and the nine helicopter pilots who would chopper the delegation over the potential barrier dam sites and planned national park area.[13]

Masland reported on the tour in a long letter to Dock Marston. After returning to their motel in Page, Masland showed the assembled group film footage of some of his earlier expeditions, and Udall displayed maps of three potential park units. The group overwhelmingly preferred the largest of the proposed park areas but understood that the Navajo people would not part with any portion of their land, especially their holy Navajo Mountain. Except for Dave Brower, there was little insistence on a barrier dam, and the issue was sidelined.[14]

Masland was encouraged by the expedition in spite of its large numbers and short duration (one day). And his admiration for Udall soared. "He is an amazing person," he told Marston, with a quick mind and keen memory. Physically, he was fit and tireless. "I emphasize that his attitude at all times indicated an appreciation of form and beauty and of natural wonders." Masland hoped that Udall would find a way to achieve the goals of the Central Arizona Project without building a massive dam at Bridge Canyon that would intrude upon Grand Canyon National Monument.[15]

At the end of the expedition, Masland went to Grand Canyon National Park to attend the biennial conference of the National Park Service. In a preaching-to-the-choir address titled "Conservation of Spiritual Values," he emphasized the theme that connecting with nature was equivalent to connecting with the Creator. Fellow Advisory Board member Sig Olson, soon to become vice president of the Wilderness Society, had been preaching the same message for three decades. The Park Service, Masland stated, was charged with preserving the lands under its jurisdiction as inviolable. But it also had a responsibility to educate the public on threats to existing sanctuaries and the need to establish new parks for spiritual and recreational uplift before the land was gobbled up by commercial predators and a growing population. If the Park Service, united conservation groups, and concerned citizens exerted enough pressure, Congress would act in the public interest. Like Horace Albright, one of his mentors, Masland clung to the view that the national parks should be both kept inviolate and made accessible to the public.[16]

Masland told the biennial conference crowd that he had been spiritually reborn during his first trip down the Colorado River in 1948, that it had awakened in him a dedication to preserving it and other pristine, God-given natural sanctuaries. It had led him to a "new world . . . in which people gave major thought not to their personal physical needs, but to the spiritual needs of posterity." The land of the Anasazi, near the "Holy Hill of the Navajo," was one such natural wonder "whose heart beats in time with mine," he said, and it should be preserved for future generations. "The cause for which we struggle is the preservation of God's cathedral that the jaded spirit of civilized man may, in His temple, be reborn and find new life and purpose," he sermonized. "With determined dedication, we must guard those treasures our heritage has entrusted to us." Noting that time was the enemy of preservationists, he closed by quoting a hymn written by the nineteenth-century New England poet James Russell Lowell: "Once to every man and nation / Comes the moment to decide."[17]

Masland was especially anxious that Udall and the Park Service reach a decision on protecting portions of the canyon lands. In mid-July 1961, he and Udall made another reconnaissance trip there, this time with some thirty others. In addition to Udall's wife, Lee, and oldest son, Tom, the inspection team included the US secretary of agriculture, Orville Freeman, and his son; Utah's governor and congressional delegation; NPS personnel; river and backcountry guides; and numerous members of the press. For three days, they motored down the Colorado River in thirteen boats, launching from Moab, Utah, camping at Dead Horse Point, above Cataract Canyon, and then cruising upstream to Anderson Bottom on the Green River. Whether riding the river or at evening campsites, there "was no disharmony, no grumbling, no laggards," Masland observed. All members "were excellent campfire companions," he informed Marston. "When a lone Republican speaks of an assemblage of Democrats in such terms the statement should not be minimized."[18]

Udall took time to explore the slickrock canyons, clefts, and crags on foot, and his energy and enthusiasm impressed Masland as they had during the trip to Rainbow Bridge. Udall, he told Marston, "is tireless, agile, almost foolhardy—most assuredly not lacking in courage." His admiration for the down-to-earth Lee Udall also continued to grow. She charmed him by saying, "Frank, you are neither a Democrat nor a Republican. You are a Conservationist." Pleased with her characterization, in letters to Stewart he occasionally signed himself "The Chairman of the Conservation Party."[19]

On the final evening, the two cabinet secretaries held an unusual press conference. Against a background of hulking cliffs, a starry sky, "campfire light flashing on the cottonwoods, and the murmur of the river in the background," they announced plans for a gigantic new park. "I do not believe there was a person on the trip who was not impressed by the grandeur of the country, by its loneliness, its beauty and its form," Masland wrote. Moreover, the potential park area would not require congressional appropriation for purchase because it would fall entirely within public land administered by the Bureau of Land Management. "With complete unanimity all agreed that as a National Park it would rank second to none." Unfortunately, Masland misread the degree of enthusiasm on the part of Utah's conservative governor and congressional delegation.[20]

He filed a favorable report on the proposed new park with the Advisory Board. The report pleased Udall. "It has warm sensitivity to the values involved, and it caught the essential spirit of our adventure and the problems we encountered," Udall responded. "It will be one of the papers that will have historical value long after both of us have gone down the road."[21]

When Udall requested his input on the boundaries of the contemplated park, Masland mapped out a sprawling area of a million acres, larger than the state of Rhode Island. When he presented his plan, he recalled Udall saying, "That's a hell of a lot of land. We'll see what we can get."[22]

Marston attempted to cool Masland's enthusiasm by predicting that Udall would eventually disappoint him. "It is good to hear all the fine things about Udall," he wrote. "My increasing age makes me sure that anyone who is a Democrat has 2 ½ strikes against him when he comes to bat." Marston was wise to be skeptical of Democrats, Masland responded, but Udall at heart was a committed conservationist. And apart from a barrier dam to protect Rainbow Bridge and the department's focus on recreation, he was in accord with Udall's conservation agenda.[23]

Masland and other Advisory Board members were concerned that recreation was the tail wagging the Park Service dog. Wirth was especially mindful of the need to win popular favor by promoting recreational activities. In the mid-1950s, the Park Service had approved a plan for a 632-mile scenic road through the Allegheny Mountains. Modeled after the Blue Ridge Parkway in Virginia and North Carolina and Skyline Drive in Shenandoah National Park, established during the New Deal, the proposed Allegheny National Parkway would be carved through portions of West Virginia, Virginia, and Kentucky and would be administered by the Park Service. Although Wirth supported the project, the Advisory Board, including Masland, wanted to deemphasize road-building efforts and failed to give its recommendation. Owing to the outcry from preservationists, Congress never approved the parkway.[24]

The surge in domestic travel and outdoor activities after World War II prompted Congress to establish the Outdoor Recreation Resources Review Commission in 1958 to study and coordinate future needs at the federal, state, and local levels. Chaired by Laurance Rockefeller, the ORRRC recommended the creation of a new federal agency called the Bureau of Outdoor Recreation. Wirth did not want to surrender his control over recreation and sought jurisdiction over the new agency, but the Bureau of Outdoor Recreation was established in 1962 as a separate entity within the Department of the Interior.[25]

Since the Park Service apparently no longer had responsibility for recreation, Masland questioned whether the Advisory Board could focus solely on park issues. Assistant Secretary of the Interior John Carver Jr. responded with a resounding "no." He wanted the board to remain involved in recreation issues. Recreation, he explained, was the "new magic word in Government." Udall had relied more heavily on the advice of the Advisory Board than any previous secretary and had valued the board's views on issues that affected the Park Service and Interior Department. "Preservation is the touchstone of the work of this Board, but in these changing times the Board cannot deal with preservation in absolute terms."[26]

In addition to his demanding and fulfilling work chairing the Advisory Board, Masland delivered speeches and corresponded frequently with conservation leaders and former river runners. "Life is indeed rewarding and full," he informed Sig Olson. "What a wonderful world it would be if the Damoclean sword of Communism didn't hang over our heads."[27]

Swords of sorts also hung over the Colorado River and the Canyonlands National Park project. "The threat to the River is perennial," he complained to Marston. "Being where it is and being the only river in that section of the world, it provides an irresistible temptation to all Chambers of Commerce, so called Service Clubs and those State and Federal Bureaucracies that are out of a job when out of a river, and so the assault will never cease. . . . It is the quite logical perpetual battleground of the West." Humankind's two worst inventions, he continued, were television and the bulldozer. Television destroyed individualism while the bulldozer "has laid the land to waste. Nothing, not even the Grand Canyon is sacrosanct."[28]

He also despaired over the future of the canyon lands. The Navajo people were unwilling to sell or exchange any of their established Navajo Tribal Park preserve for a new, federally administered national park. Without their cooperation, the new national park would shrink in size, and a large slice of natural beauty would belong to the Navajo rather than federal jurisdiction. And the Navajos might open sizable swaths of their park to roads and commercial enterprises. Moreover, Utahans, including the governor and members of the congressional delegation, objected to locking up for aesthetic purposes a gigantic chunk of public domain that might be used for hunting, grazing, and mineral extraction. In 1961, Senator Frank Moss (D-UT) had introduced legislation proposing a Canyonlands National Park of 330,000 acres. Udall and Masland were disheartened by the Navajo Nation's uncooperative stance and Moss's undersized park proposal.

Masland received little encouragement from the Advisory Board for an expansive canyon lands park. During his last meeting as chair of the Advisory Board, in May 1962, Utahan Harold Fabian told him he was tilting at windmills in his quest for a million-acre park. Fabian preferred a park of about three hundred thousand acres, with no hostile uses (such as dams), plus a large buffer zone of several thousand acres where hunting, grazing, and mining would be permitted. Other members agreed, leaving the board to consider three options: a park of some 300,000 acres with no hostile uses; a park of 330,000 acres with hostile uses; a park of 330,000 acres with grazing, but with hunting and mining to be phased out after twenty years. Masland, like Wirth, preferred the third option because it included more land, but John Oakes and Fred Smith championed park purity. Smith, the meeting minutes noted, "felt the Board should not let down the bars even at the expense of not getting some of the land desired." The board passed a resolution recommending a park bill with no adverse uses.[29]

Masland still held out hope for a larger park. At Udall's request, he returned to canyon country for ten days in late May and early June 1962 to help reconfigure the core areas for a park. With an entourage of guides, Jeeps, and packhorses, he visited the Maze Area and Horse Canyon Area to the south and Panorama Point and Hatch Point to the west. "There is nothing anywhere in the Canyon Country, the equal of the view from Panorama Point," he told Udall. "This includes Dead Horse, Grand View and, heresy or not, Grand Canyon." If he had to choose only "one spot in the vast Canyon country and say, 'this is the place,' it would be Panorama." To only a slightly lesser degree, he continued, the vista from Hatch Point "meets the eye and fills the soul." As far as Udall was concerned, Masland was preaching to the choir. Unfortunately, the Utah congressional delegation had yet to see the light.[30]

Masland was aghast because Moss's proposed bill would not include Panorama or Hatch Point, prompting him to press again for a sizable buffer zone. The core or "inner sanctum" area should encompass Moss's 330,000 acres plus Panorama and Hatch Points, even if it meant allowing grazing. An adjoining area of some seven hundred thousand acres, he advised, should be set aside as a national reserve, with hunting and grazing permitted upon authorization by the secretary of the interior. Udall agreed with the "inner sanctum" approach but proposed waiting until after the November congressional elections to pursue their bold plan.

Masland considered 1961 an eventful year, mainly because the establishment of a new park in the canyon lands appeared promising. Encouraged about the prospects, he wrote Udall in December, "I am delighted beyond words that you are moving in this area. No single act during the years I have been on the Board could cause me the gratification that I would derive from the success of your efforts in this matter."[31]

Masland also held out hope that the Navajos would budge on surrendering some of their Tribal Park domain. He believed that the tribe, along with tourists and businesses such as the Navajo Trading Post operated by Ralph and Madelene Cameron, would derive greater benefit from a park administered by the Park Service. Udall, he explained to Madelene Cameron, was sympathetic to the "purposes and ambitions" of the Navajos. His successor might not be. "I think you know how I feel toward the Navajo," he continued. "I don't need to tell you that in any deal I think the Navajo should get the better of it—they deserve it. Knowing that, when I tell you that I believe the Tribe should consciously endeavor to work out an arrangement with the Secretary that will permit your slickrock country to become a National Park that you can count on it that I think this can be done to the advantage of all parties concerned and especially to the advantage of the Navajo." He left vague why cooperation would benefit all parties except to say that the Park Service would provide greater administrative and economic stability and less tolerance for commercial uses. At bottom, however, Masland was placing emphasis on land preservation over land accessibility.[32]

Masland was crestfallen when the Navajo Tribal Council refused to yield to the overtures of the Interior Department. "One of the most primitive areas in the United States will be gone," Masland moaned to Udall. "It is unique geologically and for that reason, as well as because it is one of our great primitive heritages should be in our National Park." The steadfast positions of Utahans and Navajos forced Masland and Udall to downsize their plans for a canyon lands park.[33]

While in the canyon lands in 1962, Masland and photographer Charles Eggert produced *The Sculptured Earth*, a publicity film extolling the magnificence of the Southwest. Udall invited Masland to join him in co-hosting the premiere of the film in Salt Lake City, but Masland begged off owing to Virginia's hospitalization for spinal surgery. "The film was superior in every way, and my only regret was the absence of the man who made it possible," Udall wrote in appreciation. "For the first time," he continued, "I strongly feel we'll get the park, and the impact of this film on Utah public opinion will surely be profound." The film, however, did not speed up legislative action or lead to the grandiose park that Masland and Udall envisioned.[34]

When Masland's six-year term on the Advisory Board ended in June 1962, Udall sent a warm letter of appreciation. "The energy, time and dedication you contributed have left an indelible mark on the National Park System," he wrote. Masland's successors on the board would be hard pressed "to match the remarkable record of progress achieved during your years as Chairman. Cape Cod is a reality with Point Reyes on the threshold. The number of other proposals which have advanced toward ultimate approval borders on the phenomenal in contrast to any previous period." Udall made special mention of the proposed park in Utah's canyon lands. "I am particularly mindful of your personal contribution to the Canyonlands cause and will always cherish the experience of our trip through that magnificent country." He urged Masland to continue to battle for park and wilderness values and to be available for counsel and special assignments.[35]

Masland thanked Udall for his gracious comments and said he would "preserve and treasure" the letter. His colleagues on the Advisory Board and Park Service were exceedingly friendly and talented, he acknowledged, but their achievements were "made possible by your interest, dedication and determination." As Advisory Board chair, he had come to realize "how important it is to the wellbeing of the Park Service, and, therefore, to the preservation of our National Heritage to have a Secretary who possesses an inherent love of nature and a recognition of the need to preserve the spiritual values of our National Heritage." He assured Udall that he stood ready to assist whenever asked.[36]

While awaiting congressional action on the Canyonlands Park proposal, Masland continued to push its merits. When the noted editor Paul Brooks of the Houghton Mifflin publishing house expressed an interest, Masland persuaded him to visit the area and to write an article supporting its designation as a park. "Canyonlands can use good publicity and lots of it. It would be most timely." He recommended specific landscapes and provided Brooks with copies of his reports to Udall on his own recent trips. He also agreed to critique a draft of Brooks's essay "Canyonlands: A New National Park," which appeared in the influential *Atlantic Monthly* in March 1963.[37]

The proposed park was discussed again at an Advisory Board meeting in late March 1963. Masland was invited to attend as a special consultant to Secretary Udall and the Park Service. Conrad Wirth and his assistant secretary, John Carver, were also there. Chairman Fabian extended a special welcome to Masland, stating that "his illustrious presence again is welcomed officially at our meetings as long and as often as he wishes." Considering the proposed Canyonlands National Park to be of "paramount importance," the board passed a resolution urging the establishment of a park of at least 330,000 acres that would include Panorama and Hatch Points. It also recommended congressional approval of the proposed Voyageurs National Park in Minnesota and the Wilderness Act. Carver cautioned the group, reminding them to deal gently with Congress, especially the powerful Wayne Aspinall, if they wanted new parks and passage of the Wilderness Act. Aspinall, he reminded them, believed that Congress had jurisdiction over the public lands.[38]

That fall, Masland made his seventh expedition to the southwestern slickrock country and proposed park area. After visiting with the Navajos, he reaffirmed that the tribe had no intention of ceding, selling, or trading any of their land for inclusion in a national park. In his correspondence with Udall, he suggested appropriate sites for park headquarters, interpretive centers, and campgrounds. He also reiterated his argument that Panorama and Hatch Points should be included within the park's boundaries, even though Udall had informed him that the inclusion of those areas would not be acceptable to the Utah governor or congressional delegation. He assured Masland that once a downsized park had been established, he would preserve Panorama and Hatch via an executive order or some other means. Disappointed, Masland grumbled privately to Mary Abbott that Udall would be forced for political reasons to sell "down the river" the plan for an outsized park.[39]

In March 1963, Masland was gratified when the US Board on Geographic Names approved his suggested names for eleven geographical features that he had explored during his many visits to southern Utah. His friend Joe Eisaman believed that one of those many arches should be named for Masland, but the rules prohibited naming features after people who were still living.[40]

During the last two weeks of May, Masland took yet another reconnaissance trip. Accompanied by Marston, *National Geographic* photographer William Belknap, Arches National Park superintendent Bates Wilson, and horse wrangler Art Ekker, he toured the canyon lands, Escalante, and a geological feature called the Waterpocket Fold in southern Utah. All were worthy of inclusion in the national park system, Masland reported. (Eventually, the Waterpocket Fold region was preserved as Capitol Reef National Park in 1971, and the Escalante region as Grand Staircase–Escalante National Monument in 1996.)[41]

At the eastern end of the water pocket region, the party rode by Jeep and horse to Iron Top Mesa, overlooking the Colorado River a thousand feet below. "It was a beautiful sight. It was also sickening," he later reported to Abbott. "It was beautiful since the water is rising behind Glen Canyon Dam and the silt is dropping and so all is clean. . . . It was sickening since we were witnessing the death of a river, the obliteration of all its treasures and because we knew that the beauty we saw would turn to muck and slime and tamarisk and white stain when the river falls as it is bound to do." The white stain (or bathtub ring, as it is derisively called) did indeed appear as the river fell. In fact, the plunging water level, with the corresponding silting and staining, has become so pronounced in the twenty-first century that engineers are considering freeing the river by diverting it around the dam.[42]

Masland was also sickened when he learned that, starting in July, the Department of Defense planned to fire ten or twelve test missiles per month over the proposed Canyonlands Park from its army base in Green River. Since its rocket boosters would fall in the Needles area of the proposed park, ranchers were advised to relocate stock during the testing. "Perhaps Canyonlands tourists will become expert at ducking boosters and not need to be moved along with the cattle," Masland noted sarcastically. Udall assured him that once the park was established, no boosters would be falling within its borders.[43]

In September 1964, after deliberating for more than three years, Congress established Canyonlands National Park, initially comprising 257,640 acres and later increased to 337,000 acres. Located in southeastern Utah, the hourglass-shaped park was thirty miles long and twenty miles wide. Two wild rivers, the Green and the Colorado, converged at its center. Rivers, gorges, sandstone arches, spires, domes, mazes, and buttes stood as monuments to what Masland called its "harsh beauty."[44]

Though compromises were necessary, Masland was pleased that a large expanse of the land he loved had been saved for posterity. "In the land embraced in this Park there is ample opportunity for man to commune with himself and his God," he wrote. "Here is a cathedral, built not by the hands of man placing stone upon stone, but a glorious cathedral formed by the hands of God, the cathedral of the wilderness." Masland had worked long and hard to win national park status for the cherished piece of land, and he deserves a share of the credit for its creation. Longtime Utah river pilot and Jeep guide Kent Frost insisted that Masland "did more towards making Canyonlands National Park into a park than anyone else." Masland, too, took pride in his contribution. "Since I was present at its birth," he recalled, "I have for it, the affection that a father has for his first born." And late in life he was warmed by the fact that, under various classifications, nearly the entire one million acres that he had wanted had been preserved as park or recreation area, calling it "a great and unknown park." Adding Canyonlands to the national park system was the greatest highlight of Masland's career. He also took pride in the fact that only he and the legendary Horace Albright had served three years as chair of the park system Advisory Board. He took satisfaction in being linked with other prestigious board members, like Wallace Stegner, Sigurd Olson, and Stanley Cain. As Udall's special consultant and later as a member of the newly created National Park Service Advisory Board Council, he would continue to serve the Interior Department and to help shape policy as an unpaid bureaucratic insider.[45]

CHAPTER 8

On Assignment

When Masland's six-year term on the Advisory Board ended in June 1962, Stewart Udall asked him to continue to serve the Interior Department as his unpaid special consultant, including special assignments and attendance at meetings of the Advisory Board as his personal representative. "I don't know how long it will last but while it does it is awfully nice indeed," he confided to fellow board colleague Carl Wheat.[1] Masland's influence and active involvement endured throughout Udall's eight years as secretary.

In July 1962, at Udall's request, Masland joined a select team of National Park Service officials as a delegate to the First World Conference on National Parks in Seattle, Washington. Both he and Udall viewed the conference as a means of promoting the national park idea internationally, especially in Africa. Additionally, Udall understood that the conference would meet with the approval of the president, given JFK's support for the Peace Corps, the Alliance for Progress, the US Agency for International Development, and other programs designed to assist emerging nations during the Cold War. Udall was adept at recognizing the symbolic significance of JFK's New Frontier program, including closing the so-called missile gap, promoting civil rights at home, supporting global conservation efforts, and encouraging self-determination in Africa.

As a presidential candidate, Kennedy had lambasted the Eisenhower administration for neglecting Africa. By 1960, seventeen African states had become independent. As president, JFK was especially keen to prevent emerging African states from aligning themselves with the Soviet Union or the People's Republic of China. And a closer relationship with Black African leaders would resonate with American civil rights activists. European and American conservationists had a separate concern relating to decolonization—namely, that in order to advance their economies, new Indigenous leaders might open existing African national parks and preserves to development and hesitate to establish new ones.[2]

Attempting to regulate hunting and the trade in ivory, hides, and feathers, European colonial powers had cooperated in setting aside national parks and nature preserves in Africa through the London Convention of 1900. In November 1933, a second treaty, called the Convention Relative to the Preservation of Flora and Fauna in their Natural State, fine-tuned the original agreement by prioritizing the preservation of migratory animals over establishing order and sustainability for the trade in tusks, skins, and feathers. It sharpened the distinction between two types of sanctuaries: national parks and national preserves. The main purpose of national parks, the 1933 convention stated, was to promote tourism, while the primary goal of national preserves was to protect habitat and animals. Hunting and human habitation were prohibited in both parks and preserves. Adjacent zones outside the protected areas were established for licensed hunting and trapping.[3]

Over the next three decades, more than three hundred national parks and preserves had been established, mainly in sub-Saharan Africa. As with national parks in the United States, as historian Mark Cioc has shown, Indigenous Africans were dispossessed of their lands, including their traditional hunting, grazing, and gathering grounds. And park boundaries were established without regard to animal migratory patterns or the natural habitat. Black Africans sometimes referred to these sanctuaries as "white man's parks" or "apartheid parks." Although Masland and Udall were hardly free from white paternalism, they sought to cooperate with Black representatives of emerging states by protecting existing sanctuaries and establishing new scenic and wildlife preserves to stimulate their economies through international tourism. True, parks and preserves appealed mainly to white European and American tourists, but their visits were economically beneficial to African nations.[4]

Attended by 145 delegates from sixty-three nations on six continents, the weeklong First World Conference on National Parks convened in Seattle on the last day of June 1962. Sponsored by the International Union for Conservation of Nature and Natural Resources (IUCN), the United Nations, and the US National Park Service, the conference enlightened Masland in several ways. First, it helped break down racial barriers, including his own. Apart from American Indigenous people, he had not associated with people of color and was particularly impressed by the ability of African delegates. "I came away convinced there is no such thing as a 'color bar,'" he told Abbott. The so-called bar was really a lack of opportunity, because most Black Africans had been subjects of European colonial rulers since the 1880s.[5]

The participation of Black delegates, he reported to Udall, resulted in respect for the ability of African emissaries among non-African delegates. "The Conference brought home the fact that color is not a matter of significance," he wrote. "There quickly developed a rapport based on personality, character and qualifications in which color played no part." He demonstrated little regard for the delegates from Latin America, by contrast. They showed little enthusiasm for parks or wildlife protection and the instability of their governments made park planning nearly impossible. He was also perturbed because Cuba had recently become a communist state under Fidel Castro.[6]

Second, Masland was excited by the global interest in preserving areas of natural splendor. Delegates viewed national parks as sources of national pride and revenue from tourism. Such national "status symbols," he believed, probably would not be used for resource extraction or agricultural and industrial development.

Third, the national park idea and the preservation of wild nature, he emphasized to Udall and to Jean-Georges Baer, president of the IUCN, promoted international goodwill. To Udall he pronounced the meeting "an unqualified and quite possibly an unparalleled success in the field of international relations." The delegates, he said, appreciated that Udall took the time to address the conference and to mingle and talk with them afterward. "I regard the First World Conference on National Parks not simply as historic and significant in the conservation field, I regard it as even more historic and significant in the field of human relations," he gushed to Baer. "I doubt if ever heretofore have so many people representing so many nations come together for the purpose of discussing and implementing a subject in which there was no semblance of jealousy or greed or achievement at the expense of another," he continued. Conservation, he added, "is a universal word. It represents one of the few ideas capable of bringing people together in an atmosphere devoid of intrigue and capable of creating understanding."[7]

Masland recommended several follow-up actions to Baer. The IUCN should devise an acceptable worldwide definition of "national park." Not surprisingly, he suggested one: "The designation, National Park, should be applied to those areas of outstanding beauty and scientific interest which are provided with the maximum protection possible within the political, social and economic conditions of the country." He also recommended the preservation of wilderness. In nonauthoritarian states, wilderness must be made accessible to the public. But controls should be implemented to prevent overuse and commercial razzmatazz. State parks, recreation areas, and buffer zones should be established near national parks and wilderness areas to act as "a sponge, absorbing a vast amount of the gregarious tourist population." As always, Masland stressed preservation over equity in access. Baer, however, noted that a zoning or grading system would be a tough sell with emerging states that feared that downgrading a preserve would result in a loss of national status.[8]

Masland also offered recommendations to Udall. The United States should, upon request, provide receptive developing nations with trained experts in the management of national parks. In addition, the NPS should offer foreign nationals the chance to study park management in the United States. He also believed, but left unsaid, that the goodwill resulting from US assistance in developing national parks might aid in thwarting the advance of communism. Udall promptly implemented Masland's suggestions. Masland was less willing to provide federal assistance to disadvantaged citizens in the United States because they might become dependent and support programs and politicians that he regarded as socialistic. FDR, he reasoned, had "bought" allegiance to the Democratic Party through federal assistance programs for the needy. Foreign technological assistance to create national parks, preserve wildlife, and stimulate tourism might win friends against communism, while domestic programs of uplift would create economic dependence, political party allegiance, and ultimately socialism.[9]

While in Seattle, Udall asked Masland to serve as a roving natural resource troubleshooter in the United States. His first assignment was to evaluate the effects of a nor'easter that had pummeled the mid-Atlantic states four months earlier, in March. Accompanied by raging tides and ferocious winds, the "Ash Wednesday Storm of 1962" destroyed homes, resorts, roads, restaurants, and sand dunes, killing forty people and injuring a thousand more. The New Jersey seaside towns of Cape May and Sea Isle City took the brunt of the blast. To prevent another natural catastrophe, the mayor of Sea Isle City insisted that the Interior Department construct a hundred-mile protective barrier wall. While Masland could support a small barrier dam in the American Southwest to protect Rainbow Bridge National Monument, he opposed a barrier dam for the Jersey shoreline to protect people. The barrier dam at Rainbow Bridge was based on the principle of national park inviolability and to keep a promise made by Congress. The request for a concrete wall along the New Jersey shoreline was based not on the value of human survival but on greed and foolhardiness, he believed. Homeowners, commercial interests, and resort owners, he told Udall, should have been smart enough not to build so close to the coastline. Also, they should have taken care to prevent the dunes from being stripped of vegetation. The federal government, he advised, should help cities plant beach grass and other flora on the dunes. If the government consented to a concrete wall, he said, it should do so only if the cities and the State of New Jersey each assumed one-third of the cost. Udall agreed, writing that he did not care for the mayor of Sea Isle City or his plan for a wall.[10]

Masland also kept busy with nongovernmental activities. In September 1962 he attended a special dedication ceremony honoring Abbott for her contributions to the preservation of the Adams historical homestead in Quincy, Massachusetts. One of the few invitees not related to the Adams family, he prepared a speech for the occasion, as did Abbott, but Mrs. W. S. Harris, the autocratic superintendent of the national historic site, decided that the only speaker should be the assistant secretary of state, Edwin Martin (Udall could not attend). Masland's speech, a bouquet to Abbott, was printed in the *Concord Journal* a few days later. Always eager to boost Abbott's reputation and income as an artist, Masland purchased one of her paintings of the Colorado River for $350 and donated it to the Grand Canyon National Park headquarters, where it is displayed at the South Rim Visitor Center. The brass plaque reads, "Painted by Mary Ogden Abbott for Frank Masland Jr. They ran the river together."[11]

Masland also eagerly sought to boost his own reputation by membership in the prestigious Cosmos Club. Founded by Colorado River explorer John Wesley Powell in 1878, the Washington, DC, organization operated as an exclusive social club for gentlemen who had distinguished themselves in the fields of science, literature, the arts, or public service (women gained admission in 1988). Masland had long desired membership and submitted supporting letters of recommendation from naturalist Sig Olson, former NPS director Horace Albright, and the current NPS director, Conrad Wirth, but was repeatedly denied. He believed that his six scientific expeditions to the American Southwest and his service on the National Park System Advisory Board supported his membership, but to improve his chances he had resigned from the controversial John Birch Society and, upon Albright's advice, sought to publish more. He submitted a manuscript titled "Adventure Begins at Fifty" to the University of New Mexico Press, but it was not accepted. In late 1962, the *Explorers Journal* published his article on his six expeditions to southwestern slickrock country, but this apparently failed to impress the admissions committee of the Cosmos Club. "One keeps grasping at straw after straw," he confided to Wirth, "especially when one wants something as much as I frankly admit I desire a membership in the Cosmos Club." He finally gained admission in 1971.[12]

Masland's many conservation-related activities no doubt took his mind off the repeated rejections from the Cosmos Club. Accompanied by Virginia, he spent three weeks in the Everglades in March 1963. As usual, he followed up the visit with a long report to the Interior Department on the many environmental and economic issues plaguing the national park, including poaching, an insufficient fresh water supply for birdlife, and poor management by the superintendent, chief naturalist, and concessionaire. He recommended more policing to prevent poaching and littering, more nature trails and primitive campgrounds, and more pressure on the US Army Corps of Engineers and other federal agencies to provide the park with more fresh water.[13]

Ever the elitist, he recommended more publicity targeted at attracting wealthy, preservation-minded tourists to the park. Too many visitors, he observed, were boat-trailer locals who used park facilities for fishing and partying. Other vacationers were itinerant older folks and retirees who trailer-camped for weeks and viewed the park as a cheap form of lodging and entertainment. To characterize dress at the Flamingo Bay dining room as "casual," he said, "is flattering." Other park visitors were only interested in snapping a photograph of an alligator and moving on. They were like tourists at the South Rim who quickly photographed the canyon and then bolted for the Las Vegas casinos. "This is not snobbery," he lamely declared, but reality. Unless the park could attract a clientele "of a higher cultural level," it might as well be downgraded to a national recreation area. For the wealthy elitist Masland, habitat preservation once again trumped recreational use. The main mission of the Park Service, he told Wirth, was to protect and preserve the biota, not to cater to fishermen, squatters, and recreationists. Otherwise, the motel and marina at the Flamingo visitor area should be rezoned out of the park.[14]

He also unloaded to Wirth, and later to Hartzog, about the concessionaire and the park's superintendent and chief naturalist. "Everglades needs a Superintendent who is dedicated, indomitable, who is experienced in the area of negotiations and whose men will follow because they love and respect him." He lambasted the chief naturalist for being deskbound, arrogant, antagonistic, and disliked by co-workers. The concessionaire cared only about making a profit, not about the quality of housekeeping or food at the dining room.[15]

Masland was sickened to learn that the Park Service planned to build two five-mile roads to Bear Lake and Snake Bight inside the Everglades. The roads would serve mainly anglers and would destroy flora like orchids. Instead of roads, he advised Wirth, the Park Service should add more hiking and canoe trails, primitive campsites, and campfire interpretive talks by park rangers. To provide the concessionaire with more revenue to upgrade food and housekeeping service, the NPS planned to build sixty new visitor-housing units, half of which would be economical prefabricated units. Less expensive motel units would merely attract more "tin can strewers," sneered Masland. Already, at the pricier Flamingo cabins, he complained about sex threesomes, drunken parties, loose women, and profane guests in adjoining sound-porous rooms. "Never in any Park have I encountered as low a cultural level as that at Flamingo." What the park needed, he asserted, was fancier lodging, like the El Tovar and Bright Angel hotels at Grand Canyon, to attract more cultured people. "I hope you will forgive my bitterness. I think I know the Everglades about as well as anyone, and you know the deep love I have for it." Wirth replaced the park superintendent but did not address Masland's other concerns.[16]

Hartzog, who replaced Wirth in January 1964, proved slightly more receptive. He did not back away from building two roads and more low-priced housing units, but he replaced the chief naturalist, pressured the concessionaire to improve the quality of food and housekeeping service, introduced campfire talks, and committed to more ranger patrols and the construction of more hiking, nature, and canoe trails. It was enough to win Masland's support and friendship, and Hartzog proved to be one of the most successful NPS directors, adding more than sixty assets to the system.[17]

Although the Everglades and southwestern canyon country were never far from his mind, Masland also had commitments as a trustee of Dickinson College. At his suggestion, President Edel invited Udall to deliver the commencement address and accept an honorary Doctor of Law degree in early June 1963. Udall agreed, staying with the Maslands at Kings Gap during his visit. Masland introduced Udall, who delivered an address emphasizing the connection between wilderness preservation and human uplift, a theme dear to Masland. "He and I stay away from politics and so we get along rather well," he told Abbott.[18]

Later that year, Udall asked Masland to accompany him on another trip to Africa. That fall, Udall and Thomas Kimball, executive director of the National Wildlife Federation, traveled with Masland to Nairobi, Kenya, to attend the meeting of the International Union for Conservation of Nature and Natural Resources. Like Kimball, Masland was captivated by Africa and felt passionately about the need to protect its disappearing wildlife and wilderness splendor. Both men believed that developed nations should help emerging states train people in wildlife and ecological management practices.

After the conference, Masland spent several weeks with Kimball visiting national parks and wildlife in the emerging east African nations of Uganda, Kenya, and Tanganyika, assessing the potential for the preservation of nature and economic growth through tourism. Masland argued that Western nations could prevent east Africa from falling into the communist orbit if they helped them grow economically. One way to do so was to provide consultants and financial aid to help build a transportation network and to manage their abundant scenic and wildlife resources, which would attract vacationers. With quick action and a generous financial commitment, the United States had an opportunity to make east Africa a friend and a "show case" for other emerging nations.[19]

Masland's reports to Udall glowed with optimism concerning the opportunities to make east Africa a model for democracy and capitalism. But he was less optimistic about the park program in Africa than he had been a year earlier. "I fell in love with the country and people of Tanganyika and Uganda," he told Horace Albright, but he found Kenyans antagonistic toward the United States. East Africa could become "a Garden of Eden," but it was attempting to move too rapidly toward becoming an industrial state and was doomed to socialism, he predicted to Abbott. There was little chance for the development of a two-party political system in any of the east African countries and little evidence "that anyone is performing the essential functions of orderly planning and administration." The region's main wildlife assets, elephants and hippopotami, were being decimated by hunters, and soon the large animal species would be found only in parks. And those parks needed to be expanded, because the animals were outgrowing their habitat. "Furthermore, unless the parks can prove themselves to be an economic asset, they too will cease to exist for the newly free nations are unconcerned with aesthetics and culture and only with those assets that can assist them in their wild effort to by-pass the centuries and leap from voodooism to socialism." Despite his earlier nod to international brotherhood, Masland's elitist ethnocentrism was as robust as ever.[20]

Overall, he was impressed with Africans' yearning for independence. "I find their ship has a rudder," he informed former president Dwight Eisenhower, "their eyes are on the stars, that those lean and hungry people are striving—striving for a place in the sun." At the same time, middle-class western Europeans and Americans, captives of consumer culture, were losing their moral and spiritual compass. Masland was conflicted about the effects of the so-called consumer revolution that he had helped to advance. On the one hand, it provided automobiles, televisions, washing machines, carpeting, and other popular items. On the other hand, it led to overemphasis on material acquisitions. In his influential 1958 book *The Affluent Society*, John Kenneth Galbraith pointed out that the explosion of material commodities in the West had widened the gap between rich and poor and resulted in a kind of vulgar conspicuous consumption. Masland had made his fortune marketing carpets to homeowners and businesses, but he acknowledged consumerism's harmful effect on spiritual and moral values. "Those who live from day to day in affluent unconcern degenerate," he wrote Eisenhower. "One encounters a lack of interest in things spiritual. Unprecedented affluence has led to an all too prevalent assumption that man is self-sufficient." Like latter-day environmentalists, Masland was concerned that man's greed and seemingly insatiable appetite for *things* might be destructive to the survival of humankind.[21]

Like most people, Masland was a man of contradictions. As a conservative, he admired people who lived a simple agrarian lifestyle. At the same time, he was a man of the world who had faith in capitalism, industry, technology, and progress. His views on Indigenous peoples reflect that tension. Newly independent Africans, searching for their "place in the sun," were turning their backs on their "primitive" way of life and being corrupted by civilization. So were the Navajos of the American Southwest. He wanted to improve the standard of living for the Diné, but this would jeopardize a traditional way of life. The Navajo cities of Window Rock and Gallup were modernizing, reported the guide Buck White-hat. White-hat's son, torn between two cultures, had lost his way—he hanged himself. Feeling gloomy, Masland bemoaned the advance of civilization that he had helped promote. He admired Navajos who preferred "the Trading Post life" over "the white man's commercialism," he confided to Madelene Cameron. "I realize I prefer a way of life that will inevitably come to an end. I have seen enough of primitive ways of life in this country, South America, Asia, and particularly in Africa so that I am convinced it is but a matter of time before primitive cultures are lost in civilization's tidal wave," he continued. That tidal wave "overflows other cultures, leaving them unrecognizable. It destroys God's handiwork, whether it be represented by the people he created, the other animals that once covered the earth or the earth itself." At the same time, he wanted to bring industry to the Navajos so that they could become productive capitalists instead of socialists or wards of the federal state.[22]

Masland felt that Indigenous cultures possessed many superior features that mainstream white society should emulate. But he downplayed their ability to adapt to modern society. Certainly, they could borrow what they wanted from mainstream culture, just as whites could borrow from theirs. Modern life endangered the continued survival of both Indigenous and nonindigenous people. "What bodes ill for man as a biological creature is that civilization destroys the natural processes and in doing so his ecosystem, his means of maintaining it and all means of restoring it." Thoreau was right, Masland declared, when he said that "in wildness is the preservation of man." If wilderness was not preserved, "there will soon come a time when either man will become a robot" or he will become extinct. Ironically, in the same letter in which he rued the advance of civilization, he informed Cameron that he and Virginia had added to their Fallen Arches home a twenty-by-sixteen-foot kitchen, with modern conveniences and a large fireplace. The new kitchen was adorned with Navajo woven baskets and space for a white Navajo goatskin fleece on order from the Trading Post.[23]

Like other conservatives of the 1960s, Masland used the bogeyman of socialism to disparage liberals and Democrats. Individual freedom and free-enterprise capitalism, he rashly claimed, were endangered by Kennedy and other liberals determined to establish a socialist state. As numerous historians have pointed out, conservatives were gaining momentum in the 1960s.[24] Masland and other wealthy business executives, like his friend J. Howard Pew of Sun Oil, hoped that the election of Barry Goldwater in 1964 would steer the United States back onto the right track. A fellow Pennsylvanian and kindred spirit, though a generation older, Pew had inherited and expanded a family business and had become enormously wealthy doing so; like Masland, he was also devoutly religious and deeply conservative. Goldwater, Pew told Masland, "appears to be the only Presidential candidate on any ticket in the last thirty years who was not an advocate for the Welfare State." America was built on the tradition "that the Government should do nothing that the people or the States are able to do for themselves," Pew believed. "There is a great groundswell of opinion being rolled up against the New Deal Socialism," he said, and he was going to dig deeper in his pockets than ever before to support it. Masland agreed.[25]

Though he lacked Pew's financial resources, he contributed to the cause financially and urged others to support Goldwater. "Barry is not reactionary, neither is he visionary," he advised a skeptical Abbott. "He does not have a great mind but he has a sound mind. He knows he can't fix all the evil that has been done but you can count on him to recognize evil and to do his best to see to it that integrity, be it fiscal or political or personal, shall determine policy." If nominated, Goldwater would carry the South, the West, and possibly Pennsylvania, Masland predicted. The only way he could lose the election, he wrote Dock Marston, was if "Kennedy money and chicanery" manipulated the media.[26]

In addition to boosting Goldwater's candidacy privately, Masland continued to accept assignments from Udall and the Interior Department. In early November, he delivered a speech at the dedication of a new administration and orientation building at Big Bend National Park along the Rio Grande in Texas. Addressing an audience of mainly Park Service personnel, he praised Wirth, pointing out that he had helped set the boundaries of the park in the mid-1930s. Masland began to tout a whole-earth ecological perspective that would become popular a few years later, though he could never get completely behind it. His visit to Africa, he said, brought home to him as never before that humans were part of an ecosystem and that their survival depended upon its tender care and management. But for Masland, tender care and management related mainly to public lands and rural open spaces, not urban issues. National parks, he asserted, were "essential for the development of the whole man and a hardy, clear thinking, steadfast race." Citizens should insist that Congress provide the necessary funds for park acquisition and management. And the Park Service's responsibility was "to so preserve the natural scene that it will provide an everflowing font of spiritual renewal." Masland's flirtation with ecology was essentially concerned with public lands. He never would be totally won over to the environmental view that human survival depended on regulating pollution, toxins, and overpopulation.[27]

Three weeks later, President Kennedy was dead. Following the assassination, Masland sent a letter of sympathy to Udall, describing JFK as a "great National and International leader," a kindness to Udall given Masland's real feelings toward Kennedy. Privately, he had blasted the president for supplying insufficient US air support for Cuban exiles during the failed Bay of Pigs invasion in 1961 and for pledging never to invade Cuba as part of the Cuban Missile Crisis settlement of 1962. Better to leave nuclear-tipped Soviet missiles in Cuba, he told Mary Abbott, than to promise not to use force to topple a communist government so close to the US mainland. On the domestic front, Kennedy's high-handedness in forcing US Steel to retract its announced price hike on steel dealt "a death blow to Free Enterprise." But Masland was always able to separate his political convictions from his preservationist views, and he gave the late president credit for following Udall's lead on conservation issues.[28]

Kennedy was out in front on some issues that were dear to Masland—building the US nuclear missile arsenal, giving aid, though mainly symbolic, to newly emergent African states, and recognizing threats to the environment. As historian Paul Charles Milazzo observes, Kennedy delivered a special message to Congress on natural resources policy in late February 1961, praising the bipartisan Senate Select Committee on Natural Water Resources for its warning about water pollution and promising support for a federal clean water program. That report also promoted the federal construction of multipurpose dams, especially in the American West.[29]

Masland was delighted that President Lyndon Johnson kept Udall on as interior secretary. He continued to work with Udall and the Interior Department on the acquisition of more national parks, monuments, and recreation areas, while acknowledging that Udall had to balance demands from developers for wise public resource use with appeals from conservationists for the preservation of more open space. He praised Udall for the publication of *The Quiet Crisis,* a best-selling book that explored the history of the American conservation movement that also gave impetus to the emerging environmental movement. The United States, Udall wrote, possessed unrivaled military and economic might, "yet we live in a land of vanishing beauty, of increasing ugliness, of shrinking open space, and an overall environment that is diminished daily by noise and blight. This, in brief, is the quiet crisis." No single book, Masland wrote Udall, "has so ably, interestingly, and so adequately covered the history of our inheritance, caught the ebb and flow of the tide of the conservation movement." The entire conservation community "must recognize what a stroke of good fortune it was when your friend, the late President, placed his signature on your appointment." Curiously, Masland made no mention of Rachel Carson's watershed classic *Silent Spring*.[30]

Along with expanding the park system, Masland also worked for passage of the wilderness bill. He was a member of the Wilderness Society, but there is no evidence that he corresponded with Howard Zahniser, the fellow Pennsylvanian who authored the bill and served as executive secretary of the society. Crafted and revised over nearly a decade and designed to protect millions of acres of public land designated as primitive, the legislation encountered stiff opposition from the extractive industries and from wise-use conservationists like Representative Wayne Aspinall, who did not want to lock up national forest resources. The National Association of Manufacturers (NAM) also opposed the measure. The NAM and wise-use conservationists advocated multiple uses of national forests—hunting, fishing, camping, hiking, timbering, and mining. Although lands classified as "primitive" were off-limits to timbering, preservationists worried that this might change in the future without preventive legislation.[31]

As a longtime member, director, and former vice president of the NAM, Masland took the organization to task for opposing the bill. "I wear two hats," he informed the chair of the NAM Conservation Committee. "One as an industrialist, another as a preservationist." He failed to see how enactment of the wilderness bill would "seriously impair" industry. "On the other hand," he continued, "unless we set aside substantial additional wilderness areas and retain them in their primitive condition, we will have been derelict in providing for our national spiritual needs." At a time when Americans were seeking more recreational and leisure activities, it would be wise "to consider the need to provide this vast foot-loose army with an opportunity for spiritual refreshment as well as honky-tonk recreation and that meeting this need is essential to the maintenance of the free enterprise system." Masland also protested to the NAM about the organization's misrepresentation of the bill's goals to its members. When the NAM decided to debate the merits of the bill in its seven committees, Masland pointed out that both presenters, as members of the National Forestry Association, carried the flag for the logging industry. Masland also championed the bill, eventually enacted in 1964, with members of Congress and the Advisory Board on National Parks, Historic Sites, Buildings, and Monuments.[32]

Masland supported other preservation-related legislation as well, including the NPS's Wild and Scenic Rivers Program, designed to protect portions of several free-flowing rivers, and a land and water conservation fund to raise money for the acquisition of more landscapes for scenic and recreational use. In March 1963, Masland and Sig Olson canoed a hundred miles of the Suwannee River on the Georgia-Florida border and advocated its inclusion in the wild rivers program. Masland also supported the Wild and Scenic Rivers Program because it was first proposed by Frank and John Craighead, the twin sons of his friend and Carlisle neighbor Frank Craighead Sr. Championed by Udall and introduced by John Saylor, the bill was enacted in 1968. But no measure, in Masland's opinion, was more pressing than congressional enactment of the Land and Water Conservation Fund, a revenue scheme to acquire more open space by permitting states and the federal government to share a pool of money created by taxing motorboat fuel and assessing admission and user fees at federal recreational areas. In revised form, the LWCF remains in effect in the third decade of the twenty-first century.[33]

His admiration notwithstanding, Masland did not blindly support Udall's entire conservation agenda. He was irked by Udall's clumsy handling of the forced retirement of longtime Park Service director Conrad Wirth. At a meeting of the Advisory Board in Yosemite National Park in the fall of 1963, Assistant Secretary of the Interior John Carver gave a speech saying that under Wirth, the Park Service had developed a worrisome sense of camaraderie that had the "mystic, quasi-religious sound of a manual for the Hitler Youth Movement." A few days later, Wirth was replaced by George Hartzog. Masland hosted a retirement dinner for Wirth and later sent him a warm note praising his service, especially for developing "a 'mystique' that "sets the Service apart from other agencies and that unites it as a spiritual as well as a material force." Wirth, he said, would join Steven Mather and Horace Albright as one of NPS's "three immortals."[34]

Masland was at a loss to explain Carver's speech and the timing of Wirth's retirement. He thought that Wirth was planning to step down and that Carver's remarks were mean-spirited and unnecessary. He played down Udall's complicity, implying that Carver had gone rogue. But it was unrealistic for Masland to believe that Udall had not sanctioned the thrust, if not the exact language, of Carver's remarks. Indeed, earlier that year, Udall had criticized Wirth for not being a team player. He also was upset with Wirth for not moving quickly enough to recruit Blacks and for running the Park Service as an autonomous, lily-white club. Udall asked Masland to search for a qualified minority candidate for the Advisory Board, but he was unsuccessful—not that he put much effort into the search.[35]

Masland also disagreed with Udall's stance on what some people referred to as "the biggest water fight in American history." Hailing from Arizona, Udall initially endorsed legislation proposing the federal construction of one or two hydroelectric dams on the Colorado River that would provide the pumping power to sluice water for more than two hundred miles to Phoenix and Arizona's water-starved central valley. One of the Bureau of Reclamation dams at Bridge Canyon in the proposed Central Arizona Project would create a reservoir that would send water into Grand Canyon National Monument and a portion of Grand Canyon National Park. Because the intrusion would violate the principle of national park inviolability, Masland, the Sierra Club, and other conservation organizations vigorously opposed it. In 1963, the Sierra Club's David Brower asked Masland to write or bankroll a book criticizing the Colorado River dams, one similar to Eliot Porter's *Place No One Knew*, a Sierra Club publication ruing the damming of Glen Canyon. Masland begged off, stating that the only way to save the canyon was for conservation organizations to unite in opposition to the proposed dams.[36]

Privately, and well before the Sierra Club weighed in, Masland informed Udall that he, Wirth, and Albright were worried that Udall was about to crash into the rocks if he did not find a way to navigate the political storm over the proposed dams. It seemed that Udall was destined to capsize either his canoe labeled "political future" or the one named "conservation reputation." Departmental support for a high dam at Bridge Canyon, Masland said, would produce a political "wrangle tangle" from preservationists resembling a Muhammad Ali–Sonny Liston boxing match. Masland suggested the possibility of a low dam at Bridge Canyon that would not spill water into the monument or park, a possible compromise that might satisfy Arizona water interests and conservation groups. "You have established for yourself among Conservation Organizations the reputation of being a genuine Conservationist, of possessing an inherent love for the out-of-doors and a respect for our spiritual values," he told Udall. With an opportunity to establish an unrivaled reputation, Masland implored him to steer a workable middle course. Confidentially, Udall assured him that he had no intention of endorsing a high dam at Bridge Canyon but might consider a low one.[37]

Meanwhile, as a member of the National Parks Association, Masland wrote an article for *National Parks Magazine* opposing construction of the dams. He implored conservationists "to gird their loins" for a battle to defend "the integrity of canyon, monument and park." He described the many natural glories offered by the mighty river and its tributary canyons. "And now, as I lie on my down-soft bed at home and my thoughts turn to my river days, I have heard that my bed of sand by the rapids-head may be no more; that it, together with the caves and alcoves, springs and pools, gaily-colored sculpturing, all the artistry that nature has produced in seven million years, may be buried forever, never to be seen by my children's eyes," he wrote. "Even the voice of the rapid that has roared unceasingly through all the empires that the world has ever known will vanish, even as though empires have vanished. Is there a thought here that we should heed?"[38]

Heeding the voice of the canyon and the clamor from agitated preservationists, especially Brower, Udall eventually worked out a compromise that satisfied both sides. Instead of a dam at Bridge or Marble Canyon, the pumping power to channel the water to Arizona would be provided by a coal-fired generating plant on the Navajo reservation.[39]

Fed by coal from Black Mesa strip mines on the Navajo reservation, the Four Corners and Mohave generating plants produced both electricity and unintended results. Most of the electricity went to Phoenix, transforming that modest-sized city into a megalopolis. Navajos expected to obtain power, but as historian Andrew Needham points out, only half of their homes had been electrified by the 1970s. The coal mines and power plant provided employment, but they also fouled the Four Corners area with sulfuric gases, ash tailing piles, unsightly transmission towers, and ugly power lines. Moreover, Navajos living on or near coal deposits had to be relocated. "By the early 1970s," Needham asserts, "Navajo visions of modernity had fractured." Masland too had lost his zeal for modernity, because few US industrialists or philanthropists considered it economically viable to help Navajos build factories.[40]

Eager to maintain his relationship with the Park Service, Masland offered his services to Wirth's successor, George Hartzog. He liked and respected

Hartzog, who rose through the ranks of the Park Service to become director. "I have time and health. I have one great overriding interest—the National Park Service," he wrote Hartzog. Initially, however, Hartzog paid Masland little heed and gave him no assignments. Hartzog, Masland complained to Horace Albright, "does not seem to have anything for me to do. . . . There was a period when Connie and Stew and I were quite close and between them they found more for me to do than I could handle. Times change, the years pass by, old contacts fade away and after all I am not a professional." But if his activities with the Park Service ended, he told Sig Olson, he would have no regrets. "My 'Park experience' has been the highlight of my life. I am deeply grateful." His fatalistic outlook and inactivity would soon end, as he and Hartzog began a warm working and personal relationship. "Your friendship is one of my greatest and most cherished possessions," Hartzog once told Masland.[41]

Considering him an "elder stateman," Udall also wanted to retain Masland's counsel. To keep him and other seasoned veterans actively involved, Udall, at Masland's suggestion, established the National Park Service Advisory Council. Composed entirely of former valued members of the Advisory Board, Masland, Ned Danson, Fred Smith, and a few other council members were invited to attend Advisory Board meetings and participate in discussions, but without voting authority. Nor would they be paid. In addition to Canyonlands National Park and his efforts to protect the Everglades, Masland should be credited with establishing the Advisory Board Council. Although it created another layer of federal bureaucracy, unpaid council members were wise old heads who provided sound advice, institutional memory, and a steadying influence on Advisory Board meetings. But in the summer of 1964, there was no assurance that Udall or Hartzog or the Advisory Board would have jobs following the presidential election.

FIGS. 1–4 (*clockwise from top left*) Frank Masland Jr. at summer camp in Maine. Masland Family Collection; Frank Masland Jr. as a student at Dickinson College. Masland Family Collection; Frank Masland Jr. poses with a young alligator in the Galapagos Islands, 1952. Masland Family Collection; Frank Masland Jr. portrait as president of C. H. Masland and Sons. Masland Family Collection.

FIG. 5 Frank Masland Jr. as cowhand. Cumberland County Historical Society, Carlisle, PA.

FIG. 6 Frank Masland Jr. with Native American guide in canyon country. Masland Family Collection.

FIG. 7 Frank Masland Jr. looking at pictographs in canyon country. Masland Family Collection.

FIG. 8 Slickrock, difficult terrain for horses and riders. Masland Family Collection.

FIG. 9 *(below)* Frank Masland Jr. takes a tumble. Sketch by wrangler Tom Daly. Masland Family Collection.

FIG. 10 Frank Masland Jr. and Secretary of the Interior Stewart Udall in Utah's canyon lands. Dickinson College, Archives and Special Collections.

FIG. 11 Frank Masland Jr. and US senator Barry Goldwater. Masland Family Collection.

FIG. 12 An older, bearded Frank Masland Jr. Masland Family Collection.

FIG. 13 Frank Masland Jr. honored by the Commonwealth of Pennsylvania. Dickinson College, Archives and Special Collections.

FIG. 14 Colorado River canyon with cataract boat in the foreground. Dickinson College, Archives and Special Collections.

FIG. 15 Frank Masland Jr. (center) boating in the Colorado River canyon with Dr. Joe Eisaman (left) and Otis "Dock" Marston (right). Dickinson College, Archives and Special Collections.

FIG. 16 Frank Masland Jr. poses in front of Arch in the Sky with Explorers Club flag. Dickinson College, Archives and Special Collections.

CHAPTER 9

Contrary Conservative

Frank Masland's conservation narrative is filled with contradictions, as we have seen. Throughout 1964 he worked as a consultant for Udall while laboring privately for the election of Barry Goldwater, who might have replaced Udall with a new interior secretary. Masland was a diehard conservative Republican but seemed happier working for Democratic administrations. He was nonpartisan on conservation issues but deeply partisan on other political matters. He abhorred federal programs that poisoned predators like wolves but seemed indifferent to the threat of pesticides and other toxins to humans. His antagonism to a liberal welfare state and socialism coincided awkwardly with his advocacy of federal protection for the national park system and wilderness. There was also a troubling gulf between his support for the protection of the ecosystem and his lack of enthusiasm for federal controls over water and air pollution, chemical pesticides, and nuclear waste. Like many other old-school conservationists in the 1960s, Masland cared more about public land issues than he did about human health, energy, or environmental justice issues. He also preferred to advocate through established, mainstream conservation groups, not new organizations that he considered distracting, litigious, peripheral, or extreme. And while he was critical of nearly all nonmilitary federal departments, he never wavered in his support for the National Park Service.

While awaiting assignments from Hartzog or Udall, Masland pottered around Fallen Arches performing small landscape chores and tending to Virginia, who was immobilized with arthritic knees and phlebitis. He hired a nurse to help care for her and spent his mornings at his office reading, dictating correspondence, and stewing over domestic politics and the state of world affairs. Like older people everywhere, he was preoccupied with personal health issues related to advancing age, but overall he enjoyed vigorous health. River-running partners Joe Eisaman and John Doerr suffered from Parkinson's disease and leukemia, respectively. Mary Abbott had broken her shoulder and then her rib in separate accidents with her horses. And Buck White-hat could no longer ride his mule and guide pack trips, owing to a degenerative hip ailment.[1]

Masland believed that the world he had inherited was going to hell. Domestically, the America he had known as a young man was being overrun with immigrants and rampant liberalism. Abroad, the world was being overtaken by communists. Conservative political and traditional values, as he understood them from the 1920s, had fallen into disfavor. "You and I are anachronisms," he lamented to Abbott. "There is darn little in this world of ours of which we approve."[2]

Masland did approve of Senator Barry Goldwater, hoping that his election to the presidency in 1964 would restore conservative political values and sufficiently strengthen the military to fend off the advance of the Soviet Union around the world. He advised Abbott to cool her initial enthusiasm for LBJ, who was more liberal than JFK, in Masland's view. Under the New Deal admirer Johnson, he predicted, the country would move faster toward socialism than it would have under Kennedy. Only the election of Barry Goldwater could halt the erosion of individual freedom in America.[3]

Having read his position statements and spoken with Goldwater personally, Masland made a case for the senator's presidential candidacy. He unrealistically anticipated that, if elected, Goldwater would retain fellow Arizonan Stewart Udall as interior secretary. Like Masland, Goldwater was a river runner who revered the Colorado River and the Grand Canyon. Long before running for president, Goldwater had said that he and Masland were "very close personal friends. That friendship stems from our mutual interest in the Colorado River, which both of us have explored to a considerable extent." He considered Masland to be "one of God's better men."[4] The two river runners corresponded frequently—but rarely on conservation issues, because their views clashed on western dam building and the preservation of wilderness.

Apart from wilderness preservation, Goldwater embodied a political credo that was basic to Masland and other conservatives. He favored a central government with limited powers. He championed individual freedom and vowed to seek relief for "all those who find their activities encountering the iron fist of a gigantic, centralized bureaucracy." He promised to curb the "monopolistic power" of labor unions. And he would try to reverse recent liberal US Supreme Court decisions through constitutional amendments. Masland said little about Goldwater's position on the civil rights movement, except that he would not tolerate acts of civil disobedience. A fiscal conservative, Goldwater would restrain federal spending and seek relief for high-income earners who suffered under a "Marxian" federal income tax system. It was untrue, he maintained, that Goldwater opposed Social Security. He did, however, oppose legislation to establish a socialistic health insurance system for the elderly called Medicare. And Masland ignored the fact that Goldwater had voted against the Civil Rights Act of 1964 and was not much of a preservationist, as evidenced by his opposition to the Wilderness Act.[5]

On the foreign front, Masland contended in a letter to Abbott, Goldwater would combat the communist threat through toughness and military and economic might, not "appeasement" or "passive co-existence." In other words, he would pursue a tougher version of the traditional policy of containment on every front, including Africa and Southeast Asia. No foreign aid would go to communist or unfriendly governments. Aid would be "rifled and not shotgunned," as he put it. If Goldwater was considered an extremist, Masland concluded, it was only because he was being compared to thirty years of liberalism that had resulted in "the loss of international respect, constant retreat before the forces of Communism and a steady impingement upon the freedom of the states, of local governments and of the individual." He gave little credit to the Kennedy and Johnson administrations for the emerging environmental movement. And he seemed not to care that Goldwater, like many other avid conservatives, said little about conservation issues. Despite his bipartisanship on matters of conservation, Masland could not bring himself to back a Democrat for president because he thought the party was soft on communism, labor union corruption, and moral values.[6]

Bewildered by Johnson's overwhelming victory in the 1964 election, Masland told Dock Marston that he was "certainly out of step" politically and was going into hiding. All that he had left to live by, he groused, was the US Constitution, the Bill of Rights, and the Ten Commandments. "We are stuck with Johnson and organized labor," he grumbled to Abbott. "It is a good time for prayer." In addition to prayer, he informed fellow conservative J. Howard Pew, the GOP needed sympathetic media coverage, including one television station, one weekly news magazine, and some newspapers to get out the conservative message. Because liberals consistently pandered to the desires and demands of an uninformed electorate, he wondered whether the best form of government might be "an absolute, benevolent monarchy." Not surprisingly, he came to abhor Johnson's Great Society programs, which promoted economic and social justice. LBJ, he complained, was more of a socialist than FDR and JFK combined. Masland was pleased, however, when Johnson retained Udall.[7]

Decrying as federal overreach Johnson's expensive federal commitment to fighting poverty and racial injustice, he saw no inconsistency in his support for the administration's call for stewardship of the earth. For Masland, conservation was apolitical, the responsibility of all citizens and elected leaders, regardless of party.

Besides being a harbor of opportunity for all citizens, the Great Society, LBJ stated in a 1964 University of Michigan commencement speech, would serve as "a place where man can renew contact with nature. . . . It is a place where men are concerned more with the quality of their goals than the quantity of their goods." Under federal leadership, he said, the Great Society would be pursued in cities, classrooms, and the countryside. America the beautiful, he added, "is in danger. The water we drink, the food we eat, the very air that we breathe, are threatened with pollution. Our parks are overcrowded, our seashores overburdened. Green fields and dense forests are disappearing. . . . Today we must act to prevent an ugly America." Masland agreed completely with those sentiments, but green fields and dense forests were closer to his heart than antipollution measures. He also applauded silently when LBJ sent twenty thousand Marines to put down an alleged communist rebellion in the Dominican Republic in late April 1965, and again in July when LBJ Americanized the war in Vietnam by authorizing the use of aerial bombing and US combat forces against North Vietnam and the Viet Cong. Despite agreeing with many of the administration's policies, he still believed that LBJ was leading the country into socialist ruin and that godless Bolsheviks were nearing America's gates. Masland's obsession with the threat of socialism was a lifelong political and ideological blind spot.[8]

Quite properly, Masland credited Udall for the administration's commitment to environmental stewardship, or the "New Conservation," as it was sometimes labeled. Except for the Bridge Canyon dam proposal, Masland championed Udall's ambitious conservation agenda between 1964 and 1969, which produced a record of achievement rivaled only by the presidencies of Theodore and Franklin Roosevelt. In 1964, Congress enacted Udall's proposal to establish the Land and Water Conservation Fund. With revenue derived from a federal tax on motorboat fuel and offshore oil drilling, the fund would enable state and federal agencies to safeguard landscapes and shorelines.[9]

He also endorsed appeals from Udall, the Wilderness Society, and other conservation organizations for congressional enactment of a wilderness bill. Like Udall, Masland understood that few, if any, areas in America remained undefiled; after all, Native people, early Anglo immigrants, and Hispanics had all left their imprint on the land. But there were still areas where the human imprint had been minimal or grown over by nature. Those unimpaired areas, proponents believed, helped define American uniqueness and should be preserved for future generations. Wilderness terrain, most of it in national forests, should be roadless and motorless, and it should be managed as ecological units that supported healthy relationships among humans, flora, and fauna. Masland was delighted when his friend and former Advisory Board colleague Sig Olson assumed the presidency of the Wilderness Society in 1963. The Wilderness Act of 1964, passed shortly after the death of its longtime champion Howard Zahniser, set aside as a lasting national heritage nine million acres of untrammeled western national forest terrain, with a built-in process that allowed Congress to add more parcels of land over time.[10]

When Purdue University wildlife ecologist Durward Allen made the case that wilderness was valuable mainly for scientific purposes, Masland disagreed. Wilderness was valuable principally for the spiritual enrichment it offered, he argued. "For many who do not attend church the wilderness provides the only opportunity for a spiritual experience," he wrote Allen. "I am of the opinion the opportunity to camp by a stream, to watch the sun come up, build a little fire and fill one's nostrils with the scent of sizzling bacon or to stand on a mountain top and fill one's lungs with clean, fresh air and gaze off across the valley's treetops provides a spiritual experience more essential to the quality of life of a nation than any scientific result." In a nutshell, that sentiment embodies Masland's view of nature. Connecting with nature improved the quality of human life much more than regulating pollution and toxins.[11]

Masland's view of nature and of the Christian stewardship of the earth resembled those of another anti-statist: the novelist, essayist, and poet Wendell Berry. Although there is no evidence that the two men knew each other, the much younger Berry was a fellow son of the Cumberland Valley. Born in 1934, he earned his BA and MA from the University of Kentucky and, with Edward Abbey and other aspiring authors, took a creative writing seminar with novelist Wallace Stegner at Stanford University. A full-time writer and sometime college teacher, Berry called himself "a farmer poet" and "a placed person" who lived with his wife on a fifty-acre self-sustaining farm near the Kentucky River in Port Royal, Kentucky.[12]

Like Masland and Abbey, Berry feared centralized power yet became an active preservationist. He was a strong adherent of Henry David Thoreau's maxim "That government is best which governs least." "Though I respect and feel myself dignified by the principles of the Declaration and the Constitution," Berry wrote, "I do not remember a day when the thought of the government made me happy, and I never think of it without the wish that it might become wiser and truer and smaller than it is." But federal authority was necessary, he insisted, to preserve natural beauty and wilderness and to protect the environment and humans from commercial abuses like the strip mining of coal. Unfortunately, most elected government officials, both state and federal, were more concerned with helping the rich get richer than with regulating strip mining and other commercial raids on open space and public lands. Berry and Masland regarded the bulldozer as an evil machine because it defiled the landscape. "A man on a bulldozer can scarcely make a move that does not affect either his neighbors or his heirs," Berry wrote. "All his acts . . . involve a tampering with the birthright of his race."[13]

Both men championed life on small farms and in villages like Port Royal, Kentucky, and Bustleton and Carlisle, Pennsylvania. Large cities were impersonal, dirty, and overcrowded. In small communities, neighbors looked after neighbors and depended upon one another, not federal welfare. Government handouts resulted in dependence and a loss of dignity.[14]

Masland and Berry also shared the view that citizens should be stewards of the earth. Humans, Berry once wrote, were as dependent on the earth as earthworms. Unfortunately, most citizens and corporations exploited and despoiled the earth's resources and beauty. Unbridled economic growth and reckless consumption were equally to blame for the deterioration of the environment. Americans were wasteful consumers not only of plastics, automobiles, clothing, and technological gadgets but also of nature itself. Both Masland and Berry derided tourists who considered nature's resources inexhaustible and littered the landscape with refuse of all kinds.[15]

Federal and state authorities alone could not protect nature, Masland and Berry agreed. Citizens must take responsibility. "Man cannot be independent of nature," Berry wrote. "In one way or another he must live in relation to it, and there are only two alternatives: the way of the frontiersman, whose response to nature was to dominate it, to assert his presence in it by destroying it; or the way of Thoreau, who went to natural places to become quiet in them, to learn from them, to be restored by them." Most consumers of nature, declared Berry, do not like silence and solitude because it forces them to consider age-old "questions of origins and ends. It asks a man what is the use and the worth of his life. It asks him who he thinks he is, and what he thinks he's doing, and where he thinks he's going. . . . The experience of that silence is basic to any religious feeling."[16]

Both men insisted that Christian doctrine obligated humans to be stewards of the environment. Unlike Masland, Berry was not a regular churchgoer or a member of any organized faith. In fact, he denigrated Christian faith leaders for dishonoring the Creator by being more concerned with the health of the church building fund than with the health of the earth's ecosystem. A student of the Bible, Berry was an adherent of the Gospels and the Sermon on the Mount, a self-described "solitary Christian." Like Masland, he believed that communicating with nature was a spiritual experience akin to connecting with the Creator. Americans, he noted, were "suffering terribly from a sort of spiritual nomadism, a loss of meaningful contact with the earth. . . . They lack the vital morality and spirituality that can come only from such contact; the sense, for instance, of their dependence on the earth; and the sense of eternal mystery surrounding life on earth."[17]

For many activists, as historian Thomas Dunlap explains in *Faith in Nature*, environmentalism served as a substitute religion. This was not the case with Masland and Berry. Environmentalism, like moral behavior, was part of their religious faith, not a substitute for it. "It is in nature that we find, if we seek, that God has provided unlimited opportunities for the stirring of man's mind and the uplifting of his soul. There we encounter the mysteries of life," Masland wrote a friend. "The opportunity to enjoy wilderness provides a sense of oneness with the earth and with all living things. Those who contribute to the preservation of nature have, in a sense, paid their debt to those from whom they inherited and met their obligations to posterity. . . . To a naturalist God is a living, every day fact."[18]

Masland also believed that churches of all denominations should take greater interest in the preservation of sublime natural landscapes as manifestations of God's existence and beneficence. "Of all existing agencies in our society," he wrote Sigurd Olson, "the Church has a greater stake in the preservation of wilderness than any other. . . . It is my conviction that the National Park Service and the Church have a mutuality of interest—that their objectives are the same—the preservation of the spirit."[19]

In a 1967 essay in *Science* magazine, Lynn White blamed Christianity for what he described as a mid-twentieth-century "ecological crisis"—suburban sprawl, environmental degradation, and the wanton exploitation of nature. By emphasizing human domination over the natural world, Christianity was "the most anthropocentric religion the world has ever seen." Darwin notwithstanding, White observed, "we are *not,* in our hearts, part of the natural process. We are superior to nature, contemptuous of it, willing to use it for our slightest whim." Christians, he cautioned, should understand that they are fellow inhabitants in the web of life and should act as humble custodians, not arrogant monarchs. Two decades before the publication of White's essay, Masland and numerous other conservationists had reached that same conclusion. Coming from a family of weavers, Masland understood that the fabric of life, like a beautiful carpet, contained many interwoven threads.[20]

Like most Christians, Masland believed that God had created the world and all living organisms. And, like the lapsed Presbyterian Rachel Carson, he believed that God the Creator and Darwinian evolution were not incompatible. Evolution was simply an ongoing process designed by the Creator. He also believed that God gave man dominion over the earth. But for Masland dominion meant stewardship—the responsibility not to abuse the earth or its resources. Responsibility also "recognizes the interdependence of all that is a part of God's creation, that all things hang together and if they don't, man joins the other endangered species," as he put it in a speech in 1970.[21]

Berry shared that sentiment and took issue with White's essay. He acknowledged that the Creator gave humans dominion over the earth and that they had abused the natural world. "We have an 'ecological crisis,'" he responded to White, "because we have consented to an economy in which by eating, drinking, working, resting, traveling, and enjoying ourselves we are destroying the natural, God-given world." The abuse, however, did not have to continue.

Dominion did not mean tyranny; it meant stewardship. After all, the Creator warned Adam and Eve to care for the Garden of Eden. And the Promised Land was given to the tribes of Israel so long as it was used properly. "We must not use the world as though we created it ourselves," argued Berry. "What is given is not ownership, but tenancy." The Creator's gift of good land, he added, should be accepted humbly and with a pledge to be good caretakers.[22]

Masland and Berry were not in sync on every issue. Masland had more faith in politicians—certain ones, at least—than Berry did. And he was less gloomy about the future and less suspicious of technology. After all, his carpet-manufacturing success derived in large measure from technological innovations, and he used a dictating machine for correspondence, while Berry wrote by hand and used horses, not tractors, on his farm. Berry was more tolerant of immigration than Masland was, though he maintained that the United States was nearing its "carrying capacity." Berry also opposed the Vietnam War and nuclear arms race, while Masland supported both. And Masland was a super-patriot, while Berry railed against so-called patriots who criticized other Americans for desecrating the flag but not for ravaging the earth.

Masland did not have Berry's prominence, but he had a more tangible impact on public land policy because he had the ear of Stewart Udall, NPS directors Conrad Wirth and George Hartzog, and the Park Service Advisory Board. Masland's main influence was as a member of the Advisory Board and Advisory Council. Masland also served as the eyes and ears of Udall and the Park Service as a sort of roving inspector-general.

Early in 1965, Udall asked Masland to make reconnaissance visits to several national parks to assess threats to their ecosystems. Having recovered from phlebitis, Virginia accompanied Frank on an eleven-thousand-mile, two-month trip to Santa Fe, Saguaro National Monument in Tucson, Death Valley National Monument, Organ Pipe National Monument in Arizona, and Big Bend National Park and Padre Island National Seashore in Texas, ending with two weeks in Everglades National Park. After completing the other stops on the tour, he hiked, boated, and flew over the Everglades, inspecting habitat, water levels, and bird rookeries. He lambasted the US Army Corps of Engineers for "drying up" the habitat by diverting fresh water through dams, dikes, and canals. "The whole ecology is changing. Species are threatened with extermination," he told Abbott.[23]

In his detailed report to Hartzog, he stated that the Everglades situation was "fast deteriorating." Poaching continued unabated. Alligator belly hides were selling for $5.00 per foot. Hickok Belt Company trucks blatantly parked on the outskirts of the park, ready to carry off the pilfered hides. There were not enough rangers to limit poaching. The acquisition of a helicopter, he said, would cut down on poaching and aid in the inspection of wildlife habitat. Owing to insufficient food caused by the diversion of water by the Army Corps of Engineers, wildlife species were threatened, among them alligators, manatees, wood storks, and various other bird species. Masland proposed various remedies for the water problem, the simplest being to seal the outlets of Lake Okeechobee and build a new paved canal that would allow its water to flow uninterrupted to Everglades Park. Yes, it would be expensive, but if taxpayers could pay the Army Corps of Engineers to dredge the mouth of the Miami River and deposit the topsoil for the benefit of Burlingame Island owner Arthur Vining Davis, one of the richest men in the world, he argued angrily, they could afford to build a canal to save the rare biota of the Everglades. Masland sent a similar letter to Stewart Udall.[24]

Udall provided little satisfaction regarding relief for the Everglades, but at his suggestion, LBJ appointed Masland to the president's Task Force on Natural Resources. Johnson also invited him to attend a two-day White House Conference on Natural Beauty in late May 1965. Beautifying America was a cause dear to Lady Bird Johnson, and conference invitees discussed ways to limit highway billboards, automobile junkyards, and other blights on the landscape and cityscape. She and Udall became allies in beautifying both the American countryside and cities like Washington, DC. Masland was impressed with Mrs. Johnson, who gave the opening address. She was "a very determined female," he reported to Marston. She "was warm and friendly in conversation, but one senses the steel." Like Udall, Masland would form a close association with Lady Bird in the beautification crusade.[25]

Masland was happy to be active for Udall and the Park Service in 1965. "One of these days it'll all blow up but it is good while it lasts," he told Abbott. "It is indeed ironical that I seem to be working in greater harmony, with greater effectiveness and with more pleasure with the Democrats than I was able to when the Republicans were in power."[26]

In correspondence and speeches, Masland pushed Udall's ambitious conservation agenda. In addition to the Land and Water Conservation Fund and the Wilderness Act, Udall proposals that met with Masland's approval included Guadalupe Mountains (Texas), Redwood (California), and North Cascades (Washington) National Parks; numerous new national historic sites, recreation areas, and wildlife refuges; an alliance with Lady Bird Johnson to beautify rural and urban landscapes; the Trails System Act of 1968; the Wild and Scenic Rivers System; clean air and water legislation; and an ecological perspective that informed the environment movement. "He is the best Secretary of the Interior we have had in memory," Masland told Marston.[27]

Conservationists who protested parts of Udall's agenda as too modest drew Masland's ire. In early 1966, he became upset when the Sierra Club's David Brower criticized Udall's proposed size of thirty-nine thousand acres for Redwood National Park as too scrawny. The Sierra Club preferred a larger park of nearly a hundred thousand acres. "I like Brower personally," Masland told Marston. "He is doing an excellent job for the Sierra Club. His efforts are creating a conservation conscience country. It is only when he adopts a whole hog or nothing attitude that it gums up the works." When the author Paul Brooks criticized conservatives for being timid on conservation issues in the *Sierra Club Bulletin*, Masland reprimanded him for trying to claim the cause for liberals. "Conservation is a wave that is sweeping the country," he wrote Brooks, and conservationists "should ride that wave in a well found ship with *liberal* painted on one bow and *conservative* on the other side." He clung to that view his whole life.[28]

Despite his reprimand of Brooks, Masland was troubled by Republican conservatives who were indifferent toward the proposed Redwood National Park and conservation in general, especially Ronald Reagan, the recently elected governor of California. Reagan had once claimed to be unmoved by trees, including the towering three-hundred-foot redwoods that had stood for more than a thousand years along the fog-shrouded coast of northern California. "I saw them; there is nothing beautiful about them, just that they are a little higher than the others," Reagan had said. Quite naturally, timber companies coveted the rot-resistant goliaths for lumber and were steadily harvesting unpreserved stands of them. Masland asked Horace Albright to remind Reagan that supporting beautification and national park projects was good politics and good for business. "Reagan should climb aboard the conservation wave that is sweeping across the country," he stated. "The liberal element has done so. This is good. Conservation should be a bi-partisan subject. The conservative cause will be hurt if it does not recognize this fact." Reagan, he said, should "embrace conservation simply for its own sake—and the sake of posterity but over and above that the occupant of a major political office should endorse the concept as a political fact of life." Governor Reagan understood the political power of the surging environmental movement and did support a congressional measure in 1968 establishing the fifty-eight-thousand-acre Redwood National Park. Though the park was not as large as the Sierra Club and most preservationists wanted, the compromise bill pleased Masland as the best result that could be achieved at the time. Eventually, more than a hundred thousand additional acres of the giant trees were protected by the state and national governments.[29]

Ironically, given his later assault on environmental causes as president, Ronald Reagan established a notable conservation record as governor, according to his biographer Lou Cannon. Besides supporting protection for the redwoods, he opposed massive flood control, irrigation, and hydroelectric dams on free-flowing portions of the Feather, Eel, and Dos Rios Rivers, supported the designation of several rivers in northern California as wild and scenic, and opposed a trans-Sierra highway project that would have endangered a wilderness area and crossed the John Muir Trail. As governor, Cannon explains, Reagan's position on environmental issues was guided by his resources director, Norman Livermore. Like Masland, though fifteen years younger, Livermore was a conservative Republican, business executive, Sierra Club member, and ardent preservationist. Unfortunately for environmental causes, President Reagan, following the advice of Senator Paul Laxalt (R-NV), appointed James Watt, rather than Livermore, to head the Interior Department.[30]

Like Livermore and Governor Reagan, Masland took a measured, politically achievable approach to environmental issues, hoping to avoid divisiveness and cross-purposes among various conservation leaders and groups. Firebrands like Tony Smith, president of the National Parks Association, upset him. As a member of the executive committee and vice chair of the association's board of trustees, he criticized Smith for being "dogmatic" and "arrogant" and for "usurping too much power" and failing to cooperate with the trustees and NPS. He also ripped into Smith for his declining interest in the national parks and for going public with criticism of the Park Service for dragging its feet in setting aside sizable sections of parks as wilderness areas. Smith, he argued, prioritized ecology over preservation. Smith responded by asking Masland to resign as vice chair. He complied but remained on the board of trustees. In what the association's historian John C. Miles has called a "crisis in leadership," the trustees, weary of Smith's autocratic rule, eventually forced his resignation in late February 1980.[31]

Although Tony Smith and sometimes David Brower fell short of the mark on what Masland regarded as temperate bipartisan environmental policy, Udall could do no wrong. "Poor old Stew Udall. He is catching it from all directions—and really none of it is his fault," Masland told Marston during the controversy over the proposed Grand Canyon dams. According to his biographer Philip Fradkin, Advisory Board member Wallace Stegner shared this sentiment, defending Udall as the strongest conservationist ever to serve as interior secretary. Masland praised Udall for his commencement speech at Dartmouth College in June 1965 and wrote a letter of congratulations when the conservative *Wall Street Journal* lauded him for his environmental achievements and his strong rapport with the press after a rocky beginning. "I do not know when anything that has happened in Government has given me greater gratification than the change that has taken place in the image accorded you by the press and the public," he wrote. "It is seldom the press changes its mind but in this instance it surely has and with a vengeance indeed when the old *Wall Street Journal* sees fit to confer knighthood upon the Secretary of the Interior. My best to you and Lady Lee." "That note sounds like your [*sic*] becoming my chief PR man," Udall responded. "Who knows maybe *Time* will discover me? Many thanks, old friend." Despite his complaints about government power, federal bureaucracy, and liberals, Masland enjoyed his close relationship with Udall and remained his "chief PR man" for the rest of his life. The two men were poles apart politically but kindred spirits environmentally. And though Masland was beyond traditional retirement age, Udall continued to respect his opinions as a member of the Advisory Board Council and to task him with special assignments, including a second reconnaissance trip to Africa.[32]

CHAPTER 10

Back to Africa

Udall and Masland had high hopes for the preservation of natural landscapes in Africa, even as emerging nations wrestled with decolonization, political instability, and political alignments during the Cold War. In the mid-1960s, Masland made two additional trips for Udall to the Horn of Africa, and these reconnaissance missions energized him about the potential of its parklands. They also diverted his attention from the so-called evils of the liberal state at home under the Johnson administration. Upon his return to the United States, he relished the political demise of the Johnson presidency, simultaneously regretting the accompanying domestic disarray and the approaching end of Udall's eight-year stint as arguably the nation's ablest interior secretary.

Always willing to accept Udall's assignments, he agreed in 1964 to make another trip to eastern Africa to assess the wildlife and national park potential of Ethiopia, Kenya, and Tanzania. The continent's wildlife, like bison in the nineteenth-century American West, was being hunted to near extinction. Indigenous lifestyles were also imperiled by independence movements, Masland believed. To modernize their economies, emerging nations might endanger the cultures and native habitats of the Maasai on the Tanzania-Kenya border and other Indigenous people. Westernization had been ruinous to Native peoples over the years, he told Dock Marston. Even his beloved Navajo people were abandoning their traditional ways. Masland was certainly a product of the Western tradition and believed in spreading the Christian faith, but he freely acknowledged that Christianity, arm-in-arm with Western civilization and Western wars, had killed far more people than African tribal conflicts ever had.[1]

Masland was entranced by the east African wilderness. Saving portions of it for posterity would be difficult, however, because the entire African and Asian world seemed to be falling into the godless communist sphere, in his view. Tanzania had declared its independence in December 1961 and was suffering growing pains. When the army revolted in 1964, its socialist leader, Julius Nyerere, asked the British to send in armed forces to restore order. At the same time, Africans on the island of Zanzibar revolted against their Arabian leader, raping and killing thousands of Arabs in the process. Zanzibar off the coast of east Africa, Ghana in west Africa, and Cambodia in Southeast Asia, he went on, were, like Cuba, Russian outposts. In each of these vital areas, he groused to Mary Abbott, Russia had a staging area from which to foment wars of national liberation.[2]

Eventually, the British restored order, and in April 1964 Tanganyika and Zanzibar became the United Republic of Tanzania under Nyerere. Despite the turmoil, Masland offered to go ahead with an extended visit to the region with Conrad Wirth to implement some park and economic-assistance programs. Russia and Communist China were moving into Kenya with road-building and other economic-assistance programs, he cautioned Udall. If Kenya fell into the communist orbit, Tanzania, Uganda, and central African nations would follow. The Western world's best hope of winning over emerging nations on the continent, he declared, lay in east Africa. Without prompt US aid, the entire landmass, including its people, wildlife, and natural sanctuaries, would be lost to communism.[3]

The turmoil in east Africa prompted the US State Department to cancel Masland's scheduled trip. Ethiopia, the closest ally of the US in the Horn, was experiencing a border clash with Somalia, its neighbor to the east. Somalia, with arms from the Soviet Union, sought control of the disputed Ogaden border region. Ethiopia's longtime emperor, Haile Selassie, sought additional military aid to maintain control of Ogaden. The US government hesitated to supply more military help, fearing an escalation of the fighting. Moreover, the United States was sliding into a larger commitment in Vietnam. American policymakers had to deal delicately with Selassie because he controlled the lease to Kagnew Station, the most important American military installation in Africa. Located in the city of Asmara in the Eritrea region of northern Ethiopia, Kagnew was used by the US military to communicate with ships in the area. Unbeknownst to Selassie, it also served as a secret listening outpost, intercepting messages from a variety of foreign sources. Eritrea was another unstable region because its residents, unhappy with Ethiopian annexation, sought their independence and soon would launch a rebellion.[4]

Given the regional chaos in Kenya and in Ethiopia's northern and eastern provinces, Masland was not disappointed by the cancellation of his visit. "I am indebted to you for one of my most pleasant experiences, my trip to East Africa," he informed Udall regarding his earlier visit of 1962. "I am indebted to those who prevented a return trip," he said. But he lamented that events had temporarily sidetracked American efforts to build goodwill and the region's economy through establishing national parks, protecting wildlife, and promoting tourism.[5]

In the spring of 1966, Udall again asked Masland, now seventy years old, to return to east Africa, specifically Ethiopia, even though that nation still faced border problems to the north and east. As Udall's personal representative, Masland spent nearly three weeks in May in the former Italian colony. His charge was to persuade Haile Selassie to permit the United States to send three NPS representatives to help develop and manage national parks, wildlife reserves, historic sites, and resort areas.

By Land Rover, airplane, and boat, he and Virginia crisscrossed the country, visiting towns, monasteries, historic sites, hot springs, waterfalls, river gorges, and ragged terrain populated by oryxes, kudus, crocodiles, baboons, and exotic birds. In one dusty, dirty, remote interior village he passed the John F. Kennedy Tavern. In the capital of Addis Ababa, he joined foreign and domestic dignitaries to review a four-hour parade celebrating Ethiopia's twenty-fifth anniversary of regaining its independence from Italian rule during World War II. Reverence and loyalty for the seventy-five-year-old emperor, he said, was apparent. His resolve, ability and patience were admirable, Masland observed in his private notes. The people, he noted, were friendly and good-natured. "Present were qualities we most notably have lost—pride, loyalty, respect for leaders, for flag, love of country. Also they are a deeply religious people. The church and state are the two most important factors in their eyes." Although Indigenous tribes were pagans, most Ethiopians adhered to the Coptic Church, a sect of the Eastern Orthodox Church.[6]

Masland dined with Princess Ruth, the emperor's thirty-year-old granddaughter, and the next day met with Selassie himself. Also present were the American chargé d'affaires, the Ethiopian minister of information and tourism, and interpreters. The conversation began stiffly, but eventually relaxed when the two men discussed difficulties with their grandchildren. Of a similar age, both Masland and Selassie were tall and lean and sported heavy, feathery eyebrows. After hearing Masland out, Selassie enthusiastically agreed to invite US Park Service professionals to assist with the development of national parks, wildlife preserves, historic sites, and tourist resorts and said he would direct his ministers to work out the details with Udall. When Masland turned the conversation to his travels in the country, the emperor became excited and began speaking in English instead of French. He also insisted that Masland visit Metigoshe, a national reserve of tall ancient trees, and the next day sent armed guards to escort Frank, Virginia, and the minister of agriculture, who endured the sixty-five-mile overland trek in a Jeep Wagoneer. Featuring juniper trees thousands of years old, the park reminded Masland of Sequoia National Park, but less grand. Reflecting on his Ethiopian excursion, he considered Selassie the most imposing man he had ever met and the trip near-perfect. He filed reports with Udall and the State Department but received no feedback.[7]

The US State Department and intelligence agencies did not share Masland's rosy view of Selassie. The CIA considered him a man of "declining vigor," overly concerned with "external affairs" and unable to keep pace with the complexity of governing. "The elite of the bureaucracy and the army are increasingly alienated from the regime, and the armed forces are hard pressed to put down the insurgencies in the provinces," read a CIA report on Selassie. "The outlook is for growing internal discontent, continued insurgency in the provinces, and demands on the US for more military aid." In short, Selassie's days as emperor were numbered.[8]

In March 1967, Masland received a phone call from Udall asking him to make another visit to Ethiopia. Fearing for the security of his regime and the safety of his country, Selassie had met with President Johnson in mid-February seeking additional military aid, especially helicopters. Embroiled in the Vietnam War, the Johnson administration did not want to increase its aid to Ethiopia. Neither did it wish to offend the emperor. "The maintenance of friendly relations with Ethiopia is important to our interests in Africa and especially to the maintenance of Kagnew Station, an essential US military communications installation (with important intercept functions, a fact not to be mentioned to the Emperor) located in northern Ethiopia," Secretary of State Dean Rusk informed LBJ. Rusk suggested a modest $2 million increase in military assistance and assurances to Selassie that the United States would help with nonmilitary aid programs. Acceding to the emperor's request for help in the pursuit of a parks and tourism program initiated during Masland's previous visit was a cost-effective and tactful way to please Selassie. Moreover, it did not require discussion at a high-level foreign policy meeting.[9]

Joined by the NPS head of international relations and the superintendent of Glen Canyon National Recreation Area, Masland made a second tour of Ethiopia for five weeks in March and April 1967. More physically demanding than the previous trip, the second, minus Virginia, covered more backcountry and called for the seventy-one-year-old Masland to hike, camp, sleep on the ground, and ride mules. When he arrived in Addis Ababa he was greeted and treated like a celebrity. "At the moment," he wrote to Virginia, "I'm such a bigshot I don't recognize myself. Just hope and pray I can deliver. As a personal representative of the Secretary (he calls me his ambassador), I've got to deliver." In addition to American goodwill, he hoped to deliver assurances of more financial and technical assistance for the preservation of nature.[10]

After spending his first day in Ethiopia briefing US Ambassador Edward Korry on his mission, he and his team headed to the field, first visiting the Awash game preserve, some 265 miles from Addis Ababa. Set aside a year earlier and under consideration for official national park status, the area featured spectacular waterfalls, a free-flowing river, and an abundance of baboons, sea eagles, and a variety of colorful birds. Awash was well suited to national park status. But first, as in the United States a century earlier, tribal people had to be relocated because their massive cattle herds were destroying the grassland. Masland recommended that an existing government order relocating the nomads be enforced, that access roads be constructed so that tourists could reach the waterfalls and warm springs, and (perhaps with the El Tovar on the South Rim of the Grand Canyon in mind) that a hotel be erected on the edge of the Awash River Canyon. With the implementation of these recommendations, he wrote, Awash would rival Nairobi, Kenya. It would also serve as a model for other parks and qualify for a grant of $200,000 from the US Agency for International Development.[11]

From Awash, Masland drove to the Rift Valley lakes area. Consisting of four lakes aflutter with a variety of birds, he recommended establishing the area as a nature sanctuary. Accompanied by two Ethiopian wildlife specialists, he rattled by Jeep along the Boro River to the Sudan border. The Anuak and Nuer tribes lived across the river from his party's campsite. Both tribes were sedentary and peaceful trade partners. "Both are primitive, their cultures having changed little over the centuries. Anuaks wear some clothing, Nuers seldom wear any. Both are tall, 6'6" and over, magnificent physical specimens and among the happiest people I have encountered," he wrote to Virginia in his report on the trip. They ferried him and his companions across the river in a dugout canoe to attend a dance festival and greeted them warmly. "There is no such thing as modesty or shame and it is interesting to see how quickly one becomes accustomed to nakedness," he wrote Virginia. "It was a marvelous experience, mingling so closely with them, being so totally accepted. They are among the least influenced by the outside of any of the natives. It has been my experience in East Africa and in Ethiopia, especially Ethiopia, that color of the skin means nothing."[12]

Not surprisingly, perhaps, given his favorable impression, Masland recommended that the two tribes be isolated from tourists by designating the area a wildlife and cultural reserve. "Though friendly, their way of life is as wild as the wildlife of which they are a part. Utterly natural, they are part and parcel of nature. It is as tragic to deliberately destroy a centuries old and adjusted culture as it is to destroy a species."[13] Hoping to find the proper balance between tradition and modernity, he held the same paternalistic sentiment toward the Navajo people of the American Southwest.

Masland next spent a week camping and hiking in the proposed Simien Mountains National Park region. Composed of deep valleys and towering volcanic peaks, among them the 12,750-foot Mount Mystagog, which Masland climbed, the area deserved park status for three reasons, he asserted. It possessed "unsurpassed scenery"; it held significant groves of giant heather, St. John's wort, and other vegetation; and it was the home of rare animals like the Gelada baboon, Walia ibex, and Simien fox. As the area was accessible only by foot and mule along a nearly seventeen-mile trail, Masland and the local game warden recommended the construction of a four-wheel-drive road, wildlife guard post, and lodge, leaving tourists a five-mile hike to the park. They also recommended ecological studies that would set the boundaries of the park and establish a management plan.[14]

The Simien Mountains region was "the most spectacular and the roughest country I have ever seen," Masland informed Virginia. "The High Simien is magnificent, vast, patternless eroded plateaus. Great flattops and rugged peaks. Sheer escarpments, 1000 to 5000 feet deep. Overwhelming, unfriendly, unforgiving of mistakes." On the trek up and down, the party lost a horse to a broken leg. Instead of shooting it, the Natives left it for jackals. Camping at nearly eleven thousand feet was brutally cold and windy. At night, the strong gusts would have collapsed his tent had he not clung to the pole. Hiking in high elevations did not bother him, he said, until he reached ten thousand feet. "At 12,000, I'm a bit shy of much needed oxygen. I must have done very well for the natives couldn't believe my age. Incidentally, I am beyond doubt the oldest darn fool to have invaded that country." The Natives, who carried the packs, seemed unaffected, practically running up the peaks. "I have never seen such endurance. They should win the Olympics." He concluded his letter on a tender note. "I am a very, very fortunate person, both in health and the wife God has given me, who never says no when I want to travel to the ends of the earth to do such outrageous things."[15]

On the final day of the visit, he met with Selassie for nearly an hour. They conversed easily in English. Selassie told him, "You are remarkably rugged to go through the Simien at your age." Masland then detailed his plans for Ethiopian resort and park development. The emperor expressed enthusiasm but said Ethiopia would need financial and technical assistance from the United States. When they parted, Selassie took Masland's hand and asked him to return to Ethiopia, but he knew he never would.[16]

Masland considered his trip exciting and successful. Selassie, he gushed, "is one of the world's truly remarkable men." Nonetheless, he expressed foreboding about Ethiopia's future, and rightfully so. In his report and in letters to George Hartzog, Masland pressed the Interior Department to send technicians and management specialists to Ethiopia and complained when funds were not authorized. Aiding conservation abroad, he said, was "the one area in which the United States can render financial aid that results in minimal, if any criticism on the part of the recipient or other countries." Masland left unstated but clearly implied the message that helping to preserve the natural habitat also might aid in keeping Ethiopia from falling prey to socialism. Hartzog could do little except express sympathy for Masland's appeal.[17]

As usual, Masland also vented to Abbott. The US Department of the Interior, he complained, operated on a shoestring budget. The Johnson administration could afford to send millions of tons of grain to India, where people starved because they wouldn't eat beef, "but we have no funds to assist developing nations in preserving some of our most interesting and fast vanishing wildlife species." Ethiopians were doing their part, he said, but they needed more help from the United States to manage their nature sanctuaries. "The deuce of it here is that Interior can't do anything unless State okays it. The purse strings are controlled by AID which in turn is an arm of State. And so I don't know what will happen in Ethiopia." Unfortunately, as he anticipated, the country fell into chaos in the early 1970s. Following two years of famine, Marxist rebels initiated a coup d'état in September 1974, toppling Selassie and triggering a long civil war that killed more than a million people. Most of the royal family fled the country, but Selassie was captured and imprisoned; he was murdered in prison in 1975.[18]

It is difficult to assess the effectiveness of Masland's visits to Ethiopia. Aside from demonstrating his physical vigor and his dedication to Udall and the national park movement worldwide, his personal meeting with Selassie doubtless gave added impetus to the formal designation of the Awash and Simien Mountains regions as national parks. But Selassie may have been manipulating Masland and Udall, showing interest in national parks as a means of obtaining more US economic assistance to stabilize his regime. It is likely that he was pursuing both goals.

The Ethiopian government recruited the Canadian naturalist C. W. Nicol to help establish the boundaries of the Simien Mountain region in the late 1960s, and the park was formally established in late 1969. A decade later, the United Nations designated the Simien Mountain National Park a World Heritage Site. Masland's visits to Africa, wrote NPS director Russell Dickenson in 1984, were "a significant and precedent setting early phase of our now very active cooperation with other nations on national park matters. . . . Without your personal involvement at an early formative stage of conservation in Ethiopia, it is quite unlikely that the Simien Mountains would have achieved this status."[19]

Upon his return to the United States, Masland determined that events in Vietnam were spinning out of control, much as they were in east Africa. Privately, he did not hesitate to recommend rash or reckless military moves to check the advance of what he called international communism. He decried the death of American soldiers in Vietnam, not because the cause was unjust but because the United States was fighting a limited war, as it had in Korea. Like many strident conservatives, he called for an all-out military effort in Vietnam, even if it meant war with the People's Republic of China. "All along I have felt that the thing for us to do was to go in there with our superior technology and get it over with even if that calls for the elimination of Hanoi or, . . . the elimination of the nuclear plants in Red China. Some day we will have to contend with Red China and it would be easier now than later," he blustered to Abbott. Red China had the advantage of manpower, he acknowledged. But that advantage could not "stand up against all out bombing. The greater the concentration of manpower the easier it is to bomb them. We simply can't go on playing the numbers game in Vietnam, counting score each morning to see how many of our boys died and how many of theirs. . . . We are asking our boys to die without being willing to put forth the effort to win." Masland did not see the irony of beautifying America while pulverizing the villages and countryside of Vietnam.[20]

Facing advancing age, Masland sought to connect with the American wild while he was still physically able. In July 1967, at age seventy-one, he and his fourteen-year-old grandson Jon and one of Jon's friends spent two weeks in the American Southwest, rafting the Colorado River, hiking to Rainbow Bridge, and exploring on foot, horseback, and Jeep the raw backcountry of Canyonlands National Park. "I remember it like it was yesterday, one of the highlights of my childhood," recalled Jon Masland half a century later. "My grandfather truly was a remarkable man."[21]

Masland returned from the solitude of the canyon country to be jolted by domestic race riots and heated demonstrations against American escalation of the war in Vietnam. Instead of seeking all-out victory, he scowled, President Johnson was searching for a diplomatic compromise in Vietnam. The United States had no chance of victory, he told Abbott. LBJ might be able to pull "a political white rabbit out of hat but it won't be a victory. It may win him an election, but it won't win us respect abroad nor will it win freedom for the Vietnamese." Meanwhile, Stewart Udall, Masland's top ally in the cresting environmental movement, was confiding to his journal that the war in Vietnam was senseless and the United States should withdraw.[22]

Peaceful demonstrations were constitutional, Masland wrote to Abbott, but the protests in 1967 were not peaceful, and he thought the government should take the necessary measures to prevent "anarchy on a scale probably unparalleled in history." As historian Adam Rome has shown, young antiwar protesters and members of the counterculture played a key role in the onset of the environmental movement. Blinded by his nationalism and conservatism, Masland failed to see that many of those same young war protesters, whom he reviled, were also flocking to the cause of environmental protection and wilderness preservation.[23]

Realizing that his days of service were drawing to a close, Masland savored his association with Udall. "The Secretary and I have a rather intimate, a rather fine relationship," he informed the archaeologist Emil Haury. "Recognizing the difference in our ages he frequently refers to me as 'Uncle Frank.'" He relished being called upon for special assignments like the African mission and inspecting conditions at national parks. At Udall's request he also conducted a search for a qualified person of color to serve on the national parks Advisory Board (unsuccessful) and attempted to recruit wealthy donors to subsidize Lee Udall's cause of promoting southwestern Native American art.[24]

Above all, he took pride in Udall's conservation achievements, facilitated by an obliging bipartisan Congress. In 1968 alone, Congress approved proposals by Udall and the NPS Advisory Board establishing Redwood and North Cascades National Parks and passed the National Trails System Act and the Wild and Scenic Rivers Act, which set aside segments of sixteen western rivers as free-flowing and included a built-in mechanism for adding more. It also authorized the Central Arizona Project, minus Bridge Canyon Dam or any other new dams on the Colorado River. Other successful projects during Udall's tenure that met with Masland's approval included the establishment of Canyonlands National Park in Utah, Guadalupe Mountains National Park in Texas, and other national parks; numerous new national historic sites, lakeshores, recreation areas, and wildlife refuges; clean air and water legislation; and an alliance with Lady Bird Johnson to beautify rural and urban landscapes. It was a record of achievement, said Masland, unlikely ever to be surpassed.[25]

Prior to the rollback of environmental programs during the Reagan, Bush, and Trump presidencies, it was not uncommon for a conservative or moderate Republican to be an environmentalist. Several forces combined in the 1960s and early 1970s to create a full environmental tide. Kennedy, Johnson, and initially Nixon provided presidential leadership for an environmental agenda that struck a popular chord. Interior Secretary Stewart Udall and David Brower of the influential Sierra Club served as poster boys for the environmental movement. And writers like Rachel Carson, Barry Commoner, and Paul Ehrlich increased public awareness of threats to the ecosystem and human survival such as pesticides, nuclear radiation, and overpopulation.

During most of the 1960s, a robust economy allowed Congress to provide generous appropriations to a variety of conservation causes. On the issue of clean water, as historian Paul Charles Milazzo has shown, Congress initiated action in the early 1960s. And in the early 1970s the conservative James Buckley (R-NY) worked with the liberal Edmund Muskie on antipollution legislation. During those less politically polarized "green years," Buckley and fellow congressional Republicans Silvio Conte, Rogers Morton, Pete McCloskey, John Saylor, Everett Dirksen, John Sherman Cooper, Howard Baker, and Mark Hatfield worked cooperatively with Democrats Muskie, Morris Udall, Wayne Aspinall, Henry "Scoop" Jackson, and others. Two influential conservation-related bodies—the Senate Interior and Insular Affairs Committee, headed by Democrat Scoop Jackson and Republican Thomas Kuchel, and its counterpart in the House, led by Democrat Aspinall and Republican Saylor—compromised to produce hallmark environmental legislation.[26]

Learning that Udall would depart as interior secretary at the end of Johnson's presidency in January 1969, Masland urged him to run for the US Senate. He did not want him to run against his friend Barry Goldwater in Arizona, so "Uncle Frank" urged the "Sir Galahad" of conservation to challenge the conservative Republican Wallace Bennett in Utah. On the surface, this advice seems odd, because Masland and Bennett had much in common. Both had been officials in the National Association of Manufacturers, and both were fiercely opposed to big government, labor unions, the spread of communism, and liberal policies promoting racial and economic justice. But the conservative Bennett was hostile to most preservationist causes, including establishing and, after its creation, expanding the boundaries of Canyonlands National Park. In the case of Bennett, if not of LBJ in 1964, Masland's conservationism trumped his party and conservative loyalties. Udall rejected Masland's advice to run against Bennett, informing him that he might challenge Arizona's Paul Fannin for the Senate in 1970.[27]

In the 1968 presidential race, Masland pushed Richard Nixon for the Republican presidential nomination but said nothing about the candidate's environmental vision. When polls showed that Nixon's lead over Democratic candidate Hubert Humphrey was evaporating, Masland nearly went off the rails emotionally. He was further distressed when Mary Abbott informed him that she was a dove on the Vietnam War and that she and just about everyone she knew in New England could not stomach Nixon. She sympathized with people who displayed bumper stickers reading "Snoopy for President."[28]

Her letter set him off on another political rant. Sounding almost unhinged, he asserted that the country could not withstand another four years of liberal leadership, even though that leadership had resulted in significant environmental gains: "We could quite conceivably be in a position where, if our own military doesn't take over, Russia would have no trouble doing so." In case she could not fathom his angst, he said, "I am terribly upset over the way the campaign is moving and if it goes the wrong way you may well have to write me at some coral atoll in the South Pacific." He was like the eternal pessimist, he said, who had his tombstone inscribed: "I expected this and here I am."[29]

To Masland's immense relief, Nixon won the election. Masland conceded to Abbott that Nixon possessed only ordinary ability. But only one president in the twentieth century had the attributes most people would identify with greatness, and that was Herbert Hoover, he claimed incredibly. He was not optimistic about Nixon's chances for a successful presidency, however, because he had to work with a Congress dominated by Democrats. Continued bipartisan cooperation between the White House and Congress was vital for the survival of the United States, he asserted direly. "Can we hold it together?" he wondered. "There is very little base for solidarity. We are the most mongrelized, hybridized people in history. We have little in common. We became great through the lavish utilization of natural resources, an excess of labor, inventive genius and financial acumen of a relatively small percentage of the population. We started as a Republic. We generated into a Democracy. Today we possess most of the earmarks of a Socialist State." Moreover, he lamented, the American electorate made decisions based on emotion rather than intellect.[30]

While decompressing from the stress of the presidential election, Masland hosted an Advisory Board sendoff for Stewart Udall. At that dinner and in a letter afterward, he praised Udall's leadership and accomplishments. "By any standard, you stand in the forefront of that army of men and women who from the days of T.R. have striven to assure the wisest use of our natural resources and to preserve America's natural heritage for those who come after," he told Udall. "You created an awareness of the essential need to preserve the opportunity for the spiritual renewal which can be found only beside a brook or while gazing upward at the blue above a tall tree or wandering through the heartland of a canyon or watching the sunset beyond the saw grass." He also expressed admiration for Udall's "adorable" wife, Lee. "You have had beside you the perfect helpmate, one of my favorite people." He concluded by sending his love and prayers for their future fulfillment. He was saddened by Udall's departure but looked forward to working with the new Republican administration. Until called upon by the new president or interior secretary, he would continue to busy himself with conservation projects in Pennsylvania.[31]

CHAPTER 11

Pennsylvania and the Blessed Cumberland Valley

While devoting most of his time and effort to conservation work at the federal level, Masland also contributed to the preservation of nature in Pennsylvania, especially during the administrations of Republican governors William Scranton (1963–67) and Raymond P. Shafer (1967–71). Besides serving as a conservation guru to the two governors, particularly Scranton, he worked to promote what he regarded as the interests of Dickinson College, including upholding traditional social standards and acquiring property for environmental field research.

Three decades of liberal policies by government, churches, and educational institutions, Masland argued, had undercut moral standards throughout the nation, including at Dickinson. A member of the college's board of trustees since 1945, he groused that as vice chair he had to do most of the work because the chair was eighty-two years old and the remaining forty-five board members were "useless." Dickinson faculty members believed that they could both teach and set college policy, he scowled. An opponent of the tenure system, he conceded that he was not popular among faculty members. "College Faculties today are, by and large, members of one of the most insidious and unfortunate unions that blights our land, the AAUP," he grumbled to Mary Abbott. The American Association of University Professors was a union "polluted with ideologies foreign to the welfare of the United States," he said. Many Protestant church leaders also were infused with "imported ideologies." "It is a rare church leader today," he railed to J. Howard Pew, "who devotes his time to saving souls. The term is almost archaic." Advocating an end to the Vietnam War and civil disobedience in the fight for civil rights, the National Council of Churches was even worse than the AAUP and NAACP, in his view. Those organizations, in league with liberal presidential advisers, wanted "to destroy the Free Enterprise System, substitute therefore Socialism and bring the United States completely within the world Socialist State orbit."[1]

Not surprisingly, Masland had a falling-out with Dickinson president Howard Lane Rubendall. As William Edel's successor, Rubendall had liberalized the college's social and academic policies. Masland had served on the search committee that selected Rubendall for the presidency. A 1931 graduate of Dickinson, Rubendall had previously headed both the Mount Hermon School for Boys and the Northfield School for Girls in Massachusetts. From the very beginning, Masland expressed reservations about Rubendall. The man, he told search committee chair Boyd Lee Spahr, had no administrative experience at the college level, and paying him a yearly salary of $20,000 plus $4,500 in living expenses would not sit well with the faculty. Rubendall possessed a divinity degree and was an ordained Presbyterian minister, but Masland had doubts about his piety. Nonetheless, he went along with the appointment because he did not wish to undercut Spahr.[2]

Rubendall, fifty-one years old in July 1961, assumed the college presidency at a difficult time. Much of the trouble had been brought on by Masland, who had spearheaded the campaign to oust economics professor Laurent LaVallee four years earlier (detailed in chapter 5). Faculty morale had cratered because the AAUP had censured the college for violating standards of academic freedom. Additionally, the Middle States Association of Colleges threatened not to renew Dickinson's accreditation unless it reformed its curriculum and its policies relating to academic freedom. Rubendall worked with the faculty to institute those reforms, thus lifting the censure and the threat of nonaccreditation.

By 1963, Masland had concluded that hiring Rubendall had been a monumental blunder, blasting him for virtually divorcing the college from its affiliation with the Methodist Church and its moral values. Rubendall abolished mandatory chapel attendance and permitted both the use of alcohol for students of legal age and the presence of women in fraternity houses. Such a relaxation of the social rules, Masland insisted, contributed to the moral degeneracy of the student body. His despair deepened when Rubendall, perhaps out of spite or for ideological reasons, did away with the Masland student scholarship program. Rubendall also tolerated students who lived a counterculture lifestyle and their protests against racial discrimination and the deepening American military commitment in Vietnam.[3]

Masland also claimed that Rubendall had brazenly lied to him during the interview, when he vowed not to divorce the college from the church. "I regard him as occupying the lowest rung on the human ladder," he fumed. "Drinking is freely and openly indulged in. The 'new morality' would seem to be not only condoned but embraced. Chapel has been abolished," he reported to Edel, the former president. In a detailed confidential memorandum to selected trustees, Masland spelled out the moral lapses, including women and men showing up drunk to dances, underage students attending beer parties, kegs cluttering curbsides, house directors ignoring rules, and women visiting the second floor of unsupervised fraternity houses. From time immemorial, he continued, when young males asked females "to visit the second floor of any house, anywhere on any evening, they usually had but one purpose in mind." These social reforms at Dickinson led to his resignation from the board of trustees in 1964. They also prompted him to discourage millionaires Pew and later Laurance Rockefeller from contributing financially to the college.[4]

Masland also seethed when Dickinson College gave the Priestley Award, one of its most prestigious prizes, which Masland had helped establish, to two-time Nobel Prize winner Linus Pauling in 1969. A brilliant chemist, Pauling was a critic of the Vietnam War and advocate of world peace through nuclear disarmament. To his cousin William Masland, then head of the college's board of trustees, he portrayed Pauling's positions as "subversive," because they would leave "us naked before the purposes of our enemy" and create more "civil turmoil" in the United States. Fortunately, Masland found nothing sinister about the environmental movement, although he was displeased with its growing zealousness and emphasis on urban and human health issues.[5]

In spite of his outrage over declining moral standards at Dickinson, he did help the college acquire land for use as a nature sanctuary. Animal lover Florence Waring Erdman had established a $1 million trust in her will, controlled by the Girard Bank in Philadelphia, for the protection of wildlife nationwide. In the early 1960s, the Dickinson College Science Department sought land for use as a field laboratory. After a lengthy search, it found an isolated tract of thirty-one hundred acres in Perry County, about ten miles north of Carlisle, that would ideally suit the purpose. Unfortunately, the land was owned by Clarence White, a gruff local lumber mill operator who refused to sell it. Biology professor William B. Jeffries asked Masland to intercede on behalf of the college.

White and Masland had crossed swords several years earlier, when Masland had blocked White's attempt to harvest a tract of virgin trees in the Tuscarora State Forest. But White agreed to meet with Masland. The two men learned that they had a common interest in the Florida Everglades and visited each other there in 1966. White eventually agreed to sell the property but wanted $50 per acre. Donald C. MacFarland, the administrator of the Erdman Trust, would offer only $30 per acre. With Masland acting as intermediary, the two sides settled on $40 per acre and the title was transferred to the trust as a wildlife sanctuary for use by Dickinson College.[6]

Both Professor Jeffries and President Rubendall thanked Masland for his decisive efforts. "You were successful beyond our fondest hopes with Mr. White," Jeffries wrote. "Your contacts, know-how, and determination finally brought this opportunity to fruition, and I am grateful untold generations of Dickinson students will benefit from this acquisition. . . . You should count this as one of your crowning achievements." Rubendall wrote in similar fashion. "Your contributions to the field of conservation have been so many and so varied that it would seem impossible that a new and different one could be added to the list, yet here it is, and one that only you could make." Masland also used his influence with the National Park Service to designate the sanctuary a national natural landmark.[7]

Named for Erdman's mother, the Florence Jones Reineman Wildlife Sanctuary was officially dedicated in September 1971. At Masland's request, his friend Nathaniel Reed, assistant secretary of the interior, spoke at the occasion. But Masland was disappointed that the *Dickinson Alumnus* magazine failed to mention his valuable contribution in its account of the dedication ceremony. Apparently, neither he nor Donald MacFarland had played a role in "arranging for the Dedication, securing a speaker for the Dedication or participating in the Dedication," he snarled. The failure to acknowledge their roles, he grumbled, displayed the pettiness of the college administration.[8]

Despite his dissatisfaction with Rubendall, Masland was generally upbeat regarding conservation in Pennsylvania, though he denounced the state's program of predator poisoning. As historian Thomas Dunlap has shown in *Saving America's Wildlife*, scientific and public opposition to the federally sponsored predator-control program—mainly by poisoning—had been building since the late 1920s. Western sheep and cattle ranchers, however, possessed sufficient political clout to continue the program until congressional hearings and reports from scientific committees appointed by interior secretaries Udall and Rogers Morton demonstrated that the predator-control program was ecologically harmful. President Nixon ended predator poisoning on federal land by executive order in 1972, and Congress enacted a law the same year that extended the ban on poisoning to the states.

Masland was friendly with Clarence Cottam, Starker Leopold, Stanley Cain, and other scientists who were critics of poisoning predators. But he also opposed predator control through hunting, with the exception of coyotes. In August 1963, he berated the editor of *Pennsylvania Game News* for publishing a piece titled "Hunt the Horned Owl." The wanton killing of predators, Masland fumed, was "an utterly archaic" practice, and hunters should realize that "the Eco System necessitates the protection of the natural predator if man hopes to continue to function as the most predatory of animals." Masland helped persuade state legislators to remove bounties on most predators, including hawks and most owls. He sought to ban the use of lead shot against waterfowl and to classify coyotes as a game species, preferring that they be shot by hunters rather than suffer a slow and agonizing death by poisoning. For his efforts, the Pennsylvania Fish and Game Protective Association honored him in 1965 with its Conservation Award. True to form, Masland was more outspoken on the issue of predator poisoning than he was on the poisoning of humans through toxins and nuclear waste and fallout.[9]

Overall, he believed that the state's conservation program was ably guided by Maurice Goddard, secretary of the Pennsylvania Bureau of Forests and Waters and then of the state's Department of Environmental Resources. Not as well known nationally as congressional representative John Saylor or Masland, Goddard was Pennsylvania's "Mr. Conservation." A Democrat and a former professor of forestry at Penn State University, Goddard was instrumental in expanding Pennsylvania's state park system. But he also was a wise-use conservationist, like Gifford Pinchot. As such, he was not always in Frank Masland's good graces.[10]

Specifically, Goddard was receptive to clotting Pennsylvania's untamed waters with dams, and he tolerated the spraying of DDT in state forests. To Masland's horror, a bill in the Pennsylvania House of Representatives proposed giving the Bureau of Forests and Waters the authority to spray the damaging pesticide anywhere on public or private land. It was one of the few times that Masland publicly seemed to acknowledge that Rachel Carson's dire warnings had merit. The Pennsylvania legislature seemed oblivious to Carson's pathbreaking exposé of the dangers of agricultural pesticides in her best-selling book *Silent Spring*. The introduction of such an outrageous bill by the Pennsylvania legislature, Masland fumed, showed "the militant attitude of the commercial interests." Goddard opposed the bill, but Masland accused him of lacking the courage to stand up to the chemical and forestry interests. When the bill failed to pass, the bureau proceeded "with their spraying program irrespective of the opposition of Conservation organizations and a considerable body of authoritative advice," he informed Thomas Kimball, executive director of the National Wildlife Federation. When Kimball protested the spraying, Goddard explained that the bureau was not treating lakes, ponds, or agricultural land, only forests, in order to fend off canker worms. In the future, he said, the bureau might use a pesticide sold under the brand name Sevin (carbaryl) if it proved as effective as DDT. But, as Masland's appeal to Kimball indicates, he was at least as concerned about pesticides' dire effects on animals as on humans.[11]

Masland heartily approved Project 70, a 1964 law permitting the state to issue bonds for the acquisition of land for public parks, recreation areas, and historic and fishing and boating sites. Under Goddard's guidance, several new state parks were established during the decade, the largest being the eighteen-thousand-acre Ohiopyle in Fayette County. Preserving public lands at the national, state, and local levels was always the cornerstone of Masland's outlook.[12]

In a speech titled "Why Conservation?," he praised Project 70 and said that more such programs were needed. Habitat, wild species, environmental quality, and open space all were endangered by commercial development, rapid population growth, pollution, ugliness, and indifference, he stated. Sound conservation policies were necessary to protect the physical and spiritual quality of life. The main problem facing the United States, he said, was not the Vietnam War, not communism, not the economy, but youth unrest. Rebellious youth and searching adults might find what they were looking for in nature. "In God's cathedral the jaded spirit of urbanized man may be re-created and find new life and purpose," he suggested. Parents, educators, and legislators should provide opportunities for young and physically able adults to experience the wild, and Pennsylvania should take the lead. In addition to promoting conservation in its schools and through programs like

Project 70, the commonwealth should provide opportunities along its three great rivers: the Allegheny, the Delaware, and the Susquehanna. Portions of these waterways should be preserved as wild and scenic. But other free-flowing segments and tributaries should be hemmed with public recreation areas for boating, camping, fishing, hiking, and picnicking. He downplayed the cost. "A nation that can afford billions for outer space can afford millions for open space," he said.[13]

As noted at the beginning of this chapter, Masland had influence over policy during the administrations of Republican governors William Scranton and Raymond P. Shafer. Under their administrations, he boasted, "I was Chair of just about everything that had to do with the environment and conservation." Scranton held him in high regard as a national conservationist and as the driving force behind the success of Masland and Sons, and he looked to Masland for guidance on state nature programs.[14]

Masland worked hard to make Governor Scranton an active conservationist. "I would like to see your name become associated with 'Conservation' on a state-wide and national scale," he wrote in June 1965. "You know of my activities in Conservation and that I hope to see you become a national figure in the conservation movement," he wrote two months later. "As I said when I visited you, it is a wave that is sweeping the country. Stew Udall has long recognized that. He has become the symbol of Conservation—and, though a Democrat, I don't hesitate to say that he has deserved it." President and First Lady Johnson had done the same, he added. "Conservation is like motherhood used to be before the population got out of control. No one in public life can go wrong by so steeping himself in the objectives of the movement that he may speak with recognizable knowledge. . . . You have all the qualifications to become a recognized leader in the Conservation movement—and that doesn't mean that one has to be against all dams. It does mean that no dam or any other permanent alteration of natural conditions should be built or take place until viewed from the perspective of what is best for posterity." Conservation, he concluded, was nothing less than "the preservation of the spiritual in man."[15]

In 1965 alone, Masland peppered Scranton with two dozen letters filled with advice on water resources; fishing; hunting; gravel, sand, and strip mining; and the possibility of offering conservation education in public schools. "You certainly are a wonderful communicator," Scranton replied diplomatically after receiving one such letter. "You are getting to be quite a correspondent; and I appreciate it," he said after another barrage of advice. Only twenty minutes away by auto, Masland had ample opportunity to meet with Scranton personally.[16]

He also sent the governor copies of some of his conservation speeches, hoping to inspire Scranton. As usual, he stressed the connection between experiencing nature and fulfilling a spiritual need. In a speech at Dickinson College, he described conservation as "an ethic—a spiritual interpretation of the beauty and grandeur of the universe and what this means to the life of man. It appreciates the order of nature and the delicate balance under which we live. It enriches the lives of humans." Great strides had been made in the 1960s, especially in the preservation of open space. But there was more to be done. To provide for the spiritual nourishment of future generations, he urged his audience to heed the advice of the ancient philosopher Lucretius, who counseled men to avoid the destruction of habitat and species; of John Muir, who recognized the interconnectedness of the natural world; and of Henry David Thoreau, who believed that preserving wildness preserved the world. Getting down to earth, Masland said in another speech, was more important than getting to the moon: "A fraction of the money we spend to reach the moon could restore Old Earth to some of its pristine beauty." And in the fashion of a religious evangelist, he stated in an *American Forests* magazine article, "The cause for which conservationists struggle is the preservation of God's cathedral that the jaded spirit of civilized man may, in his temple, be re-born and find new life and purpose."[17]

He also provided political advice, taking offense when Scranton said in a speech that the Republican Party should distance itself from fringe groups, an obvious reference to the John Birch Society. Pointing out that Americans for Democratic Action had a larger membership than the John Birch Society, Masland asserted that the Democratic Party owned the fringe label. "It is the party of the extreme left-wing college faculty members and students. It is the party to which those labor leaders who are far to the left of center adhere. It is the party of the lunatic theological fringe." Since the days of William Jennings Bryan and free silver in the 1890s, Democrats had been extremists, he bellowed. What could be more extreme than the Democratic Wilson administration getting involved in the Great War as a "player" instead of as an "umpire"? Democrats, he insisted, were the party of war. Had it not been for the influence of the Left during the administrations of Roosevelt, Truman, Kennedy, and Johnson, we might have avoided getting drawn into the Vietnam War. If the GOP hoped to regain control of national policymaking, it needed the support of conservatives from both parties, he declared.[18]

When Scranton was rumored to be a viable Republican presidential candidate for 1968, Masland warned him about the evils of unions and the danger of becoming associated politically with GOP presidential hopefuls Governor George Romney of Michigan and Governor Nelson Rockefeller of New York. Romney had a bland personality and a feeble grasp of domestic and foreign affairs, and Rockefeller was too liberal, he maintained. If Scranton could not secure the top spot, Masland advised, he should run as Richard Nixon's vice president.[19]

Scranton gave more weight to Masland's environmental advice than to his political counsel. And Masland did in fact help shape the governor's conservation program. At his suggestion, Scranton formed the Governor's Conference on Natural Beauty, appointing Masland as chair and inviting Stewart Udall to address it. Pennsylvania, Scranton wrote Udall, "is determined to have a cracker-jack Governor's Conference on Natural Beauty. Your close friend and admirer, Frank Masland, has agreed to be the chairman." Udall agreed.[20]

Sponsored by the Hershey Chocolate Company, the conference was held in Hershey on September 12–13, 1966. With the assistance of Goddard, conference manager John Davis of the Bell Telephone Company, and Laurance Rockefeller, who had chaired the earlier White House Conference on Natural Beauty, Masland spent the spring and summer selecting the subjects that would be addressed and the panelists who would discuss them. The purpose of the conference, he informed panelists, was "to generate awareness of the need for urban and rural beauty—to develop a program of action involving state and local government agencies—to enlist private participation and . . . to provide the means for implementing the Conference recommendations." After a day of discussion on September 12, the chairs of the panels would submit written summaries to the governor for action.[21]

After a soloist kicked off the conference with "America the Beautiful," Masland welcomed the guests, introduced the governor, and delivered opening remarks, challenging panelists to reestablish Pennsylvania's heritage of natural beauty. "The kind of environment we provide for ourselves, our children, and our grandchildren is the measure of our culture and maturity," he told the crowd. "Certainly, if each generation does not cultivate the concept of conservation and pass it on to the next, the creeping unguided megalopolis—like sand dunes advancing before the wind—will blot out the landscape." US

Representative John Saylor headed a panel on beautifying the Pennsylvania countryside, and state specialists like Goddard chaired panels on the beautification of cities, reclaiming strip mines, removing billboards, junkyards, and litter along highways, teaching conservation in public schools, protecting water resources, creating more parks and scenic roads, and other topics.[22]

The conference concluded with an evening banquet on September 13. After a student group sang "This Land Is Your Land" and Governor Scranton gave a short speech, Masland introduced guest speaker Stewart Udall. It was difficult to speak unemotionally about Udall, he said, because they had worked closely for years and shared intimate conversations around many a campfire. He cited Udall's "magnificent achievements" and said that under Udall's tutelage, "the National Park Service has made greater strides than any time in its history and the conservation movement has come of age." Moreover, Udall had made the beautification of America a national cause. Udall then said that he had accepted the invitation to speak at the conference out of friendship for Masland and his admiration for the conservation work of Saylor at the national level and Maurice Goddard at the state level. He urged his audience to put aside political partisanship and single-issue conservation causes for the good of the whole environment. It was a rich moment for Masland. Scranton, Saylor, Goddard, and the panelists proclaimed the conference a signal success. And it was apparent to all in attendance that Masland and Udall shared a deep bond and that Masland had had a hand in the secretary's many stellar achievements. Before leaving office after one term, as required by state law, Scranton acted upon one of the conference's recommendations by creating the Governor's Citizens Advisory Committee on Natural Resources, appointing Masland its chair.[23]

Masland also was active during the administration of Republican governor Raymond P. Shafer, serving on the Fish and Boat Commission and continuing to chair the Governor's Citizens Advisory Committee on Natural Resources. In keeping with a national trend initiated in Wisconsin, Masland recommended the creation of a state Department of Environmental Resources to administer and oversee the state's natural bounty. Shafer agreed, naming him to head a task force to work out the details. Upon Masland's recommendation, Goddard was named head of the new department. Legislation establishing the new umbrella agency was enacted by the Pennsylvania General Assembly and signed into law in 1970. Establishing the DER with the help of Tom Webster and Jerry Goldberg, Masland later said, was "one of my activities that I quite frankly like to look back upon with a not inconsiderable degree of gratification."[24]

Shafer also supported Masland's effort to gain national recognition for a rare plant species. State and local pride prompted Masland to campaign for national recognition of a box huckleberry specimen in Perry County as one of the oldest shrubs in the continental United States. The rare twelve-hundred-year-old shrub was discovered in the early 1800s. In a grand ceremony perhaps unbefitting a humble plant, Shafer, Masland, and other state dignitaries looked on solemnly on a hot summer day in July 1968 as NPS director George Hartzog dedicated a ten-acre huckleberry colony a national historic landmark. The appearance of several notables in the dedication of a simple but ancient plant reflects the high esteem in which the NPS and state government held Frank Masland.[25]

In 1967 Shafer appointed Masland to the Fish and Boat Commission. Masland was surprised by the nomination, he said, but the governor informed him that he wanted someone on the commission with a strong conservation background. In addition to an opportunity to promote recreation, Masland saw the position as a chance to preserve more open rivers and riverbanks: "It is not too late for us to preserve the wilderness that remains along our great rivers and to zone contiguous areas that they will continue through the years ahead." Quoting the nineteenth-century American author Robert Louis Stevenson, he stated, "There's no music like a river. It takes the mind out of doors and quiets a man down like saying his prayers."[26]

Masland served nearly eight years on the eight-member commission, one year as vice president and another as president. The commission heard appeals for the revocation of boating and fishing licenses, administered watercraft and fishing programs, enforced boating and fishing regulations, authorized agents to sell fishing licenses, raised and stocked fish, published promotional and educational literature, including the *Angler,* and acquired private property for boating- and fishing-access areas and hatcheries. Masland was concerned mainly with acquiring access and hatchery property, promoting conservation education in public schools, returning shad to the Susquehanna River by skirting them around dams, setting aside certain streams as wilderness and fly-fishing-only areas, and introducing a cane-pole fishing program to inner-city children, mainly minorities.[27]

Apart from routine matters like enforcing regulations and stocking streams and lakes, the main success of the commission during Masland's tenure was the cane-pole program and the establishment of a new hatchery at Big Spring Creek in eastern Pennsylvania, making twenty-five miles of land along its banks accessible to the public. The cane-pole program outfitted disadvantaged youth with wooden or bamboo poles with fishing line attached to the tips. This simple, inexpensive effort, noted Ralph Abele, the commission's executive director, "certainly improved the image of the Fish Commission as an agency which strives to serve all the people, regardless of race, color, creed, or social standing." Other programs, such as reintroducing shad, acquiring Boiling Springs Lake, and incorporating conservation into the public-school curriculum, were unsuccessful.[28]

Despite his influential role on conservation issues, Masland was disappointed in Shafer's leadership. The governor, he wrote, was not pushing hard enough for legislation to clean up streams, eliminate sand and gravel pit residue, repair marred strip-mining sites, regulate junkyard and billboard clutter, and provide protection for wilderness.[29]

Shafer also obstructed passage of the national Wild and Scenic Rivers Act. Sponsored in the US House of Representatives by Saylor, the bill included sixteen rivers, with several other streams to be studied for possible inclusion later. Pending a final determination, these rivers would be off-limits to commercial development. Segments of the Susquehanna and Clarion Rivers were scheduled to be part of a study group that would make the final determinations. Preserving free-flowing sections of those rivers and Pine Creek, Masland wrote, would prove far more beneficial to state residents than sacrificing them for commercial purposes. As a conservationist, a member of the Economic Development Committee, and chair of the Governor's Citizens Advisory Committee on Natural Resources, he beseeched Shafer to endorse Saylor's bill.[30]

Shafer was not persuaded. Anticipating dam and power project developments on those rivers, he asked several members of the state's congressional delegation to oppose the bill until those rivers were removed. This eleventh-hour request infuriated Saylor, Masland, and other preservationists, who appealed in vain to the governor to change his mind. "We never had a more hopeless administration here in Pennsylvania," Masland vented to Abbott. The bill passed, but without the two Pennsylvania rivers among those under study for possible later inclusion.[31]

Two commercial developments in Pennsylvania also offended his environmental and historical sensibilities. In 1971, a developer named Thomas

Ottenstein launched the so-called second battle of Gettysburg by attempting to erect a three-hundred-foot observation tower on private land abutting the Gettysburg battlefield. Masland opposed the project and urged Shafer to speak out against it. Even though it would be built on private land, Masland ripped the residents of Gettysburg for authorizing its construction. "The people of that community would seem to be governed solely by avariciousness and selfishness. They seem to be totally unconcerned with protecting and preserving one of our foremost national treasures," he complained to Shafer. In subsequent letters he pointed out that the Governor's Citizens Advisory Committee on Natural Resources had unanimously approved a resolution denouncing the tower and urged Shafer to join opposition forces. But Shafer demurred.[32]

Masland disparaged the project as "an abomination" in letters to the National Park Service, National Parks Association, Senator Hugh Scott (R-PA), Stewart Udall, Lady Bird Johnson, President Nixon, the *Gettysburg Times*, and the *New York Times*. He also blasted Ottenstein directly. "Never anywhere have I encountered such a deliberate desecration as that which you have perpetrated on this nation's most 'hallowed ground.' If you were capable of shame you would blast your tower to the ground." When that indelicate appeal got no response, Masland sent the developer a letter from a war widow stating that the tower desecrated the dead. Ottenstein returned the widow's letter with a note that read, "I do not except [*sic*] junk mail." To twist the knife, Ottenstein included with his note an advertising sticker depicting the tower standing upon a cannon and pyramid of cannonballs. Despite the strong objections of the Park Service, historians, and preservationists like Masland, the project could not be blocked because it was located on private land. Erected in 1974, the tower survived for a quarter century before the Commonwealth of Pennsylvania seized it by eminent domain and had it demolished in early July 2000.[33]

In similar fashion, Masland opposed a US Army Corps of Engineers plan to erect a flood-control dam at Tocks Island, located in the Delaware River about six miles upstream from the scenic Delaware Water Gap, a popular tourist area where the river has chiseled through the Appalachian Mountains. Yoked to the states of New Jersey and Pennsylvania, the earthen dam was to stand 160 feet above the streambed. The reservoir created by the impoundment would cover nearly thirteen thousand acres, creating a lake thirty-seven miles long (effectively a reservoir that would supply water to New York City and Philadelphia). The NPS proposed edging this reservoir with a national recreation area of more than fifty thousand acres. The lake, plus the adjoining recreation area, would provide benefits to perhaps as many as ten million visitors per year.[34]

Several factors delayed approval of the Tocks Island National Recreation Area project. The cost of the dam, adjoining acreage, and compensation for displaced property owners and businesses totaled more than $100 million at a time when the federal government was undergoing a budget crunch owing to the Vietnam War. Local private property owners derided the plan as a socialist scheme, and conservationists like Masland wanted to leave the river untamed.[35]

As chair of the Governor's Citizens Advisory Committee on Natural Resources and as a member of the Fish and Boat Commission, Masland recommended building the national recreation area without the dam. "I do not know of a conservation group that is for it," he complained. "My interest is in the Commonwealth as a whole and I regard the river as it is as a far greater asset to the Commonwealth than I do the river irreversibly altered." He also rebuked the Pennsylvania Federation of Sportsmen for not opposing the project. Several attempts to deauthorize the dam failed, but the Delaware Water Gap National Recreation Area, as the project was renamed, was created—without the dam—when the upper and middle reaches of the river were added to the Wild and Scenic Rivers Program in 1978.[36]

Shortly after the election of Democratic governor Milton Shapp in 1970, Masland fretted to Stewart Udall that the new administration in Harrisburg might undo the conservation gains that he had helped achieve under the two Republican governors. He also told Udall that he was apolitical when it came to conservation and would work with Shapp if called upon. The new governor did not share Masland's cooperative spirit. He left conservation programs essentially intact but removed Masland from committees and ignored him. Under the new regime, administrative heads were required to divulge the sources and amount of their income. Masland refused, arguing that he took no salary as a member of the Pennsylvania Fish and Boat Commission. Shapp asked for his resignation, despite letters recommending his reappointment by the Pennsylvania Izaak Walton League, the Pennsylvania Federation of Sportsmen and Conservationists, and other conservation groups. Not surprisingly, Masland became resentful. He added several lines to his résumé detailing his conservation work in Pennsylvania, ending with the line: "Fired from everything by Governor Shapp. Greatest honor accorded me."[37]

More legitimate honors soon came his way, however. In 1971, the Pennsylvania House of Representatives heralded him for his "unselfish devotion to the promotion of the betterment of the environmental quality, not only in the Commonwealth, but in the United States and throughout many foreign countries." Also in 1971, at its annual convention in Pittsburgh, the Pennsylvania chapter of the American Legion presented him with a Distinguished Service Medal for "outstanding public service, particularly in the field of conservation and antipollution."[38]

Members of the Pennsylvania Fish and Boat Commission and Department of Environmental Resources also honored Masland. Letters poured in thanking him for his service and decrying the governor's political partisanship. "Suffice it to say, I think it is tragic that a man of your rare talent and wisdom was replaced for political reasons," wrote Peter S. Duncan III of the DER. "It is a damned shame because everybody (indeed all life forms) lost by that decision," he continued. "Godspeed, Great man!"[39]

At an evening ceremony, Ralph Abele of the Fish and Boat Commission awarded him a gold badge and induction into the Order of the White Hat, the highest honor bestowed by the commission, for his "unselfish contributions to our programs and goal, and your efforts, willingly and untiringly, made in the cause of Conservation for the betterment and benefit of the people." Later that year, Abele invited Masland to join the group on a two-day camping and fishing trip on the Juniata River. In a letter of gratitude, Masland described the Fish and Boat Commission as "a great gang." Working with them and the dedicated staff of the National Park Service, he said, was "one of the highlights" of his service in the public sector.[40]

Like Laurance Rockefeller and only a few other independent, unpaid prominent conservationists, Masland had the money and time to volunteer his service simultaneously to environmental causes at the national and state levels. With his career winding down and his expertise no longer requested by the new governor of Pennsylvania, he hoped to provide a few more years of service to the NPS and the presidential administration of Richard Nixon before retiring. He would discover that the environmental tide, so powerful at the beginning of the decade, was beginning to ebb, and so was Masland's activity and influence within the Department of the Interior.

CHAPTER 12

Outside the Gate

Masland had high hopes for the Nixon administration. Now in control of the executive branch, if not of Congress, Republicans could stem the tide of liberalism while continuing to ride the wave of environmentalism, he believed. If his party failed to advance the environmental cause, he warned in a speech in the late 1960s, it would fall to the Left by default and constitute "political suicide" for the GOP. "This must not happen. As the very word itself suggests, 'conservation' is intrinsically a conservative concern, though conservatives have often been hesitant about it or excessively rationalistic in their approach. A failure of initiative here, however, could be disastrous, because, especially in America, the issue of conservation touches the deepest emotions, and moves beneath the rational level to America's consciousness of its own meaning and identity."[1]

Masland wanted to help Republicans capture the environmental moment. Reappointing Stewart Udall, he maintained, would demonstrate the new administration's commitment to protecting nature. He urged Barry Goldwater, reelected to the US Senate in 1968, to press for Udall's reappointment as interior secretary—if not Udall, then an eastern environmentalist like John Saylor. A fellow conservative Pennsylvanian, Saylor was the ranking minority member on the House Interior and Insular Affairs Committee and a staunch preservationist who had introduced the wilderness bill and Wild and Scenic Rivers bill in the House. Nixon, however, selected Governor Walter Hickel of Alaska.[2]

Hickel would disappoint Masland. Even before taking office, he stated publicly in mid-December that he opposed "conservation for conservation's sake." That statement, Masland exclaimed to Mary Abbott, "has created fear among conservationists that what we have accomplished in the last eight years will go by the board in the next four." He hoped that Hickel would settle into the job and realize that conservation had become a popular political cause. He also cautiously expressed the wish that the new secretary would call upon him for advice and use him for special assignments, as Udall had. It would be ironic, Masland said, if, as a "birthright Republican," he found himself "outside the gate" during a Republican administration.[3]

He also wanted Hickel to keep George Hartzog as director of the National Park Service. Hartzog was an able administrator, a man of character and loyalty. "I have for him the highest admiration," he told Abbott. "We enjoy a relationship I cherish." He lobbied for Hartzog's reappointment with Nixon ally William Scranton, recently named special envoy to the Middle East (after he turned down the post of secretary of state). Masland wondered whether he or Hartzog would be called to serve, as he assumed that Hickel would not want to associate with anyone close to Udall.[4]

But Hickel surprised him. Upon returning with Virginia from his annual winter vacation in the Everglades, Masland attended a weeklong meeting of the NPS Advisory Board in Washington, DC. At that affair, Secretary Hickel presented him with a National Conservation Award for his service with the Advisory Board and Advisory Council. Hickel also reappointed Hartzog as director of the NPS. Masland was impressed with the appointment of Russell Train as well, for Train shared his support for the preservation of African wildlife as undersecretary of the Interior Department. Upon meeting Hickel, Masland described him as "a most affable, interested gentleman desirous of performing effectively in the areas of conservation." He grew more hopeful that Hickel would give him something to do.[5]

Although Masland was concerned that Hickel might spurn him for his close association with Udall, he continued to laud the environmental record of the former interior secretary. In late April 1969 he hosted a black-tie dinner honoring Udall at the Explorer Hall in the National Geographic Society Building in Washington, DC. Lady Bird Johnson also attended and paid tribute to Udall. As master of ceremonies, Masland sat with the former First Lady, who had always impressed him with her charm, intelligence, and commitment to the beautification of America. Before leaving office, Udall had appointed her to the Advisory Board, and she took to her appointment, attending the week-long board meeting and participating in the discussions. "I told her at dinner that I now understood why there were so many Democrats, that she almost had me converted," he told Sig Olson. Portraying her as "the brains and the personality in that family," he told Abbott that the Johnsons still would be in the White House if Lady Bird had been president.[6]

Over the summer, prostate surgery sidetracked him from outdoor or government activities. But once he had recovered, he complained to Olson that "Hickel has nothing for me to do." Hickel was relying instead on Undersecretary Train for advice. The department was "quite different from that of McKay or Seaton or Udall," Masland lamented. "It would appear to be more 'internal,' more mechanical, more professional administratively."[7]

On the environment, the Nixon administration got off to a stunningly good start. Given its popularity as a pressing issue, the environment became a high priority for the politically shrewd president. He appointed environmental advocates to positions of influence, among them John Ehrlichman, assistant to the president for domestic affairs; John C. Whitaker, Ehrlichman's deputy; and Russell Train. Before being named undersecretary, Train had headed the Republican Task Force on Natural Resources and the Environment, which submitted a report recommending that the administration emphasize environmental issues. The overall thrust of the study, writes historian J. Brooks Flippen, was that "the administration should take the lead against environmental degradation, for the good of the country as well as for the administration politically."[8]

On his first day in office, Nixon publicly committed his administration to "protecting our environment and enhancing the quality of life." And though this was done mainly for its political advantage, over the next two years, Nixon delivered on his commitment, especially after a devastating oil spill off the coast of Santa Barbara on January 28, 1969, the largest spill ever to have occurred in US waters at the time. The disaster brought environmental degradation into the spotlight and spurred Nixon and Hickel into action. After delaying for a week, Hickel ordered a halt to oil pumping off the California coast. And Nixon appointed committees to study a variety of ecological issues. Although no comprehensive framework had yet to be formulated, in piecemeal fashion the administration advocated for more national parks, signed the Endangered Species Act, and preempted pending Democratic legislation by approving the National Environmental Policy Act (NEPA).

When Nixon created the Environmental Protection Agency in December 1970, Deputy Attorney General William Ruckelshaus was appointed chair of the new agency. "Ecology has finally achieved currency," chortled George Hartzog.[9]

Signed on January 1, 1970, the NEPA legislation mandated that government agencies consider the environmental impact of their proposed actions before making decisions and that they provide alternatives if adverse environmental impacts would be significant. The measure also created the President's Council on Environmental Quality to advise the president and oversee the implementation of NEPA. "I have become convinced that the nineteen seventies absolutely must be the years when America pays its debt to the past by reclaiming the purity of its air, its water, and our living environment," Nixon informed the press.[10]

Environmental protection measures generally had the support of a bipartisan Congress in the early 1970s. Republican senators Howard Baker of Tennessee and James L. Buckley of New York helped secure passage of the Clean Air Act and the Clean Water Act in 1970. Like Masland, Buckley was a bona fide conservative who believed that preserving nature was a psychological and moral imperative. "As for the protection of critical ecosystems and the species that depend on them," Buckley wrote, "one would think that conservatives in particular would understand Edmund Burke's caution that 'temporary possessors and life-renters should not think it among their rights to . . . commit waste on the inheritance [and] leave to those who come after them a ruin instead of a habitation.'" Buckley also endorsed the Endangered Species Act of 1973, explaining to the *National Review*, edited by his brother William, "that a Wood Thrush's haunting song may have no monetary value, but it enhances countless lives." Masland shared this sentiment, including Buckley's caveat that environmental regulations could be "needlessly rigid" and environmentalists' call for action "too demanding."[11]

During the early 1970s, Masland rode the environmental magic carpet, but he was an uneasy and unsteady rider. He was concerned that the emphasis on curbing pollution would serve as a substitute for the preservation of wilderness and public land. "Environmental concern has been substituted pretty much for conservation," he observed to Fred Smith, fellow NPS Advisory Board member and head of the Council of Conservationists. "It is much easier to generate interest in environmental problems than in conservation, though, of course, in many respects they are one and the same and certainly overlap." Masland and Sons was striving to be a good environmental steward by burning solid waste and reducing smokestack emissions. But Masland's personal focus was always on beautification and the preservation of land and wildlife.[12]

In January and February 1970, President Nixon continued to press for environmental causes during his State of the Union address and in a special message on the environment to Congress. Seeking ecological balance between humans and nature, the message to Congress set forth a multifaced agenda promoting clean air and water, management of solid waste, more parks and recreation, and overall care of the ecosystem.[13]

Masland delighted in the administration's environmental achievements but continued to fret about being outside the gate. At age seventy-five, he had slowed some physically, but not mentally or politically. Hoping to become relevant and useful again, he jumped on a rumor that he was being considered as an appointee to the President's Citizens' Advisory Committee on Environmental Quality, headed by Laurance Rockefeller. Masland contacted Fred Smith, principal aide to Rockefeller, volunteering his service, only to learn that the committee members had already been selected. Masland also ingratiated himself with President Nixon, hailing the appointment of Warren Burger as Chief Justice of the US Supreme Court and urging him to appoint additional conservative justices. "I can think of nothing more therapeutic than bringing about the retirement of Justice Douglas," he wrote Nixon, even though the liberal justice was a committed environmentalist. He praised Nixon for criticizing the UN's expulsion of Taiwan in favor of the People's Republic of China.[14]

He also pleased Nixon by raging against student antiwar protests, blaming them on socialist faculty members, communist infiltrators, liberal television reporters like Walter Cronkite, Chet Huntley, and David Brinkley, and "radical" politicians like US senators Eugene McCarthy, George McGovern, J. William Fulbright, Birch Bayh, and Lowell Weicker. He knew Weicker's father as a man of discernment and ability, he told Abbott. "It is difficult to understand how he could have produced such a vicious and inane offspring." In a telegram, he urged Nixon to send Fulbright and Bayh to Vietnam as forward observers: "They are both highly expendable." The simple solution to student unrest, he told Abbott, was to expel all student protesters, as Haile Selassie did in Ethiopia. Of course, shortly thereafter, Selassie was overthrown, jailed, and murdered.[15]

The antiestablishment bias of students prompted Masland to downplay the observation of Earth Day on April 20, 1970, even though that popular nationwide celebration thrust environmental stewardship into the spotlight. Advisors like Train urged Nixon's involvement, but the president remained standoffish. And so did Masland.[16]

As historian Adam Rome has shown, Earth Day involved thousands of participants and speakers from all walks of life. The event was so trendy that Congress adjourned for the day, television provided coverage, and even many conservatives gave their cautious support. Goldwater, for example, endorsed the crusade for a healthy environment at New York's Adelphi University—though he proceeded over the next few years to miss votes on the Clean Air Act, Clean Water Act, and Endangered Species Act, suggesting, in the words of historian Brian Drake, "that in practice his commitment to federal environmentalism was not always as strong as his rhetoric." In a speech at Harvard, Train, head of the Council on Environmental Quality, urged moderation, not radicalism, in the environmental cause. Likewise, Saylor, the foremost conservationist in the US House of Representatives, took a guarded, backhanded approach in a speech at Penn State University. "I don't know what you expected of your Earth Week kickoff speaker," he began. "If you expected him to tell you to man the barricades, burn down billboards, clog telephone lines, occupy buildings, beat up policemen, carry signs and banners, stage sit-ins or sit downs, wear gas masks, and other childish nonsense, all in the name of conservation—then you will be disappointed. Very frankly there is already too much of the revolutionary motif in the student environmental movement to suit my tastes." To protect the natural world, he urged his young audience to work with, not against, the establishment. Masland agreed completely with Saylor's sentiments.[17]

Masland attended Earth Week seminars at Dickinson College but was not invited to speak. Nor did he hype the event. And he lamented the fact that the young attendees failed to apply the lessons they had learned about earth stewardship. Two weeks after Earth Day, angry Dickinson student protesters trashed the campus following the killing of four Kent State students by the Ohio National Guard on May 4, 1970. Masland fired off an angry letter to the editor of the *Carlisle Daily Sentinel*. Dickinson's Earth Week teach-ins, he said, were among the best anywhere, but they ultimately accomplished nothing. There was no evidence that the clutter accompanying the protests had been cleaned up on the campus, town, or countryside. "I have long held that if we are to achieve a beautiful land, protect our natural resources and avoid unnecessary pollution of all sorts the [environmental] educational program has to begin in kindergarten" and continue through college, he wrote. But "many of our college students and youth in general so conduct themselves that they appear not to have graduated from kindergarten."[18]

Both Masland and Saylor misjudged the environmental commitment of working- and middle-class students, simultaneously overestimating the Left's threat of usurping the environmental cause. Even before Earth Day, Masland expressed misgivings about the enthusiastic acceptance of the environmental impulse among students, colleges, and politicians. "I am downright scared," he told Fred Smith. Although he did not say so explicitly, it is difficult to escape the conclusion that Masland believed that socialists and subversives were co-opting the movement and that both the free enterprise system and national parks and wilderness would be undermined. His fear of socialism caused him to shy away from a cause that emphasized environmental quality issues, especially in urban and suburban areas, more than the traditional emphasis on national parks, wilderness, and recreation on public land. To be sure, Masland deplored the degradation of the environment by strip mining, timber clear-cutting, federally constructed hydroelectric dams, and the bulldozing of green space, but, as we have seen, he was consistently less critical of air and water pollution, solid waste, chemical pesticides, and nuclear fallout from atomic bomb testing that degraded human health and the quality of life.[19]

Masland dismissed the youth counterculture as a threat to traditional moral values. He failed to note, however, that many of those young people decried the materialism, consumer excess, and environmental degradation of American society much as he had. He feared that overzealous students and back-to-the-land activists might cause a backlash against environmentalism, especially among conservatives already fearful of a federal regulatory state. He fretted that the coalition of traditional conservation groups that had achieved significant gains though a measured, bipartisan approach might be upended by the rise in the late 1960s and early '70s of more assertive, specialized splinter environmental advocacy groups. Like Masland and Saylor, old guard conservation groups like the Sierra Club, National Parks Association, National Audubon Society, Izaak Walton League, and others were initially suspicious of the aggressive new grassroots ecological standpoint because it might detract from the traditional emphasis on preserving public lands. "We cannot afford to let up on the battles for old-fashioned Wilderness areas, for more National Parks, for preservation of forests and streams and meadows and the earth's beautiful wild places," declared the Sierra Club's president, Edgar Wayburn. Masland wholeheartedly agreed.[20]

Masland never questioned the wisdom of the federal government when it used its authority to preserve pristine public terrain. But other conservatives did, especially in the last three decades of the century and beyond. As historian James Morton Turner has shown, conservatives not only recoiled from strict environmental regulations but also from locking up public lands, especially in the American West, that could be used for commercial development and recreation, like riding snowmobiles and ATVs. Those conservatives eventually joined the so-called Sagebrush Rebellion and wise-use movement. Masland had some reservations about the speedy implementation of some antipollution regulations but had no tolerance for either the Sagebrush crowd or the wise-use perspective.[21]

Considering old-school conservation groups too stuck in tradition and too focused on the preservation of public lands, new organizations emerged, including the Conservation Foundation, Natural Resources Defense Council, Environmental Defense Fund, and Friends of the Earth. Composed of scientists, lawyers, and lobbyists, they used the courts and citizen activism to promote human health and other quality-of-life issues, including seeking environmental justice for the poor and communities of color. Masland pooh-poohed them.[22]

Moreover, some counterculture activists proposed alternative ways of living to promote ecological balance between humans, nature, and a sustainable way of life. Anti-statist writers like Wendell Berry and Gary Snyder used their essays, poems, and public lectures to promote a simple, practical, agrarian lifestyle based on individual effort and family and community cooperation, not federal handouts, guidance, or directives. They and many other back-to-the-land advocates shunned modern technology as part of the environmental problem, not the solution. Even some activists from mainstream conservation groups, like Wilderness Society director Olaus Murie, blamed the machine for the deterioration of civilization. "The machine . . . is ruling us and we are subservient to it," Murie complained. Masland's machines had made his family rich and had served the public in peacetime and war, so he was not about to bash their use.[23]

Some members of the counterculture praised technology as being compatible with nature and the new ecological impulse. As the writer Stewart Brand put it, "humans were as gods, and might as well get good at it." Born in Rockford, Illinois, in 1938, Brand attended Phillips Exeter Academy in New Hampshire and Stanford University before joining the US Army in 1960. After his discharge from the army, he moved to California, took additional college courses, and eventually founded an iconic underground publication called *The Whole Earth Catalog*. Modeled on the L. L. Bean catalog, *Whole Earth* took a practical, individualistic, technological approach to sustainable ecological balance by emphasizing the use of tools of all sorts. The main idea, writes historian Andrew Kirk, was that "individuals working within specific local environments could make everyday choices to use small-scale technology enabling, if multiplied across a nation, a sustainable economy." Moreover, he continues, "the model of individualistic ecological living represented in the catalogs offered a corrective to the impersonal top-down activism institutionalized by the end of the 1960s." The *Whole Earth* approach should have resonated with fellow technophile Masland, but there is no evidence that he was familiar with the catalog or with Brand.[24]

Masland's faith in technology favored expensive top-down federal activism rather than bottom-up individual efforts. Technology in itself, he argued, was neutral and could be beneficial or detrimental depending on how it was used. He gave guarded approval to the Trans-Alaska Pipeline but denounced the cost and noise associated with the supersonic transport plane. "The more energetic our technology, the more wasteful products we produce: Waste paradoxically is a measure of our success," he concluded. "Correctives can be devised," he believed, including mechanisms to reduce pollution from automobiles and household detergents. "More expensive treatment of sewerage, stricter regulations for industry and transportation, more comprehensive zoning regulations to reduce uglification and urban sprawl—all such measures, equitably designed deserve conservative initiatives." Fortunately, President Nixon had appointed a science adviser to oversee a federal program of technological pollution correctives.[25]

Masland eventually concluded that some of the federally initiated environmental regulations that he wished for were not "equitably designed," especially relating to the automobile industry. And their deadline for compliance was rushed. Like many traditionalists, he had mixed feelings about the new ecological consciousness and was slow to come around to fully accepting it. He understood that overpopulation and pollution were problems, but he never got past the notion that conservation and environmentalism meant mainly federal protection of public lands and the nonhuman world. When consumer advocate Ralph Nader, in his best-selling 1965 book *Unsafe at Any Speed,* blasted the US auto industry for endangering human health by producing unsafe and air-polluting vehicles, Masland, like Nixon, dismissed him as a troublemaker. Just as Saylor considered federally constructed hydroelectric dams an energy competitor for the coal industry, Masland regarded criticism of the auto industry as injurious to the overall economy—and to his automobile carpet business. He admitted to Nader that the internal combustion engine needed to be more fuel efficient and less contaminating to the air, but why give the trucking industry a free ride? Large trucks, he insisted, were a greater threat to safety and air quality than cars were.[26]

David Brower, too, lost his luster in Masland's eyes and in the eyes of other traditional conservationists. After his ouster as executive director of the Sierra Club, Brower formed Friends of the Earth, an organization that took a more global and strident position on environmental issues than mainstream groups. Masland and other traditionalists turned against Brower, arguably the most influential conservationist in the second half of the twentieth century. Masland resented him for dividing environmentalists. He also resented Brower, wilderness writer Michael Frome, and other wilderness advocates for attacking George Hartzog and the Park Service for moving at a glacial pace in designating wilderness areas within national parks. The Wilderness Act of 1964 called for the Forest Service and the Park Service to review units under their jurisdiction and to recommend certain unimpaired backcountry areas for wilderness designation by Congress. As James Morton Turner writes in *The Promise of Wilderness,* the Forest Service moved like the hare in its review process while the Park Service plodded like the tortoise. By early 1971, as Frome has shown, only two pristine areas totaling less than ninety-four thousand acres had been reviewed by the Park Service and approved by Congress.[27]

Not surprisingly, other wilderness advocates slammed the Park Service's slothful review pace. Hartzog claimed that the evaluation took time and that other responsibilities demanded attention. There is little doubt, however, that he and his lieutenants resented the criticism and interference. "The Park Service chose to be territorial rather than commit to the principle of greater wilderness preservation," notes historian Richard West Sellars. "In truth, its deepest commitment was to another principle: to ensure public enjoyment of the parks."[28]

Masland clung to an old-school preservationist phase of conservation that was ebbing in favor of the ecological outlook. Stewart Udall's assistant secretary, John Carver, once accused the Park Service of operating like a religious cult. And Masland considered himself a member of the brotherhood. As an apostle of Horace Albright, friend of George Hartzog, and devotee of the Park Service staff, he felt aggrieved at criticism of an agency to which he had committed a third of his life. He lamely defended Hartzog and privately ripped Brower. "As you know, Friends of the Earth has visciously [*sic*] attacked Hartzog," he wrote Sig Olson. "I have no use for Dave Brower or FOE." Masland was totally in Hartzog's corner, he stated. Hartzog "is dedicated to the preservation of the Park System which, of course, means the parks and wilderness. He also has a keen recognition of the paradox present in the Act establishing the parks. . . . I know that George is not deliberately delaying the establishment of wilderness. I know he is doing all that can be done to accelerate that program."[29]

If Masland believed that Olson would lend a sympathetic ear, he was mistaken. "The staff and that includes me," Olson responded, "have been critical of George's foot dragging on wilderness. As you know this has always been my major interest and to see the NPS with only two small areas brought to congressional hearing when two thirds of the parks and monuments should have been ready is proof of his lack of enthusiasm for wilderness designation." While the Forest Service and other agencies had moved smartly "to meet the congressional mandate, George has openly refused to even try to improve the NPS record. . . . I recognize George's good points and he has many but as far as wilderness is concerned I am appalled at his lack of cooperation."[30]

Their disagreement over Hartzog did not lead to an open break, but regular correspondence between the two old friends abruptly ended after this exchange. When Masland invited Olson to join him on a wilderness survey of Alaska's wilderness for the Park Service, Olson begged off, blaming his busy writing schedule and administrative duties as president of the Wilderness Society. Olson had also recently suffered a heart attack and was advised to curtail his schedule. But the easy, friendly relationship between the two nature lovers was never resumed, and a decade later Olson was dead.[31]

While Masland was pleased that environmentalism had achieved political currency, he and other conservatives worried that traditional family values and anti-statist principles were being undercut by the counterculture and the undertow of liberalism. The turbulent changes of the 1960s prompted some historians to describe America as "coming apart" in that decade. Masland saw it as America losing its essence. The concern that America was losing its essence and the use of its public lands fueled a rising New Right that would win the presidency in 1980.[32]

As historian Allan Lichtman has shown, antipluralism, antisecularism, and opposition to the counterculture were key factors in the burgeoning New Right. Like other conservatives, Masland asserted that American greatness and dominance were determined by a common core of values deriving from the country's English, northwestern European, mainly Protestant heritage. He attributed much of that greatness or exceptionalism to its storehouse of natural resources and the interaction of American settlers with the wilderness. But by 1970, he continued, the slogan *e pluribus unum* had been turned on its head. The United States had evolved from an Anglo-American republic into a hybrid people and a hybrid government in which minority groups had more influence than the majority. "We are a mongrel race, and it is my conviction that this is one of the major causes of our difficulty. Unfortunately, the better blood of other nations did not immigrate. By and large, we got the scum," he sneered privately to Mary Abbott.[33]

Sounding dangerously like a racist eugenicist, he claimed that interbreeding had led to a fragmented nation. And a disjointed society "permits any minority to vocalize far more than would be possible in a society that consisted of only one or two ethnic groups. We lack a common trait." Throughout history, he reminded Abbott, all supreme nations had possessed a common core. "The people of this nation possessed a 'common trait' until we opened our doors to the scum of other nations." While never identifying the specific national and ethnic groups constituting this "scum," it is probable that he meant Poles, Greeks, Italians, Russians, Jews, and other so-called new immigrants from southern and eastern Europe, along with Asians and Hispanics, after the Johnson administration relaxed immigration restrictions in 1965. Ironically, he voiced these private sentiments at the same time he was heading a community workshop on bettering ethnic and racial relations in Carlisle.[34]

Two decades later, in *The Disuniting of America: Reflections on a Multicultural Society*, Pulitzer Prize–winning historian Arthur Schlesinger Jr., a liberal Democrat who had served as an adviser to President Kennedy, reached similar conclusions, minus Masland's racist overtones. Masland attributed the loss of national cohesion to the influx of nonwestern Europeans and nonwhite ethnic groups. Schlesinger linked this influx to the end of the Cold War and the loss of a common ideological enemy; the emergence of the internet and a world without borders; and, principally, the rise of ethnic pride. Schlesinger observed that from its founding, the new American nation had been multicultural and racist. Prior to the last third of the twentieth century, he argued, white and nonwhite ethnic groups alike sought to identify themselves as Americans. And public schools cooperated by teaching a common history, language, and culture.[35]

Despite its many advantages, Schlesinger argued, multiculturalism was eroding national identity by becoming cultish: "A cult of ethnicity has arisen both among non Anglo whites and among nonwhite minorities to denounce the goal of assimilation, to challenge the concept of 'one people,' and to protect, promote, and perpetuate separate ethnic and racial communities. . . . It belittles *unum* and glorifies *pluribus*." Masland, with more racial overtones and less eloquence, had expressed the same sentiments two decades earlier. But Schlesinger also warned that national cohesion was a two-way street and that ethnic groups must be welcomed by "those who already think they own America."[36] Masland never seemed to grasp this concept.

George Hartzog rescued Masland temporarily from inactivity but not from his nativist musings. In August 1970, he and Masland took a ten-day inspection tour to the national parks in Hawaii. Masland relished the Pearl Harbor National Historic Site and the scenic splendor of the parks and countryside, but he disliked the state because it was too populated, too pricey, and too "Oriental." "Hawaii is a Japanese-Chinese enclave, an Oriental inholding," he told Dock Marston. "Except for the governor all political officials are Orientals. I wouldn't want to live there."[37]

In moments of gloom, Masland wondered whether the United States would come completely unraveled. "We are a tribal nation, suffering from tribalism. We lament the tribalism of Africa. We are more of a tribal nation than any other. Every nation and every race is represented within our borders," he complained to Abbott. "We are a pot in which nothing ever melted [and] from which today there issues only the smoke of marijuana." Still, he hoped to live another couple of decades to see what would happen. "I don't expect the end of the world. I do expect the end of an era." Well into the twenty-first century, conservatives and liberals have engaged in the so-called culture wars, disagreeing about what constitutes a common core and the themes that should be emphasized in public schools and museums.[38]

Masland also fussed about whether his active service for the Interior Department had ended. He had little interaction with Secretary Hickel and groused about the Interior Department's inertia. Hickel, unlike Udall, was no bundle of energy, and Masland believed he had surrounded himself with a "kitchen cabinet" of second-rate advisers, except for Train. Open space was rapidly disappearing to development, logging, and mining, and the government needed to preserve more of it, as quickly as possible, before it was gone. Saylor agreed. "I am not only disheartened with the Interior Dept & the new Sect., but also with the White House that even refuses to do the things that don't cost money to gain public support," he wrote Masland. "If I only had a Teddy R in the White House and about 20 stalwarts in the House & Senate, we might be able to save whats [*sic*] left."[39]

Masland was pleased, however, when Hickel helped block a commercial development that would have menaced the existence of Everglades National Park. The Miami-Dade County Port Authority had purchased an expanse of big cypress swampland to build a massive airport for Florida tourists. Located six miles north of the Everglades, the proposed project included six runways, massive terminal and parking areas, and an interstate highway connecting the airport to both Florida coasts. It would also have covered much of Big Cypress Swamp, which supplied water to the Everglades. When completed, the Big Cypress Jetport would be the largest airport in the world. When conservationists, including Masland, objected, Hickel ordered an environmental impact review by noted environmentalist Luna Leopold (Aldo's son). Leopold concluded that the project would strangle the water supply to Everglades National Park and thus destroy it. To the delight of Masland and other conservationists, Hickel killed the project. Shortly thereafter, the Nixon administration reimbursed Miami-Dade County the $13 million it had invested in purchasing the land and established the 556,000-acre Big Cypress National Preserve.[40]

Hickel had saved the Everglades, but not his job. Exasperated by the secret bombing and invasion of Cambodia and the senseless murder of the four Kent State students who protested those war-widening moves, Hickel vented his feelings in a private letter to President Nixon. He blasted the White House for ignoring the views of young people. When the letter became public, Nixon fired Hickel. "If anyone ever asked for the axe, he did," Masland said of Hickel.[41]

Masland hoped that Nixon would name Saylor as Hickel's replacement to head the Interior Department. Instead, Nixon appointed Rogers Morton of Maryland. The move pleased Masland, especially when Morton kept Hartzog on as director of the Park Service. Two years later, Saylor died at age sixty-five following complications from heart surgery. Masland scribbled atop Saylor's last letter, "one of the *greatest*. An irreplaceable loss when he died too young."

Masland engaged in several nature-preservation and national park–related tasks in 1971 at age seventy-six. The previous December, President Nixon had signed into law the Susquehanna River Basin Compact, establishing a federal interstate body of commissioners to oversee the ecosystem of the Susquehanna River. The governors of New York, Maryland, and Pennsylvania or their designees would serve as commissioners. Masland served as a Pennsylvania member of the commission. He also spent the early winter months of 1971 with Virginia in Everglades National Park, as usual, spending much of that time on the water mapping out a canoe trail. He then took several days in June to evaluate the impact of human traffic on the rim and Colorado River at Grand Canyon National Park. At Secretary Morton's request, Masland and James C. Whittaker, as members of the NPS Advisory Board, conducted a performance review of all national park concessionaires. And in early July, Hartzog tasked Masland, Emil Haury, and Frank Setzler, head of the Department of Anthropology at the Smithsonian Institution, with examining complaints of unruly youth behavior in Yosemite National Park. At Yosemite, the three men toured various campgrounds and spent July 4 around a hippie campfire in a haze of marijuana smoke. Marijuana, they reported, was ever present, but pot smokers were generally too mellow to be unruly. Overall, they concluded, park rangers were doing an excellent job of policing, and the best they could do about drug use was to arrest pushers and leave users alone.[42]

After leaving Yosemite, Masland surveyed several national monuments and historic sites in the American Southwest with fellow Advisory Board members Haury and Ned Danson. "The Southwest safari," he reported to Abbott, "increased my homesickness for that red rock country and made me anxious to trade the four wheels on which I was travelling for the back of a horse." He also made a ten-day reconnaissance trip with Lady Bird Johnson. In September they toured Great Smoky Mountains National Park, Cape Hatteras in North Carolina, and other national preserves in the southeastern United States. Sharing a love for the national parks, flowers, and nature, they became close associates and corresponded for the remainder of their lives. In her report to Masland, who chaired the inspection mission, Lady Bird raved about the beauty of the parks but rued the fact that she saw few nonwhite visitors, an observation that still applies today.[43]

The following summer, Hartzog asked Masland and Haury to take a reconnaissance trip to Alaska. Native Americans, conservationists, state residents, and commercial developers had been squabbling over how to allocate the state's vast natural resources. Developers and state residents sought to tap into the region's rich oil reserves; Native peoples wanted to preserve their villages, hunting grounds, and traditional way of life; conservationists hoped to preserve giant chunks of wilderness. Environmentalists opposed construction of the Trans-Alaska Pipeline, fearing oil leaks that would despoil the wilderness habitat and kill wildlife. Not surprisingly, Masland sided with environmentalists in their quest to preserve millions of acres of resplendent nature, though he did grudgingly support the pipeline project if the oil companies agreed to pay a fine of $50,000 per day for any leaks.[44]

He and Haury spent a month covering the state "like mustard plaster." Having hopscotched the state by helicopter, they recommended the inclusion in the park system of more than a dozen areas of natural splendor, including the Wrangell–St. Elias ranges in the southeast and Gates of the Arctic on the north slope of the Brooks Range. "Our immediate and deep concern is that all steps be taken as soon as possible to set aside selected areas for protection against destructive developments, to acquire more rather than less acreage to insure the preservation of total environmental units and most importantly of all, to recognize the overriding fact that if aggressive and forward-looking action is not taken now, the opportunity to achieve these goals will have been lost forever," they reported. "We must, at every turn and through every channel available to us, press for the acquisition of maximum acreage in those units identified as having park and monument status."[45]

Using a provision of the Alaska Native Claims Settlement Act of 1971, Secretary Morton withdrew from commercial use eighty-two million acres of public land, including most of the areas recommended for preservation by Masland and Haury, the Park Service, and preservationists. Masland, Haury, and most other preservationists were disappointed that this was less land than they expected and opened some of those landscapes to multiple uses, including hunting, mining, and recreation. But as historian Stephen Haycox has shown in *Battleground Alaska*, Morton had set aside as much natural splendor as politically possible. As it turned out, in addition to those eighty-two million acres, Congress preserved another twenty-four million in the 1980 Alaska National Interest Lands Conservation Act.[46]

Masland found Alaska's scenery breathtaking; its residents, not so much. Haycox describes its people as the most anti-statist in America. Yet the anti-statist and elitist Masland was, as ever, unsympathetic to their efforts to resist federal efforts to preserve wilderness and scenic splendor. Aboriginal people, he said, were plagued by alcoholism. Nonnatives were plagued by greed. He had no desire to return to the state, he told a friend, because "I don't like the people up there. The Americans up there are in the exploitive stage. They have no concept of resource and environmental protection. Their only idea is to use available resources to get rich as quick as possible." The state flower, he said, "should be an oil drum."[47]

Despite his many achievements, including adding numerous parks and historic sites to the national parks system and appointing the first female, African American, and Native American park superintendents, George Hartzog came under fire in 1972. As noted above, David Brower, Sigurd Olson, and other environmentalists had chastised him for not moving quickly enough to designate portions of national parks as wilderness areas. When the Nixon administration reduced NPS funding, Hartzog closed the national parks, including the Grand Canyon and the Washington Monument, for two days each week until Congress appropriated money to keep them open every day. Hartzog believed that Nixon was marginalizing the Park Service and wanted no more parks. The tipping point occurred when the superintendent of Biscayne National Park, without Hartzog's knowledge, denied Nixon's friend, Florida banker Bebe Rebozo, permission to dock his pleasure boat there. When Rebozo complained to the White House, Nixon fired Hartzog. "The dismissal of George Hartzog is a major tragedy," Masland exclaimed to Marston. Hartzog, he added, was an able administrator and totally devoted to the Park Service. He also understood that Hartzog was a committed environmentalist, and his successor might not be. To Masland's dismay, Nixon replaced Hartzog with thirty-four-year-old Ronald Parker, a man without Park Service experience who had headed the White House Office of Scheduling and Advance.[48]

With the exception of Hartzog's firing, Masland supported Nixon's environmental record, even after the president's interest in environmental issues began to flag. When Hugh Sidey of *Time* magazine wrote an unflattering essay on Nixon, claiming that he lacked the human touch and, unlike both

Roosevelts, Eisenhower, and Kennedy, had no connection with the land, Masland characterized it as liberal tripe. Why did Sidey omit Calvin Coolidge and Herbert Hoover, who loved to fish and led exemplary family lives, unlike the morally challenged FDR and JFK? Nixon loved his wife and daughters, attended church, and revered Camp David and his retreats at San Clemente and Key Biscayne. Masland did not hate anyone, he told an acquaintance, but there were some individuals he despised, and liberal columnist Hugh Sidey was high on his list.[49]

Despite building a strong record in his first two years, Nixon had begun to forsake his environmental program by 1972. Strong environmental activists like Ruckelshaus and Train lost influence. Several factors, according to historian J. Brooks Flippen, account for the president's easing off the environmental throttle. First, Nixon was tired of environmentalists who never appeared to be satisfied with his many achievements. Second, Nixon was running for reelection, and he believed that economic and foreign policy issues, including ending the Vietnam War, carried more political weight with voters. Third, federal air, water, solid waste, and environmental impact studies and other regulatory measures were harming the economy and distressing industrialists and anti-statist conservative Republicans, whose support he needed.[50]

In 1973, Nixon appointed the able EPA administrator Ruckelshaus to head the FBI, replacing him with the equally competent Train. In many ways, Train and Masland were kindred spirits. Both had been born to privilege and were dedicated conservationists. As former head of the World Wildlife Federation, Train had devoted his life to the preservation of wildlife, especially in Africa, and to his duties at the Environmental Protection Agency, while Masland focused his efforts on the preservation and expansion of National Parks at home and abroad and never fully committed to the environmental impulse that emphasized human health and safety issues.

Masland took issue with Train in two areas. He scolded Train for not halting the use of cyanide guns to kill coyotes. If ranchers leasing federal land wanted to protect their flocks, he said, let them use shepherds or sheep dogs. Train also hit too close to home when he encouraged Americans to save gas by purchasing smaller cars. That meant buying foreign cars, Masland grumbled. Larger, American-made cars were safer, he said. He left unsaid the fact that American-made cars used Masland-made carpets, and the larger the car, the more carpet needed. He also opposed any effort to reduce fuel consumption by increasing the federal tax on gasoline. Instead, Masland wanted strict enforcement of the 55-miles-per-hour speed limit for cars and trucks. The auto industry, even more than housing, he insisted, was crucial to consumer spending and a vibrant economy. "Anyone who lived through the 1929 depression has an unholy fear of the consumer withdrawing from the marketplace," he told US senator Richard Schweiker (R-PA).[51]

Masland remained an apologist for Nixon even after the president began to lose interest in environmental issues, authorized the invasion of Cambodia, and covered up the Watergate criminal break-in. The president's and the Republican Party's commitment to environmentalism began to ebb when pollution controls threatened to throttle economic progress. Just as Masland had questioned the economic wisdom of reducing the size of automobiles, other business executives doubted the wisdom of air and water quality controls that affected their economic interests. Additionally, Masland was disappointed with the lackluster environmental plank of the 1972 Republican Party platform. Still, he tried to influence policy through extensive correspondence with Russell Dickenson, deputy director of the NPS, while registering few complaints about Nixon's leadership. In short, his fear of communism and American liberals like Democratic presidential candidate George McGovern outweighed his concern for Nixon's flagging environmental interest.[52]

The break-in at the Democratic headquarters at the Watergate Hotel, not the prolonged war or loss of environmental commitment, was of course what brought down the president. Masland initially downplayed Watergate as a minor episode. He was far more disturbed by Nixon's firing of George Hartzog as Park Service director, thereby destroying the morale of the NPS, than he was over Watergate. He blamed the White House staff for the break-in and cover-up and the liberal media for exaggerating the crisis in its long vendetta against Nixon. The news outlets, especially the three main television networks, he fumed to Abbott, controlled news in much the same way that Hitler had in Nazi Germany. Liberal commentators had been trying to destroy Nixon politically ever since, as a member of Congress, he had helped jail the federal bureaucrat and alleged communist spy Alger Hiss for perjury. None of the encouraging words from supporters, Nixon told Masland, had been "more welcome than those which come from old friends like you—your message of support and understanding means more to me than I can tell you."[53]

Even after the White House tape recordings revealed that Nixon had ordered the cover-up of the break-in, Masland urged him not to resign, lauding him for firing special prosecutor Archibald Cox, "a typical Left-wing Harvard professor," during the "Saturday Night Massacre." Nixon's misstep, Masland said, was minor compared to those of FDR (who had not been impeached after maneuvering the Japanese to bomb Pearl Harbor) and JFK (who had led the United States into Vietnam). He berated Richard Schweiker, a Republican senator from Pennsylvania, for calling for Nixon's impeachment. With Nixon removed from the presidency, he declared, "we become more vulnerable to the Russian threat." When Nixon resigned in August 1974, Masland again blamed his downfall on the left-wing news media, which he accused of trying to replace a conservative government with a socialist one. He credited Nixon with bringing about a ceasefire in the Middle East and improving the environment, while conveniently overlooking the fact that the president had covered up a major political crime, further eroding people's faith in their government. The best Masland could offer as criticism concerning the Watergate incident was to admit to Barry Goldwater that Nixon had not handled it well.[54]

Masland recognized that the Watergate crisis would cost Republicans control of the White House in 1976 and perhaps for years to come. But he still had hopes for environmental causes if the Republic endured. Secretary of the Interior Morton survived Nixon's downfall but seldom put Masland to use, especially after Hartzog's departure. Udall had had "an open door policy," but Morton had only asked him to visit once, Masland groused. And the new Park Service director, Ronald Walker, also failed to call on Masland. "I have never been so happy as when involved in a mission for the Park Service," he told Horace Albright. "It is a Service one learns to love undyingly."[55]

Worried that the Walker appointment foreshadowed an emasculation of the Park Service, Masland sent a letter of concern to US senator Hugh Scott (R-PA) and several other members of Congress. The Interior Department was responsible for protecting the natural resources within America's borders—resources that made those borders worth defending in the first place. In turn, the Park Service was "the guardian of those resources which are essential to the maintenance of spiritual values and development of the whole man," he wrote. He believed that there could be no greater consideration "for those in a position of responsibility than the retention of the National Park Service with no less responsibility and authority than it now possesses."[56]

With few park-related responsibilities, other than attending Advisory Board meetings, Masland had more time for leisure. Unfortunately, health and old-age issues interceded. Virginia required knee replacement surgery, restricting her travel. And his beloved Southwest—both the Colorado River and the canyon lands—was becoming overcrowded. More than ten thousand people ran the river each year. He would rather "ride a motorcycle down Fifth Avenue," he told Marston, than run the river again. One way to restrict traffic on the river, he suggested, was to ban motors and restrict the number of passengers. Eventually, the Park Service did restrict permits for commercial boaters and capped traffic on the river through the Grand Canyon to twenty-two thousand passengers per year.[57]

In 1974, Marston asked Masland to join him on one last river run. Nearly seventy-nine years old, Masland declined, proclaiming that his days of roughing it were over. "I would very much like to make another river run with you and to further explore the rough country on the back of a horse. Neither are likely," he said. "I think I prefer to live with my memories of those days when the craft and the only people on the river were our little party and the craft we occupied. Those memories are so choice I am afraid to spoil them." He would live nearly two more decades with his memories. During those twilight years, he continued to offer feisty observations on the national political scene and to make charitable, community, and conservation-related contributions as night came to the Cumberland.[58]

CHAPTER 13

Environmentalism at Bay

Apart from attending NPS Advisory Board sessions, Masland had little association with the Interior Department after Nixon resigned. "One gets so old," he muttered to Dock Marston, "that one is no longer called upon." He had scant regard for President Gerald Ford, ruing the fact that Nixon had not replaced disgraced vice president Spiro Agnew with Goldwater instead of Ford. "I am a Ford, not a Lincoln," the president once famously quipped, and Masland completely agreed.[1]

Turnover within the Interior Department troubled Masland. Following Secretary Morton's resignation, Ford appointed Stanley Hathaway, who lasted less than four months before being replaced by Thomas Kleppe in October 1975. Kleppe, Masland informed Emil Haury, was personable but there was no evidence that he was in touch with environmental issues. The National Park Service also was in flux. Ford replaced Ronald Walker, a blatant political appointee with no experience in the field, with Gary Everhardt, the former superintendent of Grand Teton National Park. Everhardt, like Ford, was personable, Masland wrote, but he was no Hartzog.[2]

Besides stewing about the future of the Park Service, Masland and Mary Abbott exchanged woeful letters about the decline of national political leadership and the moral, religious, and cultural decay of the American Republic. President Ford and other modern leaders, they tut-tutted, did not measure up to the Adamses and other Founding Fathers. Ford's measures to remedy the economic recession through tax cuts, reduced federal spending, and appeals to citizens to increase personal savings proved ineffective. Masland approved of Ford's pardon of Richard Nixon but decried the president's granting of clemency to Vietnam War draft dodgers.[3]

In a peevish mood, Masland also poured out his frustration over the state of public affairs to Senator Richard Schweiker. One of Pennsylvania's two moderate Republican senators (Hugh Scott was the other), Schweiker was not up to the task of governing, in Masland's view. Neither was Scott, but Masland singled out Schweiker for criticism. "Why would any conservative or industrialist vote for you?" he asked. "You are not only a liberal but a radical liberal who did not support Nixon or the war in Vietnam." To make matters worse, he was "in 'labor's pocket.'" Schweiker had done nothing for Pennsylvania or for the national defense, Masland went on, and might as well join the Democratic Party. "You have sold yourself, body and soul, to labor and your vote to our Nation's enemy." Schweiker responded, "I only wish I could be as sure about every problem and every answer and every person as you are. You belong in the Senate!" Formerly on a first-name basis, for the next few years they addressed each other as "Dear Sir."[4]

Democrats won the White House in 1976, making Masland more disconsolate. A devout Christian, President Jimmy Carter had a strong conservation record as governor of Georgia and was a committed environmentalist as president, but Masland was convinced that Carter's liberal politics negated his commitment to nature. He disparaged him as the "Peanut President." Perhaps because during the campaign Carter admitted to having lusted after other women in his heart, Masland described him as a "mental and moral pervert" in a letter to Abbott. He would take America further down the road to socialism; he had weakened the nation militarily by signing a second Strategic Arms Limitations Treaty with the Soviet Union; and he had committed an act of "treason" by transferring control of the Panama Canal to Panama after 1999. "I regard Carter as an unmitigated disaster," he fumed to Robert Stoddard, a Worcester, Massachusetts industrialist and John Bircher. "His actions indicate an arrogance that can only be traced to a conviction on his part that he is a born again Christian, has a direct line to the Almighty and can do no wrong," he added. Although a fundamentalist Christian himself, Masland despised evangelical politicians who believed that they were acting as the Creator's earthly agents.[5]

Throughout the 1970s, Masland agonized over rumors that the Park Service Advisory Board and Advisory Council might be phased out. Emil Haury tried to lift his spirits. "Few people will ever fully know the impact you have had on the highest level bureaucrats with the Department of Interior by keeping them apprised of the nature, functions, and traditions of the Advisory Board," he wrote. "Secretaries and Assistant Secretaries come and go, but the devoted Councilmen in the Advisory Board stay and establish the needed continuity."[6]

In 1976, Congress reauthorized the Advisory Board until January 1, 1990, renaming it the "National Park System Advisory Board" and shortening the term of membership from six to four years, to coincide with presidential terms. The fate of the Advisory Council remained in limbo. With the board becoming more politically partisan and marginalized, he feared that the Advisory Council would be eliminated. And without the council, the politically partisan board members would lack historical context and knowledge about conservation issues that wizened old-timers like himself could provide. Council member Marian Heiskell tried to assure him that his work for the Advisory Board and council would not be forgotten: "You really are an incredible man and have my great admiration for your efforts on behalf of preservation and the National Park Service."[7]

Disregarding his previous sharp criticism, and before realizing that the Advisory Board had been reauthorized by Congress, Masland appealed to Senator Schweiker (now "Dear Richard") to help save the board and council from oblivion. "I know you will question my assertion that in the field of the Government's responsibility for the preservation and nourishment of the spiritual quality of the nation and the physical well being of the people there is no agency that matches the history of the National Park Service." But the board and council brought years of wisdom and expertise to the service and to the secretary of the interior, he explained, and he asked the senator to be its congressional guardian. Schweiker informed him that the Advisory Board had been reauthorized and that the fate of the Advisory Council was in the hands of the new Carter administration. Prospects for its continuation, he added, looked promising. To Masland's great relief, the Advisory Council was finally reauthorized in 1978 by the Interior Department and the Office of Management and Budget.[8]

In May 1980, President Carter's interior secretary, Cecil D. Andrus, named Russell Dickenson the director of the NPS, a move that pleased Masland. A thirty-three-year veteran of the Park Service, Dickenson had worked his way up the ladder from ranger, to deputy director, and finally to director.

Considering him ideally suited to repairing the damaged morale of the Park Service, Masland became a supporter and frequent correspondent.[9]

Dickenson shared many of Masland's concerns about the Park Service, including the retention and use of the Advisory Board and Advisory Council and the lack of congressional funding for existing and new additions to the park system. In the late 1970s, units of land were being added to the park system under a variety of designations—as parks, monuments, preserves, historic sites, cultural centers, archaeological sites, and recreation areas. In 1980 President Carter signed the Alaska National Interest Lands Conservation Act, setting aside 104 million acres, including much of the wild and scenic land Masland and Haury had recommended for preservation in their report to Interior Secretary Morton nearly a decade earlier. But Masland, always a sourpuss when it came to Carter, gave the president little credit for prompting Congress to authorize and augment lands set aside as national monuments two years earlier. Most of that rugged and remote landscape came under the jurisdiction of the Park Service. But in a time of austerity, Congress had not appropriated adequate funding to manage those new parks and wilderness preserves. Consequently, the Park Service was forced to reduce personnel at heavily visited parks in order to manage the new units in Alaska and elsewhere in the lower forty-eight states.[10]

Like most Americans, Masland was upset about the sputtering economy. He attributed the economic decline to the lack of individual initiative and public greed dating back to the New Deal welfare state and to federal regulations that punished private enterprise. "America was great," he wrote, "when the governing principle was 'Let the buyer beware.' That necessitated each individual looking out for himself, exercising his own judgment, taking personal risks. That has been replaced by federal protection from womb to tomb. Individual initiative has been replaced by the 'gimme' attitude, an attitude for which government is responsible."[11]

At Masland and Sons, carpet sales and employee spirits sagged. Fifty percent of the company's business came from the US auto industry, and it too was unraveling. US automakers were facing keen competition from German and Japanese manufacturers, who were producing smaller, more fuel-efficient cars. Facing bankruptcy, Chrysler Corporation asked for a federal loan. Masland opposed the bailout. He blamed the US auto-making hardship on unions and on federal regulations that mandated cars that were more fuel efficient and less polluting. Instead of a $1.5 million bailout, he favored the relaxation of what he termed "unnecessary federal regulations" on cars and a quota on imports. Schweiker voted against the bailout, he told Masland, but he also opposed quotas because then there would be no incentive for US automakers to make smaller, fuel-efficient cars. Like other conservatives, Masland did not view federal regulation of imports as a form of corporate welfare. Yet he opposed welfare for the needy and federal environmental regulations that affected his business.[12]

Overall, he saw a declining United States. "We are today a second rate nation, militarily, economically, governmentally, and sociologically. The government is utterly inept and the people lack will and are dominated by greed." For Masland, the remedy for what President Carter termed a "crisis of confidence" was the election of a Republican president, a Republican majority in Congress, trust in the free enterprise system, and hope for a "religious reawakening" based on "the teachings of Christ." Masland identified with the so-called Moral Majority and tried to hurry a religious reawakening by contributing money to Jerry Falwell and to Protestant fundamentalist religious institutions like Messiah College and Liberty University. And the best way to defeat the Democrats in November 1980, he advised the Republican National Committee, was to accuse them of being socialists.[13]

The Iranian hostage crisis, the Panama Canal Treaty, and soaring inflation rates and gasoline shortages triggered by an oil embargo worked against Carter's chances for reelection. But Masland initially showed little enthusiasm for potential GOP candidates, including Ronald Reagan. Masland did not explain his indifference to Reagan's candidacy. A former Democrat, actor, and union head, Reagan had established a credible conservation record as governor of California, but his acceptance of California's toughest-in-the-nation auto emissions standards may have given Masland pause.

Masland eventually warmed to Reagan, as did other long-suffering conservatives. Historians disagree about the causes of the emergence of the New Right. Allan Lichtman tracks its origins to white Protestants of the 1920s. Kim Phillips-Fein attributes its rise to opposition to the New Deal welfare state by American business leaders. George Nash focuses on the role of post–World War II conservative intellectuals. Darren Dochuk emphasizes the activities of plain folk evangelical Christians from the Bible Belt and Sunbelt states. Matthew Lassiter highlights the role of the so-called silent majority in suburbs like Charlotte, Atlanta, and Richmond in the Sunbelt South. Lisa McGirr argues that energetic, grassroots "suburban warriors" in Sunbelt enclaves like Orange

County, California, propelled the modern Right to political ascendance under Ronald Reagan. And James Morton Turner and Andrew Isenberg note that conservative westerners, displeased with environmental regulations, helped Republicans gain control of the US Senate in 1980.[14]

Composed of business executives, intellectuals, plain folk, and upscale suburbanites, New Right men and women shared common political principles. They were virulently anticommunist, fervently nationalistic, anti-union, overwhelmingly Protestant, and strongly supportive of individual initiative, gun rights, free-enterprise capitalism, school prayer, and traditional family values. They sought to limit federal power, except when it came to fortifying the national defense and maintaining law and order. As anti-statists, they worked to limit or reverse federal control over public land, especially in the West, and to relax federal environmental regulations. Masland identified with most of these goals, though he had no patience with the New Right's disregard for the preservation of public lands, needless to say.

As a presidential candidate, Ronald Reagan embodied and championed New Right views. Although he was delighted when Reagan beat Carter, Masland had misgivings about the president-elect's nomination of James Watt as secretary of the interior. "I have a most uncomfortable feeling in the pit of my stomach with regard to the well being of our parks under the new administration," he informed fellow Advisory Board member Fred Smith. The American public, Masland noted, was fickle. The pendulum, he said, was swinging away from environmental causes, and it might become stuck in an extreme backlash position.[15]

Sure enough, he soon became disconsolate when it became clear that President Reagan was retreating from the federal commitment to protecting public lands. "The golden age of political environmentalism came to an abrupt end in January 1981 with the inauguration of Ronald Reagan as Carter's successor," historian Daniel Nelson has written in *Nature's Burdens*. Reagan was indifferent to preservation, Nelson writes, "but he delegated appointments and policy to vocal western supporters who sought to sabotage the changes of the previous century." Although ultimately unsuccessful, he adds, Reagan's agenda put conservationists on the defensive, forced many out of the Republican Party, and made the environment a politically partisan issue.[16]

Appointed secretary of the interior in January 1981, James Watt spearheaded what journalist David Helvarg has called the administration's "war against the greens." Born in Lusk, Wyoming, in 1938, Watt attended the University of

Wyoming, where he received his undergraduate and law degrees. Lean and angular, bespectacled and balding, he was bright, ambitious, and possessed of a polarizing perspective on public lands that matched his combative personality. He was a devout evangelical Christian and an ardent conservative Republican who championed limited federal authority and the economic interests of the American West.

Eastern environmentalists, Watt believed, wanted to preserve the open horizons of the American West as their own personal playground. "Conservatives," he once wrote, "must take on an entrenched elitist liberal Establishment. We must have the courage to effect change in power if we hope to stop the erosion of religious liberties and to recapture the values that have been at the very heart of the American spirit for a century and a half." To recapture the values of limited government, free enterprise, and individual rights, he had worked as a legislative aide to Senator Milward Simpson (R-WY) before joining the Nixon administration as deputy assistant secretary of the interior. A strong advocate of mining, timbering, livestock grazing, recreational activity, and hydroelectric power development on public lands, he became vice chair of the Federal Power Administration in 1975. Two years later he was named head of the Mountain States Legal Foundation. Under his legal guidance, the MSLF served to counterbalance environmental advocacy groups like the Environmental Defense Fund. Forgoing the conservative principle of judicial restraint, Watt portrayed himself as a judicial activist out to protect the rights of westerners to access public resources in their region.[17]

Colorado beer baron and ardent anti-statist Joseph Coors had founded and funded the MSLF to defend individual rights and private enterprise in the courts. Hostile to most federal environmental regulations, Coors was determined "to establish a special expertise in the law concerning the energy issues—oil, gas, coal, uranium, mining, underground and surface, agricultural, timber, livestock, crops; and particular attention to our state water rights, and the federal encroachment on them as well as management of our public lands." Coors and Masland had much in common. Both were conservative industrialists who had inherited a successful family business, and both were deeply religious, anti-union anti-statists, convinced that most college faculty members were leftists opposed to free enterprise and traditional family values. Masland, however, disdained Coors, convinced that he was determined to open wilderness and other public preserves in the West to economic development. Masland had equal disdain for left-leaning preservationists like Justice

William Douglas and Congressman Philip Burton and right-leaning antipreservationists like Coors and Watt.[18]

Watt sympathized with the so-called Sagebrush Rebellion, a movement led by development-minded westerners who sought to transfer protected public lands to the states for mining, grazing, timbering, and other commercial uses. But as historian Jefferson Decker has pointed out, it is unlikely that Watt really wanted the states to replace the federal government as landlords. Instead, Watt and the MSLF wanted "to ensure rights of access to and use of those lands—rights that were jeopardized by efforts to preserve wilderness and protect habitats." Nonetheless, the perception among most environmentalists was that Watt was in league with the so-called Sagebrush rebels.[19]

Given his support for expanded commercial development on protected public lands and his general hostility to federal environmental regulations that restricted economic development, Watt's appointment as interior secretary in 1981 was not well received by traditional conservation groups like the Sierra Club, Wilderness Society, National Parks Foundation, and National Audubon Society. If ever there was a case of the fox guarding the henhouse, they charged, this was it. Cartoonist Steven Greenberg depicted Watt about to enter a room marked "Senate Confirmation Hearings." Watt points to Bambi, Smokey the Bear, Johnny Appleseed, and Woodsy Owl and says, "When I'm Secretary of Interior I'm going to make you environmental extremists toe the line." The Sierra Club and Wilderness Society collected a hundred thousand signatures for a "What's Wrong? Watt's Wrong" petition for his removal as secretary. Congressional environmentalists also blasted the appointment. Morris Udall, an environmental advocate and the good-humored and able chair of the House Committee on Interior and Insular Affairs, said that naming Watt secretary of the interior was akin to "appointing Dracula to head a blood bank."[20] Other Reagan appointees also distressed conservation groups, including Robert Burford, a conservative Colorado rancher and state legislator who became head of the US Bureau of Land Management; John Crowell, a corporate lawyer for a forest products company, appointed assistant secretary of the National Forest Service; and Anne Burford Gorsuch, a former conservative Colorado legislator (future wife of Robert and mother of future US Supreme Court Justice Neil Gorsuch), who was tapped to head the EPA.[21]

Like the conservation organizations, Masland was wary of the Reagan selections, especially Watt, given his affiliation with the MSLF. But he reserved judgment and was initially impressed when Watt met with the Park Service

Advisory Board in April 1981. "He is forthright, fearless, articulate and I believe he is genuinely interested in the well-being of the Park Service and the Park System," Masland reported to Abbott. He was also pleased when Watt retained Dickenson as Park Service director.[22]

Early on, Masland tried to save Watt from being skewered by environmental activists. Conservation groups, leaders on Capitol Hill, and major newspapers like the *New York Times* (and less prominent ones like the *Harrisburg Patriot-News*), he pointed out, were railing against Watt's statements proposing to relieve the energy crisis by developing resources in the West, including some on protected public lands. He would not long endure under a fusillade of such criticism, Masland felt.

He forwarded advice to Watt in a four-page single-spaced letter. First, he advised Watt to pry Fred Smith away from Laurance Rockefeller to handle public relations and act as liaison with members of Congress: "I say quite bluntly . . . that you need a diplomat for in my experience no Cabinet officer has aroused more vicious and determined opposition in so short of time." Second, Watt should state publicly that he planned to allow limited development of public resources, and only on lands that were not national sanctuaries. Third, Masland suggested that Watt consider hiring George Hartzog as a consultant. Fourth, he should surrender the idea of transferring urban parks to the states; the states did not want them. Last, Watt should give the Advisory Board on National Parks, Historic Sites, Buildings, and Monuments, which was renamed the National Park System Advisory Board (NPSAB) in 1976, new purpose. He should appoint individuals with solid credentials and a commitment to the integrity of the park system. In the 1960s, the Advisory Board had met often with the interior secretary, NPS director, and congressional leaders, and its advice was welcomed and heeded. Masland reminded Watt that "God gave man dominion which means awesome responsibility for the resources he placed at his disposal and for all wildlife. I believe we should only disrupt nature when there exists a present or foreseeable need for which we must prepare." He closed by saying, "As a Jerry Falwell Faith Partner, I include you in my prayers." Watt thanked Masland for his prayers and suggestions, telling him that his support and friendship were "an inspiration." He then ignored all of Masland's advice.[23]

Within months, Masland had soured on Watt and the administration's complete disregard for the environmental program and its cavalier approach to wilderness, wildlife, and the national park system. He was disturbed by reports that Watt planned to relax federal restrictions on the use of predator poisons and the importation of hides of certain endangered animals.[24]

He also slammed Watt's plan to expand US energy production by opening one million acres of wildlife refuge in Alaska and the Atlantic continental shelf to gas and oil drilling. Masland never wavered in his belief that once public lands had been preserved for posterity, they must not be opened to development. "The American people own sufficient raw energy resources to meet our needs for hundreds and hundreds, if not thousands of years," Watt stated. The goal, he once declared, was to "mine more, drill more, cut more timber to use our resources rather than simply keep them locked up." At the same time, EPA administrator Gorsuch worked to subvert environmental regulations pertaining to air and water pollution and hazardous waste disposal. And Burford, as head of the Bureau of Land Management, failed to reduce sheep and cattle quotas designed to help public grazing lands regenerate.[25]

Watt also launched an offensive against the national parks. He sought to contain the growth and cost of the park system by ceasing to procure new units and inholdings. Until overruled by Congress, he proposed using revenue from the Land and Water Conservation Fund for park maintenance rather than for the intended purpose of purchasing more green space for public use. Maintaining the nonurban parks, Watt insisted, took priority over adding new ones to an already financially burdened system. "Build a road, build a latrine, pump in running water so you can wash dishes. Most people think that if you can drive in, walk 20 yards and pitch a tent by a stream, you've had a wilderness experience." He also wanted to farm out the interpretive mission of the Park Service to private vendors and to assign management of urban national parks to the states. He unsuccessfully sought to abolish a 1977 law mandating that the Park Service formulate a list of ten potential additions to the system. And, to Masland's horror, he appointed new individuals to the Advisory Board who were not friends of the parks.[26]

Watt retained the National Park System Advisory Council but made six appointments to the Advisory Board in July 1981 that Masland deemed totally "unsuitable." He was particularly distressed by the appointment of Charles Cushman. Cushman was a stocky, white-bearded, brash, garrulous man in his mid-thirties with a talent for rabble-rousing and theatrics. "I kind of like Chuck," recalled fellow board member and Yale historian Robin Winks. "But I also think he's mischievous, dangerous and often out of line." Masland denounced him as an antipark firebrand.[27]

Born in Los Angeles, Cushman served as a successful insurance agent before retiring on a disability and inheriting a cabin on a parcel of land within the boundaries of Yosemite National Park. A strident defender of private property and a wise-use conservationist who disparaged preservationists and environmentalists, Cushman became president of the National Inholders Association, consisting of seventy thousand members. Inholders were people who had acquired, usually through inheritance, private property within national parks. In Yosemite National Park, for example, 272 acres (out of more than 700,000) were privately held. The NPS sought to buy out inholders and to impose restrictions on the ways in which they could maintain and improve their property. Cushman considered the Park Service's interference autocratic and un-American. He also railed against the NPS for attempting to oust inholders and for attempts to make more segments of rivers wild and scenic. National Park officials, he blustered, were "Nazis" determined to destroy the economic livelihood of local communities. Accusing the Park Service of violating property rights, committing "cultural genocide," and plotting the "destruction of rural America," Cushman mobilized inholders into what historian Samuel Hays describes as "one of the most vocal sources of opposition to the National Park Service." For Masland, few public sins could be greater than attacking the NPS.[28]

Unsympathetic with Park Service goals of acquiring inholdings and other land as additions to the park system, Cushman nonetheless brazenly pitched himself to fellow Advisory Board members as a friend of the parks, noting that his father had been a seasonal ranger at Yosemite. But he soon realized that his brash personality and commitment to protecting inholdings did not resonate with esteemed Advisory Board members like former astronaut Wally Schirra and Lady Bird Johnson. Neither did his rants about eastern elitists and environmentalists. At the meetings of the board and council, he later said, he was "the skunk at the lawn party."[29]

Cushman seemed to relish his role as the skunk on the Advisory Board. He retained his position as president of the National Inholders Association and made public speeches critical of the Park Service's plan to purge inholdings. To Masland, criticizing the Park Service publicly was akin to insulting a family member. Masland asked Watt to muzzle the confrontational Cushman, arguing that he was undermining the integrity and morale of the Park Service and could not simultaneously serve two masters. Watt refused, stating that Cushman brought "a new dimension" to the board and he would not attempt to restrict Cushman's right to free speech any more than he would seek to silence Masland. He also declared that Cushman's views did not necessarily reflect those of the Interior Department. Yet his actions indicated otherwise. Not only did Watt appoint Cushman to the Advisory Board but he also named Ric Davidge, another critic of the Park Service and former lobbyist for the Inholders Association, as his assistant for the national parks and historical preservation.[30]

Flummoxed by Watt's behavior, Masland determined by late 1981 that he was a detriment to the parks and the cause of preservation. He was also put off by Watt's corrosive personality and evangelism. "For a born-again Christian, Watt is diabolically clever," Masland sputtered to Advisory Council member Nancy Rennell. "I have never encountered such egotism," he fumed to another friend. "I do not condemn Watt nearly as much as I do Reagan," he exclaimed. Reagan clearly had appointed Watt to emasculate the parks program out of gratitude to beer baron and GOP financial supporter Joseph Coors. Watt "was a Born-Again Christian convinced that he was God's earthly instrument and that as such his judgments, his decisions, his actions are in accord with God's will."[31]

Masland believed that Watt was determined to undercut the integrity of the national park system. When Masland reminded him that the Interior Department was legally obligated to prepare a list of ten potential park additions, despite the moratorium on new units, Watt suggested that the Advisory Board should do it. Winks, then the chair, asked Masland to take on the task, but Masland declined on the grounds that an assignment requiring considerable travel and exploring was too much for an eighty-eight-year-old. It was difficult enough to attend semiannual meetings of the board and council. Masland tried to enlist Paul Pritchard, executive director of the National Parks Conservation Association, but he too declined.[32]

In March 1982, frustrated by Watt's indifference to the preservationist perspective and the assault on the Park Service, Masland drafted a letter resigning from his cherished Advisory Board Council. He lectured Watt at length on the importance of preserving open space, wilderness, national parks, and public resources for future generations. "The bulldozer has replaced the covered wagon in the march of Twentieth century civilization," he declared. "We see an endless stream crossing the country from coast to coast—modern Forty Niners riding bulldozers and leaving behind them . . . a land denuded." It was the duty of the Interior Department to prevent "a cannibalistic civilization" from using up "the finite products of the Master Architect." Knowing of Watt's deep religious faith, Masland concluded by reminding him that preserving, not plundering, nature was pleasing to God. In the end, however, Masland could not make the break from an agency that was so meaningful to him. His unsent letter reflects his state of angst over the ebbing bipartisan movement to preserve the public lands being marginalized by Watt. He understood that at his advanced age he could no longer perform park reconnaissance tours, but his mind was sharp, and he could still offer counsel. But Watt considered him irrelevant.[33]

Despite his deep opposition to Watt's priorities and management style, Masland found it difficult to break off their relationship, though it had become increasingly frosty. In July 1982, he again complained to Watt about his association with Davidge and Cushman, who, he asserted, were acting for selfish economic reasons, not the national interest. He also censured Watt for opening the Atlantic continental shelf to oil and gas drilling. That move alone, he declared, would be enough to cede the environmental movement to the Democratic Party.[34]

He also ranted about Watt's assault on the national parks and wilderness to members of the Advisory Board Council, conservation leaders, and his congressman. "With John Saylor living, and in Congress, Jim Watt would not even have hair above his ears," Masland fumed to a Wilderness Society official. Without national park advocates like Saylor, Roy Taylor, and Alan Bible, he continued, "Congress remains indifferent to raids on open land and public resources." Masland feared that all the gains achieved in the previous three decades by dedicated preservationists like himself might be undone by exploiters and despoilers like Watt and his cronies.[35]

Aware of the increasingly acidic relationship between Masland and Watt, Republican Pennsylvania congressman William Goodling sought to reconcile the two conservatives. Goodling wrote Watt, reminding him of Masland's sterling credentials as a conservative and his dedicated years of service to the Park Service. He suggested that he write Masland or invite him to Washington for a chat. Watt decided to write, he told Masland, in the hope of saving their friendship. Referring specifically to Masland's concern about opening the eastern continental shelf to drilling, he noted that any "reasonable" person would recognize the need of the United States to lessen its dependence on foreign oil. "America," he said, "can no longer afford to be subjected to blackmail attempts or weakness."[36]

Watt's terse attempt at reconciliation only brought more unsolicited advice. And Masland must have realized that his scolding response would end their relationship. As an industrialist and as vice president of the National Association of Manufacturers, Masland wrote, he agreed with the need for America's energy independence. But as a "maverick, hybrid industrialist environmentalist," he also believed that resource development must be balanced with environmental stewardship. The Department of the Interior, he reminded Watt, was responsible "for protecting, preserving and *wisely* using" the nation's natural bounty "for the spiritual and physical survival (literally) of man and all life." Wilderness preservation was an especially crucial resource, he continued, "for if man is to be whole he must have available an antidote to the concrete canyons of the city." Watt, he said, would be held accountable if he withheld that "antidote" from future generations.[37]

Masland closed with words that revealed his hurt at being sidelined by Watt. He pointed out that he had served Secretaries Seaton, Udall, and Morton and that they had valued his counsel. He had hoped to provide similar aid to Watt but had been shunned. He recalled a visit shortly after Watt's appointment to the cabinet. Masland motored to Washington, but Watt gave him only ten minutes. "I had never previously been treated so cavalierly and, of course, had no intention of affording an opportunity for a repeat." He and Watt were similar, he went on, because they saw issues as black or white, with no gray areas. But he pointed out one key difference: he listened to opposing viewpoints, while Watt did not. But Watt, like many other westerners, was fed up with eastern elitists and federal bureaucrats like Masland and their dictating to westerners the proper use of public land situated mainly in their states.[38]

Shortly after sending this letter, Masland went into another snit when he learned that Watt planned to open to commercial development portions of Alaska's national parks and wilderness. "I couldn't possibly be a Democrat," he groaned to Congressman Goodling, "but why do Republicans make it so difficult for me to be a Republican?" Ever hopeful, Masland forwarded to Watt a 1953 article by Paul Sears extolling the virtues of wilderness and the danger to the human spirit of crowding out nature. Watt failed to acknowledge it.[39]

Masland gave up trying to appeal directly to Watt but continued to rail against him privately. "The Secretary pays no attention whatever to either the Board or Council," he griped. "When I think of how powerful it was in years gone by, I get sick in the pit of my stomach." If the National Parks Conservation

Association and other kindred organizations did not "exercise every conceivable means for thwarting" the attempted raids on public lands by Watt, Cushman, and Davidge, "you will be flying under false colors," he lectured its director. If Watt's hands could reach the heavens, he vented to members of the Advisory Council, the stars "would have oil on them." Writing on behalf of the Advisory Council, Masland asked Cushman to resign from the Advisory Board, but he refused.[40]

But Masland and the environmental movement caught a break. Under siege by environmentalists, liberals, and much of the media, Watt brought about his own political demise with public relations gaffes. In 1983 he refused to permit the Beach Boys to perform a concert on the Washington Mall, contending that they had an undesirable moral influence on the nation's youth. He apparently did not know that the California band was one of First Lady Nancy Reagan's favorite musical groups. A few months later, he was derided for his insensitive description of an independent coal-leasing study group he was mandated to establish by Congress: "I have a black, a woman, two Jews, and a cripple. And they have talent." Two months later he resigned and was replaced by William Clark. EPA administrator Anne Gorsuch, another public relations lightning rod who was under a congressional contempt cloud, also resigned in 1983. She was succeeded by the EPA's first director, William Ruckelshaus.[41]

Environmentalists withstood the Reagan administration's assault on the public lands and federal regulations. Indeed, from 1979 through 1983, membership in the Wilderness Society more than doubled, from 48,000 to 100,000, and the Sierra Club grew from 181,000 to 346,000. Environmentalists also countered the popularity of the Sagebrush Rebellion by portraying it as a regional movement driven by state and local governments and the extractive industries with the intention of raiding the public lands. Additionally, the Sagebrush crowd, as historian James Turner points out, did not sit well with moderate national conservatives who were less interested in states' rights than in individual property rights. In the end, President Reagan signed more wilderness areas into the system than any other president.[42]

Masland was unique among conservatives in his forceful and consistent support for the preservation of the national parks, wilderness areas, and wildlife sanctuaries. He never wavered in his belief that, once established, the ecosystems of those preserves must not be jeopardized by dams, oil rigs, bulldozers, ATVs, commercial establishments, and other threats. Like other conservative conservationists, Masland had mixed feelings about the new wave of environmentalism, with its focus on urban problems, litigation, and environmental justice for the poor and communities of color. He even resigned from the Sierra Club, insisting that it had drifted too far toward the new environmental outlook. But he maintained his membership and increased his financial donations to the Wilderness Society, with its mission of preserving and adding units of lightly trammeled nature.[43]

As a self-described "hybrid industrialist environmentalist," Masland understood the need to establish federal air, water, and solid-waste controls to protect human health and quality of life. Indeed, he admitted to a journalist that Masland and Sons had been fined by the state EPA for exceeding noise levels with its company whistle and for polluting Letort Creek with carpet dye. But he said he had never deliberately polluted and never claimed that those fines were unjust. At the same time, he saw many environmental regulations as too restrictive and damaging to business profits.[44]

Throughout his career, Masland battled dueling sentiments. He favored an activist federal government when it came to conserving nature—but not much else. He railed all his life against the establishment of a federal regulatory colossus that would endanger human liberty, free enterprise, and traditional family values. Balancing the two positions was difficult. By the mid-1970s, he and other conservatives believed that the environmental pendulum had swung too far toward regulation. Strict enforcement of federal environmental regulations eroded political bipartisanship, slowed the economy, caused consumer hardship, and portended the establishment of a totalitarian state. Masland regarded federal restrictions relating to automobile carbon emissions, fuel economy, and safety standards especially burdensome to both the overall economy and, specifically, to his carpet company. Indeed, he repeatedly reminded Reagan that a healthy US economy depended on a healthy US automobile industry. He was far more critical of the Reagan administration's assault on national parks and the wilderness movement than he was of federal environmental regulations.[45]

Neither Masland nor fellow conservative loyalist Barry Goldwater were converts to what historians James Morton Turner and Andrew C. Isenberg have termed the Republican reversal—GOP members who deserted the environmental cause. "With Reagan, the Republicans, once champions of environmental protection, began a campaign to assert new policies more favorable to business interests that put ascendant conservative values—the free market, economic growth, and individual freedom—before environmental protection," they write. Reagan Republicans downplayed threats to the environment and discounted scientific expertise, while hailing so-called free-market capitalism (in fact heavily subsidized), American exceptionalism, and human dominion over the natural world. While Masland firmly believed in these tenets of American Republicanism, he also held tenaciously to his faith in federally managed stewardship of nature, especially the public domain and its resources.[46]

Masland and Goldwater held similar ambivalent positions on the popular new environmental movement. Both paid lip service to federal regulatory measures, but not their full commitment. As noted above, in the early 1970s Goldwater had given speeches supporting clean air and water legislation but absented himself when it came up for a vote. He also missed the vote on the Endangered Species Act. A decade later, however, during the Reagan administration's assault on the environment, he voted to extend the Clean Air, Clean Water, and Endangered Species Acts. He also voted for the 1980 Superfund bill to clean up nuclear waste sites and supported federal funding for solar energy research.[47]

Goldwater also appeared to have deserted the cause of the national parks and wilderness by supporting James Watt, who delighted him. When Watt was attacked by the Sierra Club and other conservation groups, Goldwater defended him. The secretary "is doing a tremendous job," he said, and "understands the importance of our resources and intends to provide the balance in our environmental policies that have been lacking in previous administrations." Watt, he stated at another time, "is the first Secretary of the Interior that we have had in a long time who comes from the West, who really understands not only the problems we westerners face, but he also has good insights into our nation's energy needs and our land conservation and preservation goals." Despite Watt's attempt to contain the growth of the park and wilderness systems, Goldwater introduced successful bills designating nearly 6,700 acres of Arizona's Aravaipa Canyon as a national wilderness area, preserving another 750,000 acres of national forest under the Arizona Wilderness Act of 1984, and forty miles of the state's Verde River as part of the National Wild and Scenic River System. Historian Brian Allen Drake concludes that Goldwater was an environmentalist, but an inconsistent one.[48]

Masland, too, was inconsistent in his environmentalism, as we have seen. Unlike Goldwater, he never wavered in his advocacy of federal management of public land and resources and landscapes—but he did not have to answer to the voters where most of that land was located. Masland's constituency was the family business, the National Park Service, and the future generations he imagined enjoying the parks. Despite his disgust with the administration's assault on public lands, he regarded Reagan as an archenemy of socialism, and he remained a party loyalist, untroubled by the apparent hypocrisy of opposing federal activism on domestic economic and social issues while supporting it in the conservationist cause.

In his late eighties, Masland was no longer physically able to perform reconnaissance or inspection duties for the Interior Department, even if he had been asked. But he still regularly attended Advisory Board meetings and corresponded with members of the Advisory Council, and he still felt himself part of the Park Service family. Like military veterans who remained ardently loyal to their brethren and branch of service, Masland felt part of a band of brothers and sisters at the NPS. He showered Secretary of the Interior Russell Dickenson with letters of support and advice that were dutifully and thoughtfully answered until Dickenson retired in 1985.

Reflecting his elitism, one of Masland's pet peeves was the amount of boat traffic on the Colorado River and the commercialization of Grand Canyon National Park. Although he and Dock Marston had helped promote motorized rafting on the river in the 1950s, Masland had come to rue the development. Motorized rubber rafts had become so popular and prevalent that a "wilderness experience" was now the equivalent of an amusement park roller-coaster ride. With nearly as many people on the river as there were on the rim, he fumed to Dickenson, there was no more solitude and re-grounding with nature. How could one experience personal renewal surrounded by roaring motors on an artificial river choked with dams, rubber boat armadas, and crowds of boisterous people?

Masland thought the Park Service had not done enough to limit the traffic. The Grand Canyon, he asserted, was no longer grand and should be redesignated a national recreation area because the Park Service now emphasized public accessibility and tourism over park inviolability. The river had become more romper room than nature sanctuary.

Having visited nearly all of the national parks, he was absolutely certain "that none of our Parks have been so deliberately altered—nay ruined—by the hand of man for commercial purposes as Grand Canyon. It is a disgrace to the Federal Government, to the Department of the Interior, to the National

Park Service, and to the citizens of the United States." Dickenson sympathized but said that motorized rafting had become so popular that Congress would not permit the park to be reclassified as a recreational area. Masland went into another pout when the United Nations classified the Grand Canyon as a World Heritage Site. The honor, he scoffed, was undeserved because the Park Service had not kept the canyon inviolate and natural.[49]

He hoped that a similar fate did not await Canyonlands National Park. "It was intended to be a wilderness park, accessible only to those who were willing to make the effort," he said of Canyonlands. "It was never intended to be a Yosemite or Yellowstone or to be commercialized as is the Grand Canyon." If any "rock desert wilderness" should be left unsoiled, he asserted, it must be Canyonlands.[50]

Masland was energized by attending Advisory Board meetings as a member of the Council. "The years roll away when I'm with you young folks. The Advisory Board and Council and your friendship has meant much to me over the years," he told Marian Heiskell. "I wish we had more enthusiastic and dedicated members who care about the great outdoors as you," she replied. "Keep up the fight—you're terrific!"[51]

That fight, of course, had grown more difficult under Reagan, Watt, and their successors. From 1951 through 1971, two men had served as director of the Park Service. In the next decade alone, there were four, and the position became more and more politically partisan. Beginning with Nixon, Advisory Board and Advisory Council members had been seen as "green weenies" and replaced by political hacks who sometimes paid as much as $125,000 for their appointments, according to George Hartzog. Although Russell Dickenson was highly respected by career employees and the conservation community, his effectiveness was neutralized in the Reagan years. Before stepping down, Watt replaced the NPS's deputy director, a career employee, with Mary Lou Grier, a political appointee and anti-environmentalist ideologue. All budget and personnel decisions had to meet her approval before being forwarded to the secretary. Watt also named another anti-environmentalist, G. Ray Arnett, as assistant secretary for Fish and Wildlife. Amid the turmoil and turnover, Dickenson served as a stabilizing force, but employees feared that he would "leave and a worse fate would befall us." Turnover, reorganization, reassignments, and meddling also took place at lower-level agency positions, creating, as former director Gary Everhardt recalled, "a paralyzing effect on the once unshakable commitment and high morale of park people."[52]

Not surprisingly, NPS Advisory Board and Advisory Council members were also demoralized but tried to carry on by attending and voicing opinions at board meetings. "You are something. I love your determination and am very proud to know you," Heiskell wrote Masland after a 1982 meeting. "Thank God for the likes of you." If not for old-timers like Masland, she continued, the Park Service would be in even greater disarray and poorer spirits.[53]

But the political and bureaucratic mess on the Advisory Board and council had become greater than perhaps Heiskell realized. Since the Nixon administration, the board had been politicized, appointees having progressively less stature and less knowledge about park and conservation issues. The administration limited the Advisory Council to fifteen members and stopped reimbursing members for their travel expenses. New Advisory Board appointees saw council members as old geezers and hangers-on who were firmly in the environmental camp. Council members in turn viewed most board members as political hacks, unqualified for their positions, of lower social and academic stature, and complicit in the Nixon and Reagan administrations' assault on the Park Service and the environment. The board also had lost influence with Congress. "The board's source of power had been its elite, even clubby membership and the respect the notables on it received from Congress," writes historian Ronald Foresta in *America's National Parks and Their Keepers*. The worthy goal of making the board more socially diverse, which had begun with Secretary Udall, had, in short, diminished its effectiveness with Congress.[54]

The loss of standing with the Reagan administration and the estrangement from the Advisory Board had caused an us-against-them attitude among Advisory Council members. "No matter how 'they' want to look at us," wrote Marian Heiskell, "we are the guts of the Advisory Board." As political outcasts but still "clubby," council members formed a social organization called "The Outholders," a name chosen to mock Cushman's Inholders Association. The idea to form the group, Heiskell informed Hartzog, originated "one drunken evening when we learned we were booted or about to be." Headed by Heiskell, members included Masland, Wallace Stegner, Emil Haury, George Hartzog, J. O. Brew, former congressman Roy Taylor, and a few other notables. Interior Secretary Russell Dickenson joined the group after his termination in 1985. They paid modest yearly dues, carefully selected fellow members, and met occasionally for drinks and conversations about old times and park issues.[55]

Members realized that the council was doomed. Arnett, assistant secretary of the interior under Watt and then under William Clark, was behind the effort to abolish it, Masland believed. In a desperate and unseemly attempt to save the council, Masland asked Heiskell to use the *New York Times* to dig up unflattering information about Arnett and ruin him. His request was ignored.[56]

Although he had anticipated the move, Masland was saddened when the Reagan administration abolished the National Parks Advisory Board Council early in 1985. Masland regretted its demise. "Those were great days! The advent of Jim Watt was a disaster in every respect, especially as it resulted in the termination of the Council," he intoned to Roy Taylor, former chair of the House Interior and Insular Affairs Subcommittee on National Parks. "I suspect that never in government history, was there a galaxy of such knowledgeable persons in their respective roles that cost the government so little. Often the government has been penny wise and pound foolish, but never more so than when Jim Watt in his infinite wisdom, decided to bury the Council." Though rueful, Masland took satisfaction in the dedication that he and his colleagues had brought to the work. "We will always know that we served during a constructive period when the Service was building, when everything was up, when it was a pleasure and a joy. No government bureaucracy can take away from us, the sense of achievement nor the warmth of the friendships formed," he wrote Marian Heiskell. Ned Danson, Emil Haury, and other former Advisory Board friends sent similar rueful but self-congratulatory sentiments.[57]

Worried about the future of the National Park Service and the public lands, Masland hoped that a change in presidential leadership would restore morale and vigor to environmental and park issues. But the George H. W. Bush administration was more of the same. Bush's secretary of the interior, Gale Norton, had been a mining industry lobbyist, and his secretary of agriculture, Edward Madigan, had been a lobbyist for the timber industry. Rather than attempt to repeal laws protecting the environment, historian Daniel Nelson observes, they found ways to work around them. Occasionally, Bush gave lip service to environmental issues, but his speeches lacked passion and substance. "When he had something to say on nature protection," writes historian Otis Graham Jr., "President Bush reminded no one of the White House speechwriters Wallace Stegner or Stewart Udall," who had brought to life the ideas of Henry David Thoreau, John Burroughs, John Muir, and Rachel Carson.[58]

Masland entertained hope that the National Parks Advisory Board Council would be resurrected. And his hope was realized in 1990 when Congress revised the 1935 law establishing the Advisory Board and Advisory Council. Tellingly, one revision to the law required a demonstrated commitment to the national parks as a qualification for appointment to either body. But during the Bush administration both the board and the council were mainly ignored.

In his mid-nineties, Masland understood that his three decades of service and devotion to the Park Service had ended. But he remained committed to the idea of earth stewardship, especially as it pertained to the preservation of the natural world. He showed more enthusiasm for the twentieth anniversary of Earth Day than he had for the original event in 1970. Earth Day 1990, sometimes called Earth Day II, sought to reignite a commitment to earth stewardship on a worldwide basis. But conservatives were skeptical. After the collapse of the Soviet empire in 1989, argues David Helvarg, conservatives substituted the green menace for the red menace. Conservative columnist George Will, for example, claimed that Earth Day 1990 had, as "a hidden agenda," the goal of expanding the power of the state. It was a "green tree with red roots." Masland rejected that argument.[59]

Masland also showed little sympathy for the emergence of the wise-use movement in the late 1980s. That movement, unlike the earlier Sagebrush Rebellion, was national in scope and more tolerant of environmentalism. It sought to strike a balance between the use and preservation of public lands. Instead of states' rights, it focused on individual property rights, including national park inholdings, hunting in national parks, and public access to public lands with motorized vehicles. Masland took a dim view of the wise-use movement in large part because Charles Cushman was one of its more active and vocal leaders.[60]

Masland felt betrayed by President George H. W. Bush, who had claimed to be an environmentalist. He had never voted for a Democratic candidate for president, but he vowed to next time unless Bush changed his "position on oil lands in Alaska and public lands everywhere. You are not an environmentalist as claimed prior to your election. You did not speak the truth." Not only had Bush lied when he vowed not to raise taxes, but he also lied when he claimed to be an environmentalist.[61]

Masland lived his final years with warm memories and friendships but faint hope for the future of the environmental movement and the Republic.

Americans, he wrote near the end of his life, had lost faith in their government, themselves, and God. He had faith, he said, that the pendulum would "swing back and that we will become a nation of faith and believing. The question that troubles me is what agonies will we have to endure before we awaken."[62]

CHAPTER 14

Night Comes to the Cumberland Valley

Stepping away from government service, Masland devoted his twilight years to personal issues—health and advancing age, taking care of Virginia, community activities, downsizing his estate, and marveling over technological change. His own life had spanned 44 percent of the Republic's existence, he once observed. He had lived from "candlelight to satellite" and was awed by the development of electric and nuclear power, radio, television, automobile and airplane travel, space exploration, and astounding medical advances like knee replacement surgery. But advanced technology, he mused, was accompanied by downsized consumer products like cars, candy bars, and women's clothing.[1]

Environmental issues were never far from his mind. Despite being a diehard conservationist, he did not oppose nuclear power, which he saw as a clean source of energy that would help maintain the US military and economic edge over the Soviet Union. When the nuclear reactor at Pennsylvania's Three Mile Island facility near Harrisburg experienced a partial meltdown, he downplayed the accident. No lives were lost, he said, and technicians could learn from the accident to improve public safety. He conveniently failed to address the growing problem of nuclear waste disposal. And he was silent on the lethal effects of uranium dust on Navajo miners. He also said nothing about the human impact of the toxic chemicals beneath Love Canal near Buffalo, New York, or the tendency to site toxic-waste facilities near Black and Brown communities.[2]

Some human-based environmental issues did concern him. In Carlisle he cooperated with other concerned citizens for a new sewage waste-treatment system that would not pollute local streams and endanger human health. But, as always, he was most concerned with public land and green space issues. Pennsylvania, he wrote a friend, had been "singularly blessed by the Great Architect," but open space was disappearing. He worked to preserve green areas in Carlisle and the Cumberland Valley, recommending the preservation of clean, unharnessed streams like the Letort, Yellow Breeches, Big Spring, and Conodoguinet. In letters to the editor, he decried the loss of farmland to commercial development and opposed plans for the construction of a sports museum in Carlisle because it would bring billboards, neon, and the further loss of farms. He decried the fact that Carlisle, near interstate highways, served as an entrepôt for the trucking industry. From atop South Mountain, the valley below was dotted with warehouses, resembling a massive assortment of caskets. He reminded residents that individuals were custodians, not owners, of land. He also worked successfully for the establishment of Thornwald Park, a thirty-two-acre natural sanctuary on the edge of the city with picnic areas and hiking trails.[3]

Masland had nearly come unhinged in the early 1970s when he learned that the general manager at Masland and Sons had agreed to consider selling the company retreat at Kings Gap. A local developer planned to construct four hundred homes and an eighteen-hole golf course. When Masland objected, the company gave him the responsibility of disposing of the estate. Preferring that it be kept as a sylvan preserve, Masland, chairman emeritus of the board of trustees, offered in 1971 to convey the compound, valued at $1 million, to the National Park Service Foundation as a tax-free gift. George Hartzog, then in his last year as Park Service director, indicated an interest and sent a Park Service representative to evaluate the property.[4]

Located on twelve hundred acres and accessible by a meandering, four-mile, recently black-topped access road, the two-story stone building was roomy and handsomely appointed and rendered "an atmosphere of tasteful refined dignity," noted the Park Service evaluator. Irrespective of its elegance and bucolic setting, the inspector concluded that the property was not large enough to merit use by the NPS. Masland tried to convince interior secretary Rogers Morton otherwise, to no avail.[5]

Masland then turned to the state of Pennsylvania. Using Maurice Goddard as liaison, he agreed to sell Kings Gap to the Nature Conservancy for

$400,000. In a bit of accounting hocus-pocus, the Masland Foundation made a corresponding tax-free charitable grant to the Nature Conservancy, which in turn then flipped the property to the Commonwealth of Pennsylvania. "I do not know what your plans may be for Kings Gap," Masland wrote Goddard, who then headed the Department of Environmental Resources. "Virginia and I drove up there last night for our last dinner. Nostalgia and sentiment persuaded us to spend the night there." He appealed to Goddard not to harvest the hardwood trees and to continue to carry on the annual Easter service for residents. "I realize, Maurice, that from this point on what happens at Kings Gap is up to you and no longer up to me but my love for the place will be unending." In 1977, the state transformed Kings Gap into an Environmental Education Center, and it remains so today.[6]

Masland had a long history with Goddard. During World War II, when Goddard was a forestry professor at Penn State University, the two had successfully lobbied to save from lumbering a large expanse of white oak and hemlock trees in Tuscarora State Forest, where Masland leased a small hunting cabin. In December 1979, Clifford Jones, who had succeeded Goddard as executive director of the state Department of Environmental Resources, notified Masland that that area would be named in his honor. It was an attempt, he wrote, "to show publicly our appreciation and to honor a person who, for years, has dedicated a lifetime to the conservation of natural resources in Pennsylvania. I can't think of any action that gives me more pleasure and satisfaction." In a summer 1980 ceremony, the state dedicated as "forever wild" the 1,270-acre woodlot, called the Frank E. Masland Jr. Natural Area. "In a long life no honor has come my way that has meant as much to me as having that choice area of white oak and hemlock carry my name," Masland wrote to Robert McConnell, the editor of *Pennsylvania Forestry* magazine, who presided over the dedication ceremony. "There is music in the words 'forever wild' and for one who has devoted a great portion of his life to the preservation of wilderness, the very thought that an area carrying my name will be forever wild stirs me to the depths."[7]

Other accolades followed. The National Park Service bestowed an honorary ranger award. And upon completing its performance at the Pennsylvania National Horse Show in Harrisburg, the NPS mounted police lined up in front of Masland's box and saluted. It was an emotionally stirring experience, Masland noted to Ned Danson.[8]

In November 1990, one month shy of his ninety-fifth birthday, the National Parks Association presented him with the Marjory Stoneman Douglas Award at a recognition gala at the Westin Hotel in Washington, DC. Named for the author of the popular and influential *Everglades: River of Grass*, the award was established to "honor individuals who often must go to great lengths to advocate and fight for the protection of the National Park Service." "Just about everyone was there," Masland chortled to Marian Heiskell, including Marjory Douglas herself. Paul C. Pritchard, president of the association, described Masland's service as "awesome," an example of "what each one of us can do for our environment." Specifically, the association honored him for establishing the boundaries of Everglades National Park at its founding and for subsequently mapping out its primitive canoe and foot trails. "For over 50 years," the program noted, "Mr. Masland has been a leading environmentalist, devoting much of his effort to preserving national and state parklands."[9]

As a gray eminence, Masland mentored young Pennsylvania conservationists like Thomas Webster and Peter Duncan III. A Princeton graduate and resident of the Cumberland Valley, Webster served with Masland on the governor's Department of Environmental Resources task force. He regarded Masland as a "surrogate father" who had "probably imparted more wisdom to me than [to] his own family!!" Duncan, who would become deputy director of the DER and had served with Masland on the Fish Commission, remembered him as a nurturing and "fascinating guy" and also as a father figure.[10]

Masland also contributed to historical preservation. He donated, or sold at a reduced rate, carpeting for various historic buildings, including Independence Hall in Philadelphia, Ford's Theatre in Washington, DC, and the governor's residence in Harrisburg. He persuaded Masland and Sons to give to the village of Carlisle an empty field large enough for a sandlot baseball diamond (named Masland Field). He contributed hundreds of books and his papers to Dickinson College, numerous volumes on the history of the Colorado River and explorer John Wesley Powell to the Cosmos Club, his extensive correspondence with fellow river runner Dock Marston to the Huntington Library in southern California, and several letters he had acquired written by Simon Cameron, secretary of war during the Civil War, to the Army War College in Carlisle. He also purchased, restored, and gifted Simon Cameron's horse-drawn coach to the State Museum of Pennsylvania in Harrisburg. He donated Norm Nevills's cataract boat to the Utah Historical Museum and memorialized Nevills with a plaque that still overlooks the Colorado River at Navajo Bridge.[11]

Masland had aged well. He was trim and fit into his nineties but suffered some hearing loss. Though still vigorous and mobile, he had known for some time that his river running, horseback riding, and hiking days were over. "I get terribly homesick for the redrock country and the river," he told a friend. "I'd give anything to climb aboard an Indian pony again." None of his other experiences, he said, measured up to "those involving the river and the desert country—the water, the land, the animals but above all my companions are ever fresh and cherished memories."[12]

As he aged into the late 1970s and early 1980s, Masland lost associates, friends, and loved ones. Lula R. Diehl, his secretary of thirty-nine years, retired. Noted conservationist Sigurd Olson, whose environmental views most closely approximated his own, died of a heart attack at age eighty-two while snowshoeing near his home in Minnesota. After suffering from Parkinson's disease for years, Joe Eisaman died from a stroke. Dock Marston, Masland's closest male friend, died at age eighty-five after a fall at the Bohemian Club in San Francisco, where he resided. Marston never finished his manuscript on Colorado River runners, on which he had been working for decades. When he received a copy of Marston's manuscript, Masland described it as written in an "engineer's style" and understood why it was never published. "While he may have been a romantic at heart," Masland wrote, "he studiously avoided any suggestion of it in his manuscript." Tom Martin, former river boater-turned-historian, revised and published Marston's manuscript years later.[13]

In mid-May 1981, Mary Abbott, age eighty-seven, "ran her last rapid," as Masland phrased it. The death of close friends, especially Abbott, distressed him. "With Dock and Joe and Mary gone, that's the last of my age group," he wrote. Abbott, he went on, "was very near and dear to me, one of the most wonderful persons I have ever known."[14]

At a time when he was nursing his grief over the deaths of Mary and other close companions, Masland was also nursing Virginia with the help of a caregiver. Virginia had suffered from multiple maladies—arthritis, phlebitis, uterine cancer, spinal disc surgery, a heart attack, and replacement of both knees. Eventually wheelchair bound, she fell and broke her leg so severely that it had to be amputated. In mental decline, unable to speak, and bedridden, she listened as Frank read to her nightly from the Book of Common Prayer. Her sons and daughters-in-law visited but could offer only companionship and love. (David was a physician, but of the gastrointestinal tract.) Hospitalized, Virginia died in Carlisle on September 13, 1984. Her sizable estate, consisting mainly of Masland company stock, had been placed in a trust, with dividends going to her husband.[15]

Masland felt lost without Virginia. Early in 1985, he had spent two weeks in the Everglades "with nothing but lonely memories. I was miserable," he reported to William Edel, the former president of his alma mater. Few friends remained to offer solace. Most of them, he said, "lie beneath the ground."[16]

Although mournful, he remained feisty on political and conservation issues. To Lady Bird Johnson, one of his few remaining friends, he groused about conditions on the Colorado River. Fifteen thousand people rafted the river each year, far too many, in his view. "A large number run the river for the joy ride. Many are nude. . . . Beer parties are common today. My dear Lady Bird, I have lived too long. I recall the parks when they were pristine." He also lambasted a National Geographic television special on river running that showed "great, wallowing, blundering rubber rafts with shrieking motors to drown out the noise of the rapids." Conditions in the Everglades were deplorable as well. Wildlife was rapidly disappearing, especially birds. He and Superintendent Dan Beard had laid out the boundaries and determined visitor overlooks back in 1950, he said. But by the mid-1980s, the park "had become a great disappointment to me. I will not go back." (Fortunately, he did not live long enough to see further decimation of wildlife caused by voracious and proliferating pythons released into the wild by thoughtless pet owners.)[17]

Masland had a bittersweet relationship with Dickinson College. He relished his years there as a student and as an alum (though he never graduated). He donated money, books, his leather football helmet, scholarships, and considerable service as a longtime trustee. But he deplored the college's liberal faculty, its separation from the Methodist Church, and what he regarded as its spiritual and moral waywardness. He was outraged when Dickinson students booed Ronald Reagan's conservative and controversial attorney general, Edwin Meese. The student protest, he claimed, was led by the female chaplain, who was "a disgrace to Methodism."[18]

He hoped that his relationship with his nephew William Masland, who chaired the Dickinson board of trustees, could repair his damaged relationship with the college. "I am truly sorry things have worked out as they have—that my relationship with Dickinson could not have been a happy one. It once was. . . . My whole family Masland and Sharp was tied tightly to Dickinson," he stated. Counting monetary contributions, scholarships, and Reineman Wildlife Sanctuary and other land, he assessed his donations at $1.1 million. "I pass on with one hope unfulfilled. Rapprochement with my alma mater," he noted in a 1983 handwritten memorandum. "It could so gracefully come about under the administration of Bill Masland. . . . When I realize that a charlatan such as Sam Witwer received an honorary degree I admit to a lack of understanding." But Masland did not grasp the fact that he had made himself a pariah with the administration for resisting social change, especially the separation from the Methodist Church, and with the faculty for his role in unfairly terminating the teaching career of economics professor Laurent LaVallee twenty-five years earlier.[19]

Gradually, Masland pulled out of his funk. In 1985 he joined a cousin on a cruise to the British and US Virgin Islands. That trip helped lift his spirits because it did not remind him of Virginia. He also was cheered by visits from his sons and grandchildren, and in December 1985 sons Mike and David honored him with a ninetieth birthday party, gifting him with a foxtail attached to the antenna of his Ford Bronco.

Old friend Ned Danson wrote with the news that an elderly former NPS associate had remarried and suggesting that Masland might do the same. But Masland shrugged off the suggestion of future romance. "After 67 years with the same wife," he responded, "I have no desire to experiment. I will never cease missing my Virginia."[20]

In the spring of 1986, Masland took another cruise to the Caribbean Leeward Islands and Venezuela's Orinoco River and Angel Falls. In spite of his avowal to Danson, on that expedition he met a sixty-year-old widow from Scottsdale, Arizona, named Lisa Kittler, and they began a whirlwind romance. But it ended suddenly after two years.[21]

Masland's close association with the family carpet business also ended rather abruptly. The company had unionized and gone public in the 1960s, and neither he nor his son Mike nor his nephew William held executive positions in 1986, when Burlington Industries launched a hostile takeover. Burlington offered $68 per share. When that offer was rejected, Burlington raised it to $73 per share, or a total of $117 million, and company executives agreed to sell. As one of the largest shareholders in the company, Masland, already a millionaire, now had more money than he knew what to do with, as he told his grandson Jonathan.[22]

Besides making cash gifts to his grandchildren and their spouses, he used his largesse to preserve nature. As a member of Pennsylvania's Fish Commission more than a decade earlier, he had organized a financial drive to purchase Boiling Springs Lake. When that drive fizzled, he contributed $200,000 to buy the property to preserve it from commercial development. He renamed it Children's Lake and transferred title to the Pennsylvania Fish and Boat Commission, which was to "preserve it in perpetuity so that the little children will in the future, as they have in the past, feed the ducks and geese out of their hands." The seven-acre lake not only furnished recreational enjoyment; it was also the source of Yellow Breeches, a clear-flowing trout stream that meandered through Fallen Arches and the Carlisle countryside.[23]

Masland's appearance changed with advanced age. He remained trim but required a cane, wore glasses, and grew a full beard. His hair, edging around his ears below his balding dome, turned white. As a nonagenarian, he was socially active. He joined a small local group called the Eclectic Society to discuss historical, social, and philosophical issues, and another select local group, the Samaritan Fellowship, to distribute aid to disadvantaged families seeking help. He also formed an informal group of aging outdoorsmen called the Old Bastards Club. He and other OB members, among them Tom Webster, Peter Duncan, Ralph Abele, and a few others, swapped hunting and fishing stories, reminisced, and worked to influence authorities on local and state conservation issues.[24]

At age ninety-two, Masland delivered his last speech. He had to read it, he told the Rotary Club, because his memory was failing. He was like the man who headed upstairs to get something but when he got to the top couldn't remember what he was after. He headed back downstairs, hoping to trigger his memory. He stopped to rest on the landing but then couldn't remember whether he was going upstairs or downstairs. His speech on conservation covered familiar themes—preserving wilderness, protecting the ecosystem, and safeguarding the beauties of the Cumberland Valley, especially its barns, farmland, clean streams, and forested hillsides. Trees, he stated, were a renewable resource, but not if the ground was covered with buildings, roads, warehouses, and parking lots. "If our mountain lands are denuded, it is also inevitable that those living in the valley will suffer. Not only spiritually, but economically and materially." People, he continued, did not own land: "Of land, we are custodians." "For fifty years, I have been involved in preserving and protecting our land. Why? It was my way to attempt to pay my debt to those who came before and to my God for the privilege of living in freedom and beauty." In preserving nature, the older generation serves young people, he said. "There is no experience more certain to cause youth to turn to nature when in need of recreation than the memory of a camp by the side of a lake and the smell of breakfast bacon." Preserving nature, he concluded, is a great challenge. The reward was gratification.[25]

For a time, he drove his Ford Bronco short distances. At age ninety-three, with his brother-in law Bill Sharp, he motored fifteen miles to the 1,270-acre Frank E. Masland Jr. Natural Area in the Tuscarora Mountains, where the two men visited the site of a small cabin where they had camped each year before the opening of fishing and hunting seasons. They reminisced about grouse and deer hunting and catching brook trout the evening before the season opened, eating them for breakfast the next day. Shortly after that nostalgic trip, Masland was behind the wheel when he blacked out, smashed into a telephone pole, broke his nose, and spent a few days in the hospital. His sons insisted that he stop driving.[26]

No longer able to drive to the Allison United Methodist Church in Carlisle, Masland sought spiritual inspiration from Protestant radio and television evangelists, including Billy Graham, Jim Bakker, Jerry Falwell, and D. James Kennedy. As representatives of the Christian Right, these men railed against pornography, sexual liberation, drug use, homosexuality, communism, coddling criminals, and the ban on school prayer. Only Falwell met with Masland's full approval. After viewing Graham's televised California religious crusades, he suspected that many of the converted who came forward to repent of their sins were actually "decoys" or audience plants. He wrote a "Say It Ain't So" letter to Graham, but it went unanswered. But he continued to listen to Graham's message and request copies of his sermons and pamphlets.[27]

Graham was a man of character, but Reverend Jim Bakker was not. He fell from grace and popularity for paying hush money to a woman with whom he had illicit sex. He also was imprisoned for financial fraud. With Bakker jailed, Masland followed the televised ministry of Jerry Falwell, who formed the Moral Majority and urged his followers to get involved in politics. D. James Kennedy of the Coral Ridge Ministries of Fort Lauderdale, Florida, was Masland's favorite media minister. But he fell out of favor for frequently asking Masland for money and for not denouncing Hispanic immigration as a greater threat to national security and mores than communism.[28]

In his twilight years, Masland fell into grumpy, dark moods. His health was failing, friends and loved ones had died, notable Protestant preachers had feet of clay, and public land preservation seemed to be in decline. In addition to grumbling about the influx of Hispanic immigrants, he complained about the "anti-American" liberal press and the antibusiness effect of federal regulations. Not even the fall of the Soviet empire in 1989–90 could cheer him up.

He spent his days at Fallen Arches reading, writing, and sitting on the porch watching nature. He employed a housekeeper, Doris Dashiell, to help with the cleaning and marketing, and his new secretary, Brady Pyers, transcribed his dictated letters and arranged his occasional travel by air and limousine. No longer willing to deal with leasing his land, he deeded the bulk of it to sons Mike and David and grew flowers and trees instead of vegetables. Generally, he was clear in his mind, but he began to repeat himself in letters to Lady Bird and other correspondents. He also mused about aging and the passage of life. He loved the greenery, trees, and flowers at Fallen Arches but also longed for the desert country. In a poem titled "Homesick," he wrote:

I do not regret the life I live
It ties me down and lifts me high
But always will I wish that I
Could live another life,
That I might live it in the Desert
Land beneath the sky[29]

He also longed for regular female companionship. Fortunately, he encountered an old friend, Florence Corey, and she lifted his spirits. After a brief courtship, they were married, at ages ninety-three and seventy-nine, respectively, at the Allison Methodist Church. They lived happily together at Fallen Arches until Masland died there on July 30, 1994, at age ninety-eight. He was buried next to Virginia in the Holly Springs Cemetery in his blessed Cumberland Valley.[30]

After paying an inheritance tax of $500,000, Masland's estate totaled $2.5 million, plus Fallen Arches and its contents. Cash, heirlooms, and mementoes went to loved ones. He established a college tuition trust fund for each of his great-grandchildren. He bequeathed $125,000 to the Carlisle YMCA and $112,000 to the Allison Methodist Church to honor Virginia with a music fund. (He would have rolled over in his grave to learn of the sale of the church, its congregation folded into two other churches, recalled grandson Frank IV.) He also donated $50,000 each to two predominantly African American churches in Carlisle and $75,000 to the Samaritans to provide as many as two hundred turkeys each year to disadvantaged local families at Thanksgiving. Other sums went to Messiah College and Methodist Church mission causes.[31]

More than two hundred people attended his memorial service at the Allison Methodist Church on August 4, 1994. An old friend, retired bishop D. Frederick Wertz, and the current minister, Karen Layman, co-officiated. Two ministers were needed, they joked, to get Masland past Saint Peter at the pearly gates. They recounted his numerous achievements as an industrialist, conservationist, adventurer, philanthropist, correspondent, active member of several civic, educational, and religious organizations, and beloved family man. Masland regarded death, according to Bishop Wertz, as just another "new and glorious adventure." He concluded with the poem "Eventide," which Masland had written as a carpet executive before his adventures in the American Southwest. "It has been a good life and a full life," it began, and went on to tell of listening "to the soft undertones of the marsh breeze accompanying the whistling wings of high-flying ducks ushering in the sunrise and sitting on a hillside sharing lunch with his dog," Wertz said. It concluded: "I have stood on a mountain top / And filled my lungs with air that seemed to be the breath of God himself, / And gazed across the distant hill, / Knowing it was good just to be out of doors and to be alive. I sit before the hearth. What if the pipe is going out and the embers grow cold? / I have lived."[32]

He did not live to witness the demise of the company that he had helped build into a carpet colossus. Shorn of its carpet-making division, Masland and Sons went through several changes of ownership, including reacquisition by the Masland family, its interior auto parts division—flooring, dashboards, trunk and cargo bed liners—an attractive asset. The International Automotive Components Group acquired the Carlisle plant in 1996 and closed it eleven years later, in December 2007. The buildings have been razed and the twenty-six-acre site, once home to a thriving industry, sits vacant, awaiting repurposing.[33]

Most Americans, then and now, do not share Masland's reactionary political views. Shortly before his death, a Harrisburg journalist stated that compared to Masland, even Barry Goldwater's views would be considered left of center. But Masland should be mainly remembered as a nature-loving, God-fearing preservationist, not as an industrial tycoon or conservative ideologue. He once informed his son David that, upon his death, he wanted no physical memorial. His memorial, he said, was "the cathedral of the wilderness," including Canyonlands and Everglades National Parks, Kings Gap, and a clutch of nature sanctuaries in Pennsylvania. As a conservative and a man of faith, he believed that in nature he was connecting with the Creator and doing God's work in preserving wild and scenic places and ecosystems for future generations. Novelist and fellow environmentalist Wendell Berry, also a man of deep religious faith, wrote that "our destruction of nature is not just bad stewardship, or stupid economics, or a betrayal of family responsibility; it is the most horrid blasphemy. It is flinging God's gifts into His face, as if they were of no worth." Masland shared that view, expressing the hope that "when the roll is called up Yonder St. Pete will open the gate if for no other reason than my love of the land and my attempts to preserve it, as God created it, for generations to come."[34]

Masland generally did not allow his right-wing political views to interfere with his commitment to nature. Much like John Saylor, Russell Train, Wendell Berry, James Buckley, and Barry Goldwater, he saw preserving nature as the one area in which an activist federal government was justified. As a hard-line conservative Republican, Masland worked doggedly, as a member of the NPS Advisory Board and Advisory Council, as an adviser to Pennsylvania governors William Scranton and Raymond Shafer, and as a private citizen, to seek a bipartisan approach to environmental issues, especially the preservation of wild and scenic lands. Early on, he became active in the bipartisan national movement that became known as environmentalism in the mid-1960s and early '70s. He provided names for many of the arches and natural sandstone structures that he had visited in the American southwest. As a representative of the Interior Department, he visited east Africa on three separate occasions to promote the parks, wilderness, and wildlife there.

Though he disagreed with their liberal political views, Masland admired Stewart Udall and Lady Bird Johnson for their heartfelt and cooperative commitment to the preservation of the natural world. His life's work showed that a conservative industrialist could work with liberal Democrats for the greater good of nature and the planet, a scenario that appears archaic in the politically polarized twenty-first century.

Masland's long life serves as a showcase for the fluctuating twentieth-century conservation movement. He identified closely with the preservationist phase, focusing on safeguarding public lands, national parks, natural beauty, wilderness, wild creatures, and natural habitats. He was less focused on conserving natural resources for use by future generations and on the court battles, lobbying, and economic severity associated with federal environmental regulations related to human health and urban problems.

Although he would doubtless raise eyebrows and wrinkle foreheads for his strident political views today, during his lifetime, conservatives and liberals alike respected Masland as an advocate for nature. Barry Goldwater once wrote Frank's son Mike, "I have known your father for a good many years and I have the greatest admiration for him. He has done as much as any other man in the United States to perpetuate and preserve the beauties of our Country through the National Parks and all of us will be forever grateful to him." "Frank was the quintessential guardian of parks, open spaces and our natural resources," wrote Lady Bird Johnson. "He possessed a great love of nature and a strong belief that beautiful places should be available for every American to enjoy. We worked together on many projects. His stewardship, vision and perseverance were remarkable. I was deeply proud of his accomplishments, and to have crossed paths with this exceptional industrialist and adventurer." And while Masland was still alive, Park Service director Russell Dickenson wrote, "As was so often the case, you were on the [environmental] scene when actions were taking place that led to important decisions. The nation is certainly in your debt for the many tasks you have performed, on your own time and with little public credit."[35]

The Grand Canyon River Guides Association remembered him as a "tribal elder" among cataract boat river runners. As a member of the NPS Advisory Board, Masland played a signal role in the creation of Canyonlands National Park, much as John Muir had done with Yosemite National Park, Enos Mills with Rocky Mountain National Park, and Sigurd Olson and Ernest Oberholtzer with the Minnesota and Ontario boundary waters region. He was also instrumental in setting the boundaries for the establishment of Everglades National Park and for mapping out its primitive canoe and foot trails. His visits and treks to the backcountry helped pave the way for the creation of Simien Mountains National Park in Ethiopia. And, like other dedicated preservationists, he advanced the environmental movement and affirmed the principle of national park sanctity by opposing more dams on the Colorado River. And his bipartisan environmental perspective, once shared by John Saylor, Russell Train, and others has been abandoned by the Republican Party since 1980.[36]

As a consultant to Pennsylvania governors, Masland helped establish the Pennsylvania Department of Natural Resources and numerous nature sanctuaries. He relished his conservation achievements and accolades at the national and state levels. "An ardent environmentalist, Masland was helping to save the environment long before there was an environmental movement," asserted an editorial in the *Harrisburg Patriot-News*. It quoted Masland, at age ninety-four, stating, "We, in this generation, in our greed act as though we own the land. We are but tenants. Our responsibility is to preserve it for use and pleasure and recreation for future generations." Masland's activities and "outspoken advocacy in the field of conservation are an inspiration and example of what we can do to leave the world a better place," it concluded.[37]

He was proudest, he once stated, of the "forever wild" 1,270-acre Frank E. Masland Jr. Natural Area along Laurel Run in the Tuscarora State Forest. His pride and satisfaction derived, no doubt, from the sign posted there, which reads: "Named in honor of a man who dedicated a lifetime to the enhancement of human lives through the conservation of our natural resources." That small patch of trees in Penn's Woods, he once noted proudly, would serve well as his "headstone for eternity."[38]

NOTES

In the notes, the abbreviation FMP refers to the Frank E. Masland Jr. Papers, which are held in the Dickinson College Archives and Special Collections in Carlisle, Pennsylvania; OMP refers to the Otis R. Marston Papers, held in the Huntington Library Special Collections in San Marino, California.

INTRODUCTION

1. Masland, "By the Rim of Time," 7.
2. On the postwar environmental movement, see Hays, *History of Environmental Politics*; Rothman, *Greening of a Nation*.
3. R. Nash, *Wilderness and the American Mind*, chap. 9, "The Wilderness Cult," 141–60.
4. Numerous scholars have traced the evolution of the environmental movement. See Hays, *Beauty, Health, and Permanence*, 3, 13; Rome, *Bulldozer in the Countryside*, 5–13; Sale, *Green Revolution*, 14–18. On the quest for environmental justice, see Spears, *Rethinking the American Environmental Movement*.
5. The best study of the conservation movement during the Progressive era remains Hays, *Conservation and the Gospel of Efficiency*. For more on Roosevelt, see Brinkley, *Wilderness Warrior*. On Pinchot, see Miller, *Gifford Pinchot*; Flippen, *Conservative Conservationist*, 7.
6. On Muir, see Worster, *Passion for Nature*; Fox, *John Muir and His Legacy*. On McFarland, see Morrison, *J. Horace McFarland*. On the wilderness movement, see Allin, *Politics of Wilderness Preservation*; Frome, *Battle for the Wilderness*; R. Nash, *Wilderness and the American Mind*; Sutter, *Driven Wild*; Louter, *Windshield Wilderness*; Turner, *Promise of Wilderness*.
7. For an excellent analysis of the Hetch Hetchy controversy, see Righter, *Battle over Hetch Hetchy*.
8. Ibid., 4–6, 12.
9. Runte, *National Parks*, 103–4; Morrison, *J. Horace McFarland*, 175–77.
10. For overviews of the evolution of environmental ideas during the twentieth century, see Rothman, *Greening of a Nation*; Hays, "From Conservation to Environment"; Hays, *Beauty, Health, and Permanence*; Koppes, "Efficiency/Equity/ Esthetics"; Gottlieb, *Forcing the Spring*; Shabecoff, *Fierce Green Fire*.
11. For recent works on conservative conservationists, see Flippen, *Conservative Conservationist*; Drake, *Loving Nature*; Smith, *Green Republican*; Bliese, *Greening of Conservative America*.

CHAPTER 1

1. Masland IV, "Descendants of John Masland."
2. Masland IV, "Weavers and Warriors"; Masland, "Ten Generations."
3. Masland, "Masland and Sons"; Scranton, *Figured Tapestry*.
4. Masland, "Slightly Autobiographical," 3.
5. Frank Masland IV, interview by author, June 20, 2017; Masland, "Ten Generations," 20–21.
6. Frank Masland to Florence Masland, January 3, 1977, box 9, folder 31, FMP.
7. Frank Masland IV, email to author, March 9, 2018.
8. Yearbook and other information relating to Friends' Central School courtesy of Jim Davis, archivist, email to author, August 28, 2017.
9. Frank Masland to Mike [Frank III] and David [Masland], September 8, 1975 (quotation), courtesy of Frank Masland IV; Masland, "Slightly Autobiographical," 4, 7–8.
10. Masland, "Slightly Autobiographical," 8.
11. For the Cumberland Valley and Carlisle, see Durand and Richard, *History of Cumberland County*; Donehoo, *History of the Cumberland Valley*. For Masland's Edenic view of the valley and city, see Masland, "The Blessed Valley," *Shuttle*, October 1953, 2; Carol Talley, "Carlisle: 'We Simply Don't Realize How Good It Is,'" *Carlisle Sentinel*, February 26, 1983.
12. Colwell, *Bitter Fruits*; Hoffer, *Twentieth Century Thoughts*; Federal Writers' Project, *Pennsylvania*.

13. See "The Dickinson Story," Dickinson College, https://www.dickinson.edu/info/20048/history_of_the_college/1404/the_dickinson_story.

14. *Dickinsonian*, September 30, 1914.

15. *Dickinsonian*, October 28 and November 11, 1914; February 10, 1915.

16. *Dickinsonian*, February 24, 1916.

17. *Dickinsonian*, December 9, 1915; Macleod, *Building Character in the American Boy*.

18. Undated, unidentified newspaper clipping, privately held, courtesy of Frank Masland IV.

19. Untitled clipping, *Philadelphia Inquirer*, May 31, 1916, and other unidentified, undated newspaper clippings in box 16, folder 11, FMP.

20. Masland, "Slightly Autobiographical," 10–12.

21. Masland, "An Evening on the Lake," box 14, folder 85, FMP.

22. Backes, *Wilderness Within*, 60–61.

23. Agnes Trickett to Masland, January 17, 1917, privately held, courtesy of Frank Masland IV; Pam Knowlton, registrar, Dickinson School of Law, e-mail to author, September 12, 2017.

24. "Our War," editorial, *Dickinsonian*, April 19, 1917.

25. Frank Masland Sr. to Lt. Commander F. L. Starr, Fourth Naval District, Philadelphia, September 21, 1917; Lt. F. L. Starr to Frank Masland Sr., October 30, 1917; Frank Masland Sr. to Lt. F. L. Starr, October 31, 1917, all in box 4, folder 3, "Personal," Masland Business Records. Frank Masland Jr. wrote of chasing but not sinking an enemy U-boat in "Written by the 'Skipper'" in 1919 or 1920, box 14, folder 86, FMP.

26. Frank Masland Sr. to Secretary of the Navy Josephus Daniels, December 4, 1918; Frank Masland Sr. to Lt. Rowand Pierce, January 21, 1919, both in box 4, folder "1919," Masland Business Records.

CHAPTER 2

1. Masland, "quasi-autobiographical letter" to Mike and David Masland, September 8, 1975, privately held, courtesy of Frank Masland IV.

2. Barry, *Great Influenza*, 321–32.

3. Wiecks, "1918 Influenza Epidemic"; Liartis, "Spanish Flu."

4. *Carlisle Evening Sentinel*, March 13, March 15, and May 10, 1919 (quotation). The *Evening Sentinel* eventually became the *Sentinel*.

5. *Carlisle Evening Sentinel*, June 13, 1919 (quotation), April 9, 1920; *Carlisle Herald*, August 13, 1919.

6. Masland, "The Blessed Valley," *Shuttle*, October 1953, 2; Masland, "quasi-autobiographical letter," 2.

7. Masland "Masland and Sons," 15.

8. Masland, "quasi-autobiographical letter," 2–3.

9. Masland, "Masland and Sons," 27.

10. Ibid., 17–22; Hoffer, *Twentieth Century Thoughts*, 116–17.

11. Masland, oral history interview, September 10, 1982, box 14, folder 46, FMP. On FDR and conservation, see Brinkley, *Rightful Heritage*; Watkins, *Righteous Pilgrim*.

12. Quoted in Swanson, "From Depression Street," 83.

13. *Carlisle Evening Sentinel*, September 19 and 20, 1932.

14. Pinchot's telegram to Herbert Hoover was reprinted in the *Carlisle Evening Sentinel*, September 21, 1932. On Pinchot as a Depression governor, see Miller, *Gifford Pinchot*, 317–18.

15. Swanson, "From Depression Street," 90.

16. Masland, "Masland and Sons," 25–26; Maurice Masland obituary, *Carlisle Evening Sentinel*, April 9, 1930.

17. Masland, "Slightly Autobiographical," 20–21.

18. Benjey, *Glorious Times*; Frank Masland IV, email to author, May 12, 2020.

19. Phillips-Fein, *Invisible Hands*, 5.

20. Dulles and Dubofsky, *Labor in America*, 256.

21. Ibid., quotation at 258. For Roosevelt's first hundred days and the New Deal in general, see Kennedy, *Freedom from Fear*, 131–60.

22. National Recovery Administration, *Code of Fair Competition*.

23. C. Marlin Bell to Masland, February 3, March 7, May 5 and 21, July 13, and December 17, 1934; May 13, 1935; September 2 and November 21 and 25, 1936; and July 10, 1937; Masland to Stanley Root, Philadelphia Regional Office of the NLRB, May 9 and 21, 1934; C. Marlin Bell, "Special Report," July 13, 1934, all privately held, courtesy of Frank Masland IV.

24. Koppes, "Efficiency/Equity/Esthetics,"135.

25. Brinkley, *Rightful Heritage*, 180–82, 255. For the CCC in Pennsylvania, see Speakman, *At Work in Penn's Woods*.

26. Brinkley, *Rightful Heritage*, 238–67. For Ickes, see Watkins, *Righteous Pilgrim*; Koppes, "Efficiency/Equity/Esthetics," 141.

27. Maher, *Nature's New Deal*, 1–11, 224–26; Koppes, "Efficiency/Equity/Esthetics," 141.

28. Masland, "Masland and Sons," 28; Paul Masland to Frank Masland Sr., November 17, 1941, box 2, folder 4, Masland Business Records.

29. Frank Masland, "Notice," *Shuttle*, October 31, 1940, box 2, folder 4, MBF.

30. Steven Burg, "Catharine MacCaffray, June 20, 2002," in the Elizabeth V. and George F. Gardner Digital Library, http://gardnerlibrary.org/stories/catherine-maccaffray-women-world-warii.

31. Masland, "Masland and Sons," 28–29.

32. Ernst and Ernst Accounting Firm to R. P. Masland, June 25, 1943; R. P. Masland to Frank Masland Sr., Frank Masland Jr., et al., September 21, 1943; Financial Reports for November 30, 1943, 1944, 1945, all in box 2, folder 5, Masland Business Records.

33. Kallman, "German POWs in Carlisle," 10, 34–35, 58 (quotation).

34. Ibid., 34–35, 40; Masland, "Remarks at the Funeral of Lottie Ruhl," January 27, 1982, box 15, folder 196, FMP.

35. Kallman, "German POWs in Carlisle," 48–49.

36. Masland, "The Meaning of the Atomic Bomb," *Shuttle*, August 1946, 3.

CHAPTER 3

1. Masland, "Masland and Sons," 30–32.

2. Masland, "Slightly Autobiographical," 17.

3. Masland, "Christianity," folder 93; "A Thought for the New Year," folder 35; "Welfare State," folder 48; "Test of Our Faith," folder 54, all in box 14, FMP.

4. Masland, "To a Tree," *Shuttle*, June 1950, 3. Muir quoted in Maher, *Nature's New Deal*, 26. For conservative intellectuals, see G. Nash, *Conservative Intellectual Movement in America*; Phillips-Fein, *Invisible Hands*, chaps. 2 and 3.

5. Leopold quoted in Shabecoff, *Fierce Green Fire*, 90.

6. Masland, "Masland and Sons," 40; Masland IV, *Weavers and Warriors*, 12.

7. Masland, "Slightly Autobiographical," 20–21.

8. David Masland (grandson), email to author, April 8, 2018.

9. Frank Masland IV, interview by author, June 20, 2017.

10. Ibid.

11. Ibid.; Masland to Mary Abbott, December 23, 1969, box 8, folder 6, FMP; Masland, "To a Tree," *Shuttle*, June 1950, 3.

12. Masland, "A Comment on the Refugee Problem," September 28, 1958, box 15, folder 168, FMP; report of private detective Alfred B. Verbecken to Frank Masland, August 20, 1959; Masland, memorandum for the file, August 23, 1959, privately held, courtesy of Frank Masland IV.

13. Millard, *River of Doubt*; Miller, *Gifford Pinchot*, 301–5; Masland, "Running the Colorado Rapids"; Masland, "Land of the Anasazi."

14. Frank Masland IV, interview by author, June 20, 2017; David Masland, email to author, April 8, 2018.

15. Clark, "Fast Water Man"; Reilly, "Norman Nevills"; Staveley, "Norman Nevills"; Masland to Norm Nevills, May 28, June 20, 1946, April 10, 1947, and February 10, 1948; Nevills to Masland, January 24 and February 5, 1948, box 15, folder 10, Nevills Papers.

16. On Nevills and his cataract boats, see Clark, "Fast Water Man"; Reilly, "Norman Nevills."

17. Virginia Boynton, "Frank E. Masland Jr.," 2003, http://www.maslandtech.com/familytree/images/travelers/Travelers%20V.htm.

18. Masland, "By the Rim of Time," 5; see also Marston and Martin, *From Powell to Power*, 437.

19. The other passengers were Moulton Fulmer of Muncie, Indiana, and two couples: Wayne and Lucinda Hiser of Toledo, Ohio, and Bestor and Florence Robinson of Oakland, California. Bestor Robinson had recently concluded a two-year stint as president of the Sierra Club. Masland, "By the Rim of Time," 8.

20. Ibid., 7, 19.

21. Nancy Streator to Norm Nevills, August 5 and December 6, 1948, box 19, folder 41, Nevills Papers; Reuling, "Nancy Streator Reuling" (interview by Roy Webb), 27.

22. Masland, "Rainbow Below the Rim," 61, 118–19; Masland to Nevills, August 18 (quotation), November 16 and 26, 1948, box 15, folder 11, Nevills Papers; Frank Masland to Otis Marston, August 18, 1948, and Virginia Masland to

Mrs. Otis Marston, August 23, 1948, both in box 142, folder 2, OMP.

23. Sutter, *Driven Wild*; Louter, *Windshield Wilderness*; Masland to Pritchard, May 10, 1982, box 4, folder 43, FMP.

24. Shabecoff, *Fierce Green Fire*, 88–89.

25. Masland, "Some Thots [*sic*] re Canyonlands National Park, Utah," box 10, folder 4; Masland to Johnson, August 10, 1953, box 10, folder 30, FMP; Frank and Virginia Masland, *Sweet Mystery of Life* (privately printed, 1983), courtesy of Frank Masland IV.

26. See Dunlap, *Faith in Nature*; Fox, *John Muir and His Legacy*; Worster, *Passion for Nature*; Backes, *Wilderness Within* (Olson quoted on 209).

27. Masland to Marston, August 21, 1950, box 142, folder 5, OMP.

28. Masland to Marston, January 2, 1951 (quotation), box 142, folder 6, OMP; Masland to Mary Abbott, September 11, 1950, box 7, folder 90, FMP.

29. Masland, interview, September 10, 1982, p. 6, folder 46, box 14, FMP; Masland to Mary Abbott, September 11, 1950, carton 1, folder 23, Abbott Papers; Reuling, "Nancy Streator Reuling," 27; Johnson, *Central Arizona Project*; Hundley, "Clio Nods."

30. Masland to Nevills, August 30, November 10, and December 21, 1948; Nevills to Masland, September 16, October 4, November 16, and December 5, 24, and 28, 1948, box 15, folder 10, Nevills Papers.

31. See Marston to Masland, September 22, 1948, May 15, 1949, box 142, folder 2, and May 28, 1949, box 142, folder 5; Masland to Marston, August 18 (quotation) and 30, 1949, box 142, folder 4, all in OMP. Tom Martin has piloted Marston's manuscript to publication; see Marston and Martin, *From Powell to Power*; Thomas Martin, email to author, July 7, 2020.

32. Masland to Marston, January 10, 1966; Marston to the US Board on Geographic Names, September 4, 1966, both in box 144, folder 1, OMP. Despite his reservations concerning Nevills's reputation as a river pilot, Marston asked Masland to write a warts-and-all biography of Nevills, but Masland begged off.

33. Masland, "Diary of 1949 Trip," box 14, folder 49, FMP; Masland to Marston, August 28 and 30 (second quotation), 1949, box 142, folder 4, OMP.

34. Masland to Marston, October 17, 1949, box 142, folder 4, OMP; Frank Masland IV, interview by author, June 20, 2017.

35. Shortly before his death, Nevills gifted Masland with *The Mexican Hat*, his flagship cataract boat, which he had decommissioned. Masland displayed the boat in the sportswear division of his Carlisle factory. He also considered writing Nevills's biography, as noted above, but decided that it would be too much work. See Masland to Marston, November 23, 1950, box 142, folder 5, OMP.

36. Marston to Masland and Masland to Marston, October 17, 1949, box 142, folder 4, OMP; Marston and Martin, *From Powell to Power*, 440.

37. Marston to Masland, October 20 and November 21, 1949; Marston to H. C. Bryant, December 8, 1949, both in box 142, folder 4, OMP.

38. Masland to Marston, November 2, 1949, OMP.

39. Masland to Abbott, March 10, 1952 (quotation), box 8, folder 9, FMP. Besides Masland and Abbott, other committee members included Barry Goldwater of Phoenix, Arizona, Rosalind Johnson of Berkeley, California, and Frank Wright of Blanding, Utah. The details of preparing, producing, and presenting the plaque and tribute may be found in the numerous letters between Masland and Abbott in box 8, folders 8, 9, and 10, FMP, and in the correspondence among Abbott, Preston Walker, and others in box 3, folder 52, Nevills Papers.

40. Masland to Abbott, August 23 and 28, 1950; Abbott to Masland, September 15, 19, and 28, 1950, box 7, folder 90, all in FMP.

41. Abbott to Masland, April 30, 1950; Masland to Abbott, September 24, October 20, and December 1, 1952, box 8, folder 1, all in FMP.

42. Masland, "Diary—1950," box 14, folder 49, FMP; Masland, "Goat Run."

43. Masland, "Goat Run," 28–29.

44. Masland to Marston, August 11, 1952, box 142, folder 7, OMP. For the dedication ceremony, see Reilly, "Norman Nevills," 200; "Nevills Plaque Is Dedicated," *Desert* magazine, October 1952, 5–7.

45. Masland to Abbott, August 7, 1952, box 8, folder 1; Bryant to Masland, May 22, 1952, box 2, folder 62, both in FMP.

46. Harvey, *Symbol of Wilderness*, xv.

CHAPTER 4

1. Masland to Mary Abbott, February 24, box 8, folder 1, FMP.

2. Masland to Mary Abbott, June 10, 1953, box 8, folder 1, FMP; Schlesinger, *Crisis of the Old Order*.

3. See Beard, *Special Report: Everglades*.

4. Masland to Marston, December 8 and 16, 1949, folder 4; March 28 and August 21, 1950, folder 5; January 2, 1953 (quotation), folder 8, all in box 142, OMP; Craighead to Masland, January 2, 1950, and numerous other exchanges between the two men in box 3, folder 27, FMP. Masland and Dan Beard reminisced about their early days in the Everglades in Masland to Beard, December 13, 1955, Beard to Masland, May 6, 1959, and Masland to Beard, May 27, 1959, box 2, folder 67, FMP.

5. Doerr to superintendent of Everglades National Park, January 27, 1953, box 3, folder 27, FMP.

6. On Saylor, see Smith, *Green Republican*.

7. Masland, "Down the Colorado by Submarine," box 14, folder 51; Laura Bell, "River Runners Set for New Adventures," *Las Vegas Sun*, May 23, 1954, box 16, folder 10, both in FMP.

8. Marston, "Log of Arch Hunt, Cummings Mesa, Arizona, September 1954"; Jorgen Visback, log, "Arch-in-the-Sky," September 1954, box 10, folder 17; Bill Belknap, "Boulder Camera," *Boulder City News*, October 7, 1954; Laura Bell, "Adventurers Pinpoint Giant 'New' Sandstone Arch in Southwest," *Las Vegas Sun*, October 6, 1954, box 16, folder 10, all in FMP; William Belknap, "Arch-in-the-Sky," manuscript, box 16, folder 310, Belknap Papers.

9. Masland to Marston, October 12 and December 3, 1954, box 142, folder 9, OMP; Masland to Mary Abbott, November 17, 1954, box 8, folder 2, FMP; and, both in box 10, folder 17, FMP, Masland, "It's Rough Country over There," *Shuttle*, January 1955, 25–30; Jorgen Visback, telegram to Masland with poem, October 12, 1954.

10. Masland to Abbott, November 21, 1955, box 8, folder 2, FMP.

11. Masland quoted in the *Philadelphia Inquirer*, September 16, 1956, clipping attached to Masland to Marston, September 24, 1956, box 142, folder 11, OMP; "Shooting the Wild Colorado," *Argosy*, June 1956, box 16, folder 9, FMP.

12. Masland to Mary Abbott, July 3, 1956 (quotation) box 8, folder 2; Otis Marston, "Cruise of Grand Canyon, 1956," box 15, folder 53, both in FMP; Masland to Marston, December 28, 1956, box 142, folder 11, OMP.

13. Iverson, *Diné*; White, *Roots of Dependency*; Moon, *Tall Sheep*; Blue, *Indian Trader*.

14. For more on this history, see Fixico, *Termination and Relocation*.

15. For more on the history of the Carlisle school, see Witmer, *Indian Industrial School*.

16. Masland to Rev. H. B. Liebler, September 5, 1951, box 10, folder 38; Liebler to Masland, September 25, 1951, box 5, folder 6, both in FMP.

17. Quoted in Moon, *Tall Sheep*, 211–12.

18. Buck White-hat to Masland, January 27 and December 13, 1956; Bahe Ketchum to Masland, September 20, 1958; Toby Owl to Frank Masland, February 27, 1960, all in box 5, folder 6, FMP.

19. Iverson, *Diné*, 219–20.

20. Moon, *Tall Sheep*, 88–99; Weisiger, *Dreaming of Sheep*, xv.

21. Iverson, *Diné*, 223; Moon, *Tall Sheep*, 144–51.

22. Turner, *Promise of Wilderness*, 67–68; Woodhouse, "Regulating Off-Road."

23. Masland to Douglas McKay, April 5, 1955, and January 20, 1956 (quotation); memorandum to McKay and Glenn L. Emmons, "Some Thoughts Concerning the Navajo Problem," December [?] 1955, all in box 5, folder 6, FMP.

24. Masland to McKay, January 20, 1956, FMP; see also Spence, *Dispossessing the Wilderness*.

25. Masland to McKay, January 20, 1956.

26. Linenberger, *Navajo Unit*.

27. Masland to Otis Marston, June 10, 1953, box 142, folder 8, OMP; Masland to Abbott, June 10, 1953, box 8, folder 1, FMP.

28. Quoted in Harvey, *Symbol of Wilderness*, 149; see also Richardson, *Dams, Parks, and Politics*, chaps. 4 and 5; Richardson, "Interior Secretary as Conservation Villain."

29. Masland to Marston, March 30, 1954, box 142, folder 9, OMP.

30. For more on Smith, see Winks, *Laurance S. Rockefeller*, 88–95.

31. Masland to Mary Abbott, February 28, May 11, and August 3, 1955, box 8, folder 2; Masland to Douglas McKay, May 11, 1955, and

McKay to Masland, May 25, 1955, box 8, folder 2; Masland to John Saylor and other members of the Pennsylvania congressional delegation, May 11, 1955, and Saylor to Masland, May 12, 1955, box 10, folder 9, all in FMP; and, all in box 142, OMP, Masland to Otis Marston, December 9, 1954, folder 9; January 24, February 28, April 13 and 25, and May 2, 1955, folder 10.

32. Abbott to Masland, June 16, 1955; Masland to Abbott, August 3, 1955, both in box 8, folder 2, FMP.

CHAPTER 5

1. For more on these dynamics, see Drake's introduction and chaps. 1–3.

2. Goldberg, *Barry Goldwater*, 53–54; Drake, *Loving Nature, Fearing the State*, 19–28.

3. Goldberg, *Barry Goldwater*, 83–84, 138–39, 158–60.

4. Smith, "Worshipping at the Grand Canyon."

5. Drake, *Loving Nature, Fearing the State*, 83.

6. Cooke, "Patterns of Voting in Pennsylvania"; Healy, "Interparty Competition in Pennsylvania"; "Unified G.O.P. Is Aim, Masland Says," *Carlisle Evening Sentinel*, March 16, 1954.

7. Masland, "A Look at the History of the Masland-Dickinson Relationship," box 15, folder 151; William Edel to Masland, August 24, [1957?], box 11, folder 40, both in FMP.

8. "Record Shows College Tried to Give LaVallee a 'Break'"; "LaVallee Testimony Before House Group at Probe on March 1" (unidentified, undated newspaper clippings in three installments); "Dickinson College Instructor Quizzed on Status as Red," all in box 16, folder 12, FMP.

9. "Record Shows College Tried."

10. "Student Senate Backs LaVallee," unidentified, undated newspaper clipping, FMP.

11. "Dickinson President Gets Plea: Colleagues Demand Professor Reinstated," unidentified, undated, newspaper clipping, FMP.

12. "Dickinson Faculty Hears LaVallee's Reactions to Bases for His Suspension," unidentified, undated newspaper clipping, FMP.

13. Masland to Marston, April 19, 1956, box 142, folder 11, OMP.

14. Jace Bennett, "Refusal to Testify Defended by Ex-Carlisle Professor," *Harrisburg Patriot-News*, July 5, 1956; Jace Bennett, "LaVallee Fired for Ignoring Questions from Trustees," *Harrisburg Patriot-News*, n.d., box 16, folder 12, FMP.

15. "Dickinson College Trustees Dismiss Dr. L. R. LaVallee"; "LaVallee Hits Board Verdict," unidentified, undated newspaper clippings in box 16, folder 12, FMP.

16. For Buckley's views, see Farber, *Modern American Conservatism*, 39–76.

17. Masland to Edel, October 1956, box 11, folder 40, FMP; Masland to Marston, September 24, 1956, box 142, folder 11, OMP.

18. Stone, "John Birch Society"; Westin, "John Birch Society."

19. Welch to Edel, February 23, 1957, box 11, folder 40; Masland to Welch, December 26, 1957; Welch to Masland, January 6, 1960, box 7, folder 375, all in FMP.

20. Masland to Welch, March 3, 1960, box 7, folder 375, FMP; Robert Welch, "The Unhelpful Fringes," editorial, *Life*, May 12, 1961, 12; "John Birch Society," *Life*, May 12, 1961, 124–30.

21. Welch quoted in *Life*, March 12, 1961, 126–27; "Masland Interview Defines Work of John Birch Society," *Dickinsonian*, April 14, 1961, 1, 3; Masland to Abbott, April 5, 1961, box 8, folder 4, FMP.

22. Masland to Otis Marston, June 20, 1961, box 143, folder 4, OMP; Masland to Abbott, November 29, 1957, box 8, folder 2, FMP.

23. Masland to David Masland, December 23, 1975, box 9, folder 28, FMP.

24. Masland to Welch, May 8, 1962, box 7, folder 375, FMP.

CHAPTER 6

1. Masland to McKay, August 5, 1955, box 8, folder 2; Masland to Conrad Wirth, June 30, 1961 (quotation), box 6, folder 2, and January 22, 1981, box 6, folder 3, all in FMP.

2. Mackintosh, "NPS Advisory Board."

3. See, all in Record Group 79 at the National Archives, Wesley A. D'Ewart, assistant secretary of the interior, memorandum for the record, January 18, 1956; McKay to Masland, April 13, 1956; Masland to McKay, April 16, 1956; Masland to Doerr, May 8, 1956; Department of the Interior press release, May 16, 1956; Masland to Wirth, May 15 and 18, 1956, all in box 002, entry A

1615; and Doerr to Wirth, January 30, 1956, box 1, entry 36.

4. Hays, *Beauty, Health, and Permanence*, 6–7.

5. Senator Arthur Watkins to Secretary of the Interior Fred Seaton, August 28, 1957, box 2, entry 36, Record Group 79, National Archives.

6. The 1956 Advisory Board was made up of Walter Huber, Carl Wheat, Harold Wagner, Turpin Bannister, J. O. Brew, E. Raymond Hall, John Oakes, Fred Smith, and Masland.

7. Heiskell was the granddaughter of Adolf Ochs, longtime publisher of the *New York Times*, daughter of his son-in-law, publisher Arthur Hays Sulzberger, and wife of Orvil Dryfoos, who took over as publisher upon Sulzberger's death. When Dryfoos died, Marian married Arthur Heiskell. For her correspondence with Masland, see box 4, folder 18, FMP.

8. Foresta, *America's National Parks*, 71–72; Wirth, *Parks, Politics, and the People*, 164; Hartzog, *Battling for the National Parks*, 206–9; Mengak, *Reshaping Our National Parks*, 133–35; Everhart, *National Park Service*, 55.

9. Hartzog, *Battling for the National Parks*, 206.

10. Schulte, *Wayne Aspinall*; Sturgeon, *Politics of Western Water*.

11. Masland to Wirth, December 17, 1956, box 6, folder 2; FMP; Frank Masland to Otis Marston, December 18, 1956, box 142, folder 11, OMP.

12. Advisory Board meeting minutes, December 1–7, 1956, and Appendix A, box 1, entry 37, Record Group 79, National Archives; Smith, "Worshipping at the Grand Canyon."

13. Smith, "Warren Ost and the Formative Years."

14. DeVoto, "Let's Close the National Parks"; Stevenson, "Shocking Truth"; Advisory Board meeting minutes, March 28–30, 1956, box 2, entry 37, Record Group 79, National Archives.

15. Carr, *Mission 66*, 208.

16. Masland to Smith, February 15, 1957, Smith to Masland, February 18, 1957, box 1, folder 33, FMP; Masland to Marston, May 10, 1957, box 142, folder 12, OMP.

17. Sellars, *Preserving Nature*, 180–91; "Is the Advisory Board Fully Alert?," *National Wildlands News*, June 1960, 1, box 9, folder 2, Devereux Butcher Papers, 1932–1985, American Heritage Center, University of Wyoming, Laramie; Masland to Wirth, May 31, 1960, Wirth to Masland, June 3, 1960, box 6, folder 2, FMP.

18. Sellars, *Preserving Nature*, 186–90 (quotation on 190); Ise, *Our National Park Policy*, 566.

19. Sellars, *Preserving Nature*, 180–81; Backes, *Wilderness Within*, 259–65.

20. Abbey, *Desert Solitaire*, 43–44.

21. Ibid., 46–47.

22. Cahalan, *Edward Abbey*, 8, 34, 179.

23. Ibid., chap. 1, "Appalachia," and "Pimpmobile," 235; and, all by Abbey, "Planting a Tree," in *Down the River*, 61–63; "Shadows from the Big Woods," in *Journey Home*, 223–26; "The Right to Arms," in *Abbey's Road*, 32; and "Arizona: How Big Is Big Enough?," "Theory of Anarchy," "Immigration and Liberal Taboos," "A Writer's Credo," and "The Future of Sex: A Reaction to a Pair of Books," in *One Life at a Time*, 20–24, 25–28, 41–44, 164, and 199–205, respectively.

24. Abbey, *Desert Solitaire*, 46; Abbey, "Freedom and Wilderness, Wilderness and Freedom," in *Journey Home*, 227–38 (quotation on 229); Cahalan, *Edward Abbey*, 73.

25. Abbey to Masland, March 8, 1987, box 1, folder 1, FMP; Masland to Abbey, March 27, 1987, series 2.2, box 2, Abbey Papers. Masland's fan letter to Abbey is absent from both the Abbey Papers and FMP.

26. Masland to Marston, May 5, 1958, box 143, folder 1, OMP.

27. Masland to Marston, March 4 (first quotation), June 19, August 8 (second quotation), 1957, all in box 142, folder 12, OMP.

28. Masland to Marston, October 4, 1957, OMP.

29. Masland to Marston, November 27, 1957, OMP.

30. Wheat to Littell, January 2, 1957; Wheat to Masland, January 2, 1957; Masland to Wheat, January 14, 1957, all in box 5, folder 6, FMP.

31. Masland to Wheat, January 14, 1957, FMP.

32. Spence, *Dispossessing the Wilderness*; Jacoby, *Crimes Against Nature*.

33. Littell to Wheat, January 25, 1957; Wheat to Masland, January 31, 1957; Masland to Wheat, February 13, 1957; Hugh Miller, regional director, NPS, to Paul Jones, chair, Navajo Tribal Council, June 21, 1957; Conrad Wirth to Masland, June 26, 1957, all in box 5, folder 6, FMP. For more on Littell, see Iverson, *Diné*, 207–10.

34. Brower to Masland, July 11, 1958, box 5, folder 6, FMP.

35. Ben Thompson, chief, Division of Recreation Planning, NPS, to Masland, January

24, 1958; Masland to Carl Wheat, March 12, 1958; Masland to Conrad Wirth, March 12, 1958, all in FMP.

36. Masland to Mary Abbott, March 17, 1959, box 8, folder 3, FMP.

37. Masland to Abbott, March 26, 1959, FMP; Hartzog, *Battling for the National Parks*, 206. The other members were E. Raymond Hall, John Krout, Earl Reed, Robert Sproul, and Robert Stearns.

38. *National Parks Magazine*, August 1959, 2–5; and the issue of December 1959, 12–13, attached to Paul Harvey to Masland, December 11, 1959, box 4, folder 35, FMP.

39. Masland to Carl Burke, December 2, 1977, box 4, folder 40, FMP.

40. Backes, *Wilderness Within*, 292–93.

41. Turner, *Promise of Wilderness*, 54–59.

42. Quoted in Backes, *Wilderness Within*, 294.

43. Masland to George W. Fry, superintendent, Isle Royale National Park, October 19, 1960, box 3, folder 27, FMP.

44. Masland to Marston, August 12 and November 27 (quotation), 1959, box 143, folder 2, OMP; and, all in FMP, Masland to Ned Danson, August 12 and October 23, 1959; Danson to Masland, August 21, 1959, all in box 3, folder 8; Masland to Mary Abbott, October 30, 1959, box 8, folder 3; and all in box 10, folder 39, Masland to F. M. Burrill, US Board on Geographic Names, November 23, 1959; Masland, "Report on Navajo Safari 9/19/59 to 10/1/59"; Christy G. Turner II, "Mystery Canyon Survey: San Juan County, Utah, 1959," *Plateau* 32, no. 4 (1960): 73–80.

45. Masland to Wirth, February 29 and March 31, 1959; Masland to John Ross, president of the Navajo Tribal Council, May 11, 1960, all in box 5, folder 6, FMP.

46. Marshall, memorandum to Brower, "RE: Sipping Away of Indian Wilderness," July 12, 1960, FMP.

47. Masland to Brower, July 28, 1960, FMP.

48. FMP.

49. Masland to Marston, April 18, 1960, box 143, folder 3, OMP; Masland to Mary Abbott, September 4, 1959, box 8, folder 3, FMP. Goldwater quoted in Drake, *Loving Nature, Fearing the State*, 96; see also Harvey, "Defending the National Park System."

50. Masland to Wirth, November 3 and 4, 1959, box 6, folder 2; Masland to Horace Albright, with copy of telegram to six conservation groups, April 20, 1960, box 5, folder 7; Masland to members of the Advisory Board, memorandum #4, n.d., box 3, folder 27, all in FMP.

51. Masland to Abbott, August 26, 1961, box 8, folder 4, FMP.

52. Masland to Wirth, August 28, 1959, box 6, folder 2, FMP.

53. Masland to Marston, October 17, 1960, box 143, folder 3, OMP; Christy Turner II, "Further Baldrock Crescent Explorations: San Juan County, Utah, 1960," *Plateau* 34 (April 1962): 101–12, box 5, folder 6, FMP.

54. Masland to Wirth, November 14, 1960, box 10, folder 5, FMP.

55. Masland to Mary Abbott, August 15, 1960, box 8, folder 4, FMP.

56. Phillips-Fein, *Invisible Hands*, chap. 4.

57. Masland to Seaton, December 13, 1960 (first quotation), box 5, folder 34; Masland to Wheat, December 15, 1960 (second quotation), box 5, folder 60, both in FMP.

58. Masland to Horace Albright, November 18, 1960, box 2, folder 61; Masland to Wirth, May 3, 1960, box 6, folder 2, both in FMP.

59. Masland to Abbott, November 14, 1960, box 8, folder 4; Masland to Horace Albright, June 1, 1961, box 11, folder 11; Smith to Masland, November 9, 1960, box 5, folder 37, all in FMP.

60. Masland to Mary Abbott, November 14, 1960, box 8, folder 4, FMP.

CHAPTER 7

1. Fred Smith to Masland, December 2, 1960, box 5, folder 37; Masland to Carl Wheat, December 15, 1960, box 5, folder 60, both in FMP; see also Smith, *Stewart L. Udall.*

2. Masland to John Carver, April 26, 1962, box 2, folder 87, FMP.

3. For Masland's worry over Udall's support for the Bridge Canyon dam, see Masland to Mary Abbott, January 3, 1961, box 8, folder 4; Masland to Harold Fabian (quotation), March 8, 1961, box 4, folder 35, both in FMP.

4. For Udall's report to the congressional committee, see Udall to Wayne Aspinall, August 27, 1960, box 72, folder 4, Udall Papers; Masland to Wirth, November 14, 1960, box 10, folder 5, FMP.

5. Masland to Carl Wheat, March 3, 1961, box 5, folder 60, FMP; see also a similar laudatory letter to Advisory Board member Sigurd Olson, March 9, 1961, box 19, folder 60–61, Olson Papers. Masland also came to admire Udall's wife, Lee, for her verve and love of the outdoors, especially the desert Southwest canyon country. See Masland to Lee Udall, January 10, 1963, box 5, folder 52, FMP.

6. Masland to Udall, December 9, 1960, box 5, folder 51, FMP.

7. Masland to Udall, February 6, 1961, box 5, folder 6, FMP.

8. Udall to Masland, February 13, 1961, box 5, folder 51, FMP.

9. Masland to Danson, February 3, 1961, box 3, folder 8; Masland to Olson, March 13, 1961, box 5, folder 7; and similar letters to John Oakes, e.g., March 21, 1961, box 13, folder 45, all in FMP. See also Masland to Otis Marston, March 4 and 7, 1961, box 143, folder 4, OMP.

10. Masland, memorandum to members of the Advisory Board, March 3, 1961, box 4, folder 36, FMP.

11. Stegner to Udall, September 21, 1961, box 190, folder 21, Udall Papers.

12. Masland to Olson, March 13, 1961, box 11, folder 2, FMP.

13. Masland to Otis Marston, May 11, 1961, box 143, folder 4, OMP.

14. Ibid.

15. Ibid.

16. Masland, "Conservation of Spiritual Values," box 15, folder 172, FMP. See also Backes, *Wilderness Within*, 60–61, 119, 150–51, 185–86, 209, 310.

17. Masland, "Conservation of Spiritual Values."

18. Masland to Udall, March 27, 1961, box 5, folder 51; Masland, memorandum to members of the Advisory Board, July 17, 1961 (first quotation), box 190, folder 5, both in Udall Papers; Masland to Marston, July 14, 1961 (second quotation), box 143, folder 4, OMP.

19. Masland to Marston, July 14, 1961, box 143, folder 4, OMP. Masland recalled Lee Udall's comment in a letter to her dated January 10, 1963, box 5, folder 52; see also Masland to Stewart Udall, December 17, 1963, box 5, folder 52, both in FMP.

20. Masland, memorandum to members of the Advisory Board, July 17, 1961, box 5, folder 7, FMP.

21. Udall to Masland, July 14, 1961; Masland to Udall, July 17 and 21, 1961, all in box 5, folder 51, FMP.

22. Udall quoted in Masland to Peter L. Parry, superintendent, Canyonlands National Park, August 2, 1984, box 10, folder 4; Masland to Udall, November 22, 1961, box 5, folder 51; Masland tweaked the boundaries of the proposed park in letters to Udall on May 15, July 21 and 27, and October 18, 1961, all in box 5, folder 51, FMP.

23. Marston to Masland, August 2, 1961; Masland to Marston, August 7, 1961, both in box 143, folder 4, OMP.

24. Advisory Board meeting minutes, Washington, DC, April 30–May 3, 1962, box 2, entry 37, Record Group 79, National Archives.

25. Sellars, *Preserving Nature in the National Parks*, 195.

26. Advisory Board meeting minutes, April 30–May 3, 1962 (see n. 26).

27. Masland to Olson, June 9, 1961, box 19, folder 1961–1962, Olson Papers.

28. Masland to Marston, January 31, 1962, box 143, folder 5, OMP.

29. Advisory Board meeting minutes, April 30–May 3, 1962 (see n. 26).

30. Masland to Udall, June 4, 1962, box 5, folder 51, Udall Papers.

31. Masland to Udall, December 5, 1961, box 5, folder 6, FMP.

32. Masland to Cameron, September 13, 1962, box 5, folder 6, FMP.

33. Masland to Udall, August 8, 1962, copy in box 19, folder 61–62, Olson Papers.

34. Udall to Masland, September 18 and October 3; Masland, telegram to Udall, October 16; Stewart Udall, handwritten note to Masland dated "Mon" [November 3, 1962], all in box 5, folder 51, FMP.

35. Udall to Masland, August 11, 1962, FMP. Harold Fabian, Masland's successor as Advisory Board chair, wrote a similarly glowing letter of praise. See Fabian to Masland, June 26, 1962, box 5, folder 60, FMP.

36. Masland to Udall, August 20, 1962, box 5, folder 51, FMP.

37. Masland to Brooks, June 4, August 15 (quotation), August 21, and November 2, 1962; Brooks to Masland, August 2 and 29 and October 26, 1962, box 1, folder 21, all in FMP; Brooks, "Canyonlands: A New National Park."

38. Advisory Board meeting minutes, Washington, DC, March 25–27, 1963, box 3, entry 37, Record Group 79, National Archives.

39. Masland to Udall, September 11 and October 8, 1962; Udall to Masland, September 18, 1962, all in box 5, folder 51, FMP; Masland to Abbott, October 15, 1962, box 8, folder 4, FMP.

40. J. O. Kilmartin to Masland, March 6, 1963, copy in box 143, folder 6, OMP.

41. Masland to Marston, April 2, June 3, 1963, box 143, folder 6, OMP.

42. Masland to Abbott, July 1, 1963, box 8, folder 4, FMP.

43. See Masland's notes on his conversation with Udall, April 23, 1963; Masland to Udall, June 6, 1963; Masland to Udall on the trip, July 9, 1963, all in box 5, folder 52, FMP.

44. For the political battle, see Smith, "Canyonlands National Park Controversy."

45. Masland to Peter L. Perry, superintendent, Canyonlands National Park, August 2, 1984 (first quotation); Masland, "Some Thots re Canyonlands National Park" (second quotation), both in box 10, folder 4, FMP; Frost quoted in Kent Frost, oral history interview, 1973, Special Collections, Brigham Young University, Provo, UT, 14; Masland to Russell Dickenson, November 12, 1980 (final quotation), box 3, folder 19, FMP.

CHAPTER 8

1. Masland to Wheat, March 28, 1963, box 5, folder 60, FMP.

2. See the essays in Paterson, *Kennedy's Quest for Victory*; Noer, "New Frontiers and Old Priorities" and May, "Passing the Torch"; Mahoney, *JFK: Ordeal in Africa*; Jackson, *US Foreign Policy in the Horn*, chap. 4, "Self-Determination and the New Frontier."

3. Cioc, *Game of Conservation*, chap. 1, "Africa's Apartheid Parks."

4. Ibid.

5. Masland to Abbott, July 25, 1962, box 8, folder 4, FMP.

6. Masland to Stewart Udall, July 12, 1962, box 5, folder 52, FMP; R. Nash, *Wilderness and the American Mind*, 363; Adams, *First World Conference on National Parks, xxxii.*

7. Masland to Udall, July 12, 1962, box 5, folder 52, FMP.

8. Masland to Baer, July 12, 1962; Baer to Masland, July 24, 1962, both in box 1, folder 65, FMP.

9. Masland to Udall, July 12, 1962, box 5, folder 52, FMP.

10. Masland to Udall, August 8, 1962; Udall to Masland, August 11, 1962, both in box 5, folder 51, FMP.

11. *Shuttle*, Fall 1962, 2–3; "Old House: Adams National Historic Site, Special Dedication Program," September 7, 1962; Masland to Abbott, with attached speech, September 7, 1962; Abbott to Masland, September 13, 1962; Masland to Abbott, December 11, 1962; Masland, "Tribute to Miss Abbott," *Concord (MA) Journal*, undated copy attached to Abbott to Masland, November 8, 1962, all in box 8, folder 4, FMP.

12. Masland to Albright, October 25, 1962, March 12, 1963, box 2, folder 61; Masland to Wirth, May 8 and 16, 1963, box 6, folder 3, all in FMP; Masland, "Land of the Anasazi: My Travels in the Slickrock Country," *Explorers Journal* 40 (October 1962): 14–16; Washburn, *Cosmos Club of Washington.*

13. See Masland to Wirth, March 15, 1963, box 6, folder 3, FMP.

14. Masland to Wirth, March 15, 1963, box 3, folder 28, FMP.

15. Ibid.

16. Masland to Wirth, March 15, April 3, July 8 and 16; Wirth to Masland, July 26, 1963, all in FMP.

17. Masland to Hartzog, January 16 and November 12, 1964, March 29, 1965 (two letters), all in FMP. Masland noted Hartzog's compliance with his suggestions in the margins of his letters.

18. Masland to Udall, March 11 and 27, 1963, box 5, folder 52; Masland to Abbott, July 1, 1963, box 8, folder 4, FMP; *Dickinsonian*, June 3, 1963.

19. Masland, "African Report 1963"; "Memorandum Number One: Kenya-Tanzania 1963"; "Memorandum Number Two, 1963," copies of all three documents in box 20, folder 146, Hartzog Papers; Masland to Kimball, August 28, 1963; Kimball to Masland, January 3, 1964, both in box 1, folder 84, FMP.

20. Masland to Albright, October 8, 1963, box 2, folder 69; Masland to Abbott, October 7, 1963, box 8, folder 4, FMP.

21. Masland to Eisenhower, September 1, 1966, box 6, folder 32, FMP.

22. Masland to Cameron, January 13, 1964, box 5, folder 6, FMP.

23. Ibid.

24. See especially Phillips-Fein, *Invisible Hands*; Lichtman, *White Protestant Nation*; McGirr, *Suburban Warriors*.

25. Masland to Pew, June 29, 1964; Pew to Masland, September 1, 1964, both in box 13, folder 11, FMP.

26. Masland to Abbott, October 7, 1963, box 8, folder 4, FMP; Masland to Marston, June 3, 1963, box 143, folder 6, OMP.

27. Masland, address at the dedication of the administration-orientation building, Big Bend National Park, November 3, 1963, box 15, folder 175, FMP.

28. Masland to Udall, November 27, 1963, box 5, folder 52; Masland to Abbott, April 18 and November 8, 1962, box 8, folder 4; both in FMP.

29. Milazzo, *Unlikely Environmentalists*, 57.

30. Masland to Udall, December 17, 1963, box 5, folder 52, FMP.

31. Harvey, *Wilderness Forever*; Frome, *Battle for the Wilderness*; Allin, *Politics of Wilderness Preservation*.

32. Masland to Jon Daniels, NAM Conservation Committee, November 15, 1961 (quotation), Masland to Charles R. Sligh, president, NAM, November 17, 1961; Masland to Daniel Cannon, NAM Executive Committee, January 17, 1962; John Saylor to Masland, June 12, 1962, all in box 5, folder 63, FMP.

33. Masland to Udall, December 26, 1963, box 5, folder 52, FMP.

34. Smith, *Stewart L. Udall*, 174 (Carver quotation); Masland to Wirth, November 21, 1963, box 6, folder 3, FMP.

35. See Masland to Wallace Stegner, December 12, 1963, box 5, folder 42; Masland to Carl Wheat, February 6, 1964, box 5, folder 60, both in FMP; Smith, *Stewart L. Udall*, 155–56.

36. Masland to Otis Marston, August 26, 1963, box 143, folder 6; Masland to Brower, March 3, 1964, box 143, folder 7, both in OMP; Coate, "'Biggest Water Fight in American History'"; Pearson, *Still the Wild River Runs*; Pearson, *Saving Grand Canyon*.

37. Horace Albright to Masland, February 26, 1964; Masland to Albright, March 4, 1964, box 2, folder 61; Masland to Udall, March 3, 1964; Udall, by hand, to Masland, dated "Fri," box 5, folder 52, all in FMP.

38. Masland, "Exploring the Colorado," 5, 15.

39. Masland to Udall, March 3, 1964; Udall, confidential note to Masland dated "Fri" [March 1964], box 5, folder 52; Masland to Conrad Wirth, November 15, 1963, box 6, folder 3; Masland to Sigurd Olson, March 17, 1964, Masland to John Oakes, June 1, 1964, box 13, folder 45, all in FMP.

40. Needham, *Power Lines*, 15.

41. Masland to Hartzog, February 24, 1964 (first quotation), box 20, folder 146; Hartzog to Masland, October 22, 1969 (third quotation), box 21, folder 149, both in Hartzog Papers; Masland to Albright, June 23, 1964, box 2, folder 61; Frank Masland to Sigurd Olson, July 23, 1964 (second quotation), box 5, folder 7, FMP.

CHAPTER 9

1. Masland to Abbott, May 4, June 4, and December 2, 1964, box 8, folder 5, FMP.

2. Masland to Abbott, October 15, 1962, box 8, folder 4, FMP.

3. Masland to Abbott, February 10, 1964, box 8, folder 5, FMP.

4. Goldwater to M. L. Lee, July 31, 1958, copy in box 6, folder 41, FMP.

5. Masland to Abbott, July 8, 1964, box 8, folder 5, FMP.

6. Ibid.

7. Masland to Marston, November 11, 1964, box 143, folder 7, OMP; and, all in FMP, Masland to Abbott, December 2, 1964, December 13, 1965, box 8, folder 5; Masland to Pew, November 20, 1964, box 13, folder 11; Masland to Peter Duncan, March 26, 1975, box 1, folder 41.

8. Smith, *Stewart L. Udall*, 194–95.

9. Masland to Clarence Cottam, July 31, 1962, box 19, folder 1961–1962, Olson Papers; Masland to Udall, December 26, 1963, box 5, folder 52, FMP.

10. Masland to John H. Daniels, chairman, Conservation Committee, NAM, November 15, 1961; Masland to Charles Sligh, November 17, 1961, both in box 5, folder 63, FMP.

11. Masland to Allen, January 7, 1972, box 21, folder 153, Hartzog Papers.

12. See Berry, *Gift of Good Land*; Berry, *What Are People For*; Berry, *Long-Legged House*; Sutterfield, *Wendell Berry*; Wriglesworth, *Distant Neighbors*.

13. Berry, "Some Thoughts on Citizenship and Conscience in Honor of Don Pratt," in *Long-Legged House*, 92 (first quotation); Berry, "The Loss of the Future," in ibid., 66, 70 (second quotation).

14. Berry, "The Tyranny of Charity," in *Long-Legged House*, 12; "Loss of the Future," 66.

15. Berry, "Nature's Consumers," in *Long-Legged House*, 37–52.

16. Ibid., 50; Berry, "Native Hill," in *Long-Legged House*, 232–33.

17. Berry, "Some Thoughts on Citizenship," 100.

18. Masland to Robert McCormack, December 10, 1979, box 2, folder 2, FMP.

19. Masland to Olson, June 18, 1962, box 19, folder 61–62, Olson Papers.

20. White, "Roots of Our Ecological Crisis," 1205, 1206; see also Lytle, *Gentle Subversive*, 88.

21. Masland, speech, "Balance of Nature," September 1970, box 15, folder 127, FMP.

22. Berry's letter to Lynn White is quoted in Sutterfield, *Wendell Berry*, 42; Berry, *Gift of Good Land*, 267–68.

23. Masland to Abbott, May 6, 1965, box 8, folder 5, FMP.

24. Masland to Hartzog, "Everglades," March 29, 1965, copy in box 5, folder 7; Masland to Udall, August 18, 1965, box 5, folder 52, FMP.

25. Masland to Marston, May 28, 1965, box 143, folder 8, OMP.

26. Masland to Abbott, May 6, 1965, box 8, folder 5, FMP.

27. Masland to Marston, December 28, 1966, box 143, folder 7, OMP; see also Smith, *Stewart L. Udall*.

28. Masland to Marston, December 27, 1965, box 143, folder 7, OMP; Masland to Brooks, February 8, 1966, box 2, folder 61, FMP.

29. Reagan quoted in Cannon, *Governor Reagan*, 301; Masland to Albright, November 28, 1966, box 2, folder 61, FMP.

30. Cannon, *Governor Reagan*, 298–99.

31. Masland to Horace Albright, November 21, 1963, December 28, 1966, box 2, folder 61, FMP; Miles, *Guardians of the Parks*, chaps. 10–11.

32. Masland to Marston, May 26, 1964, box 143, folder 7; Masland to Marston, August 18, 1966, box 144, folder 1, OMP; Masland to Udall, June 21, October 12, and November 12, 1965, box 5, folder 52, FMP; Udall quoted in Fradkin, *Wallace Stegner and the American West*, 217.

CHAPTER 10

1. Masland to Marston, May 26, 1964, box 143, folder 7, OMP.

2. Masland to Abbott, February 10, 1964, box 8, folder 5, FMP.

3. Masland to Stewart Udall, June 11, 1964, box 5, folder 52, FMP.

4. Jackson, *US Foreign Policy in the Horn*, 56–81.

5. Masland to Udall, September 10, 1964, box 5, folder 52, FMP.

6. Masland, "Notes on Ethiopian Trip, May 2–22, 1966," box 14, folder 58, FMP.

7. Ibid.

8. "Special Memorandum Prepared in the Central Intelligence Agency, March 31, 1966," in Schwar and Shaloff, *Foreign Relations of the United States*, 537.

9. Memorandum from Rusk to Johnson, February 11, 1967; Rusk, memorandum of conversation titled "Ethiopian Request for More U.S. Military and Economic Assistance, February 14, 1967," both in Schwar and Shaloff, *Foreign Relations of the United States*, 560–61 and 564–66, respectively.

10. Masland to "Dear" [Virginia Masland], undated but identified as letter #1, box 14, folder 56, FMP.

11. Masland, "Notes on Second Ethiopian Trip, March 11 to April 16, 1967," box 14, folder 57, FMP.

12. Ibid.; Masland to Virginia Masland, letter #5, box 14, folder 56, FMP.

13. Masland, "Notes on Ethiopian Trip."

14. Ibid.

15. Masland to Virginia Masland, letter #9, box 14, folder 56, FMP.

16. Masland to Virginia Masland, letter #12, FMP.

17. Masland, "Report of Mission to Ethiopia, March 11 to April 16, 1967," box 15, folder 218, FMP; Masland to Hartzog, November 10, 1967, box 20, folder 146, Hartzog Papers.

18. Masland to Abbott, January 9, 1968, box 8, folder 5, FMP; Jackson, *US Foreign Policy in the Horn*, chap. 7, "Revolution in Ethiopia."

19. Nicol, *From the Roof of Africa*, 18–41, 342–59; Dickenson to Masland, September 25, 1984, box 3, folder 21, FMP.

20. Masland to Abbott, January 9, 1968, box 8, folder 5, FMP.

21. Jon Masland, email to author, February 7, 2018.

22. Masland to Abbott, August 3, 1967, box 8, folder 5, FMP; Smith, *Stewart L. Udall*, 255–71; George Hartzog to Masland, January 15, 1968, box 20, folder 146, Hartzog Papers.

23. Masland to Abbott, August 3, 1967, box 8, folder 5, FMP; Rome, "'Give Earth a Chance.'"

24. Masland to Haury, July 9 and 10, 1968, box 4, folder 14, FMP.

25. Masland to Udall, October 15 and 19, 1968, box 5, folder 53, FMP; Smith, *Stewart L. Udall*, 279–85.

26. See Milazzo, *Unlikely Environmentalists*; Coodley and Sarasohn, *Green Years*.

27. Masland to Udall, July 9, 1968; Udall to Masland, July 11, 1968, both in box 5, folder 53, FMP.

28. Masland to Abbott, July 1, 1968; Abbott to Masland, October 22, 1968, box 8, folder 6, FMP.

29. Masland to Abbott, October 25, 1968, May 13, 1969, FMP.

30. Masland to Abbott, November 12, 1968, FMP.

31. Masland to Udall, December 19, 1968, box 5, folder 53, FMP.

CHAPTER 11

1. Masland to Abbott, November 28, 1961, box 8, folder 4; Masland to Pew June 29, 1964, box 13, folder 11, both in FMP.

2. Masland to Spahr, November 17, 1959, box 12, folder 3, FMP.

3. Masland to Stewart Udall, September 29, 1964, box 5, folder 52, FMP.

4. Masland to Edel, April 23, 1965, September 29, 1972, box 11, folder 40; Masland, confidential memorandum to selected trustees, August 7, 1963, box 15, folder 121; Pew to Masland, September 1, 1964, box 13, folder 11, all in FMP.

5. Masland to Bill [Masland], April 3, 1969, box 12, folder 88, FMP.

6. Masland to MacFarland, August 13, 1965; MacFarland to Masland, August 27, 1965, January 19, 1966; Masland to Clarence A. White, December 29, 1965, and numerous other letters dealing with the negotiations, all in box 2, folder 13, FMP.

7. Jeffries to Masland, February 7, 1966; Rubendall to Masland, February 8, 1966; Masland to Harthon Hill, deputy director, NPS, August 23, 1971, all in FMP.

8. Howard Kolus, "The Florence Jones Reineman Wildlife Sanctuary," *Dickinson Alumnus*, December 1971, 2–7; Masland to MacFarland, January 5, 1972, both in FMP.

9. Masland to George H. Harrison, August 28, 1963, copy in box 19, folder 1962–1963, Olson Papers; and, all in FMP, Masland, memorandum of meeting with deputy director of the Pennsylvania Game Commission, April 9, 1964, and memorandum for the file, December 23, 1964, both in box 2, folder 3; Masland to Horace Albright, December 28, 1966, box 2, folder 61; *Pennsylvania Game News*, June 1965, 41, copy in box 16, folder 5.

10. For more on Goddard, see Morrison, *Walk on the Downhill Side*.

11. Masland to Kimball, May 11, 1965; Goddard to Kimball, May 11, 1965, both in box 1, folder 84, FMP.

12. Masland to Goddard, September 12, 1973; see also Masland's speech of October 21, 1981, both in box 1, folder 47, FMP.

13. Masland, "Why Conservation?," December 14, 1965, folder 179; see also Masland, "Conservation—A Moral Duty," May 17, 1965, folder 177, "Conservation Is an Ethic," May 8, 1967, folder 194, and "What Is Conservation," January 20, 1965, folder 184, all in box 15, FMP.

14. Masland to Russell Train, chair, executive office of the President's Council on Environmental Quality, December 10, 1975 (quotation), box 2, folder 36; Masland to William Scranton, July 13, 1965, box 7, folder 60; Masland, draft of introductory remarks, box 15, folder 178, all in FMP.

15. Masland to Scranton, June 29, 1965; Masland to Scranton, September 7, 1965, both in box 7, folder 60, FMP.

16. Scranton to Masland, August 25 and September 27, 1965, FMP.

17. See the speeches cited in n. 13 and Masland, "Grass Roots," February 18, 1966, box 15, folder 180, FMP; Masland, "First Among the Haves,"43.

18. Masland to Scranton, August 16 and 26 (quotations), 1965, box 7, folder 60, FMP.

19. Masland to Scranton, August 10 and September 13, 1965, December 6, 1966, and January 30 and March 6, 1967, FMP.

20. Scranton to Udall, January 17, 1965, box 7, folder 60; Masland to Udall, August 18, 1966, box 5, folder 53, both in FMP.

21. Masland to George Mooradian, January 22, 1966; Masland to Davis, March 22, 1966; memorandum from Masland, February 8, 1966, all in carton 29, folder 20, manuscript group 208, Pennsylvania State Archives.

22. Masland, "Opening Remarks," and "Program: Governor's Conference on Natural Beauty," September 12, 1966, both in carton 31, folder 7, Pennsylvania State Archives.

23. Masland, introduction of Stewart Udall, September 13, 1966, carton 31, folder 6, Pennsylvania State Archives; *Summary Report: Governor's Conference on Natural Beauty, September 12–13, 1966* (Hershey: Community Center, 1966), quotations at 11–12; "Governor's Conference Aims for More Beauty in Pennsylvania," *Shuttle*, October 1966, 14.

24. Morrison, *Walk on the Downhill Side*, 228–29; Masland to Ralph Abele, May 3, 1982, box 1, folder 1, FMP (quotation). For the pioneering effort in Wisconsin, see Huffman, *Protectors of the Land and Water.*

25. *Perry County (PA) Times*, July 11, 1968, box 16, folder 10, FMP.

26. Bruce Whitman, "Frank Masland: A Conversation on Conservation," *Harrisburg Patriot-News*, September 19, 1967, carton 2, folder 23, Record Group 72, Pennsylvania State Archives.

27. Minutes, Pennsylvania Fish and Boat Commission, October 23, 1967, April 29, July 22, and October 14, 1968, January 6, 1970, May 3, 1971; Robert Bielo to Masland, May 24, 1967, Masland to Bielo, July 25, October 28, and November 27, 1968, all in carton 2, folder 23, Record Group 72, Pennsylvania State Archives; Masland to Bielo, January 7, 1969, June 18 and August 11, 1970, carton 2, folder 24, Pennsylvania State Archives.

28. Abele to members of the Fish and Boat Commission, October 11, 1972, box 2, folder 1, FMP.

29. Masland to Shafer, November 19 (quotation) and December 17, 1969, May 8 and June 18, 1970, all in box 7, folder 61, FMP.

30. Masland to Shafer, August 8, 1968, carton 118, manuscript group 209, Shafer Papers.

31. Masland to Shafer, August 9, 1968, carton 118, manuscript group 209, Shafer Papers; Masland to Abbott, November 5, 1969, box 8, folder 6, FMP; Smith, *Green Republican*, 216–20.

32. Masland to Shafer, August 12, September 8, and December 10, 1970, box 7, folder 61, FMP.

33. See, all in Hartzog Papers, box 21, Masland to Scott, October 30, 1970, February 2, 1971; Masland, letter to the editor, *New York Times*, February 20, 1971, folder 150; Masland, letters to the editor, *Gettysburg Times*, November 2, 1970, May 21, 1971, copies in folder 151; and, all in FMP, Masland to Richard Nixon, January 25, 1971; Masland to Ottenstein, May 21 and July 29, 1974; Ottenstein to Masland, September 1, 1974, all in box 4, folder 5; Masland to Udall, May 4, 1971, box 5, folder 53; Masland to Lady Bird Johnson, July 21, 1972, box 1, folder 68, and numerous other letters in box 4, folder 5.

34. Smith, *Green Republican*, 232; Albert, *Damming the Delaware.*

35. Smith, *Green Republican*, 232–36.

36. Masland to Conrad Wirth, November 7, 1960, box 6, folder 2, Masland to Wirth, May 6, 1963, box 6, folder 3; Masland to Michael Frome, December 22, 1970; Masland to Paul Felton, June 4, 1971; Masland to Leonard Greene, June 29, 1971, all in box 2, folder 35; Masland to Stewart Udall, February 26, 1971, box 5, folder 53, all in FMP.

37. Masland to Udall, March 9, 1971, box 5, folder 53; Masland to Shapp, July 3, 1972, box 7, folder 62; Masland, résumé, box 14, folder 48, all in FMP.

38. *Harrisburg Evening Sentinel*, July 23, 1971, copy in box 21, folder 151, Hartzog Papers.

39. Duncan to Masland, January 17, 1975, and numerous other letters of gratitude in box 2, folder 1, FMP.

40. Masland to Abele, January 8 (quotation) and 15 and October 24, 1975; Abele to Masland, January 14, 1975, September 21, 1976, all in box 1, folder 1, FMP.

CHAPTER 12

1. Masland, speech, "Conservation:igh Priority," n.d., box 15, folder 198, FMP.

2. Masland to Goldwater, November 8, 1968, box 6, folder 42; Masland to Nixon, November 25, 1968, box 7, folder 28, both in FMP; Smith, *Green Republican.*

3. Flippen, *Nixon and the Environment*, 23; Masland to Abbott, December 20, 1968 (first quotation), January 2 and November 5, 1969 (last quotation), box 8, folder 6; Masland to Sigurd Olson, April 30, 1969, box 5, folder 7, all in FMP; see also Flippen, "Mr. Hickel Goes to Washington."

4. Masland to William Scranton, April 10, 1969, box 7, folder 60; Masland to Abbott, November 5, 1969, box 8, folder 6, both in FMP.

5. Masland to William Scranton, April 25, 1969, box 7, folder 60, FMP.

6. Masland to Olson, April 30, 1969, box 5, folder 7; Masland to Abbott, November 5, 1969, box 8, folder 6, both in FMP.

7. Masland to Olson, August 20, 1969 (first quotation); Masland to Olson, September 18, 1969 (second quotation), both in box 5, folder 7; Masland to William Scranton, April 10, 1969, box 7, folder 60, all in FMP.

8. Flippen, *Nixon and the Environment*, 21–22.

9. Ibid., 25–26.

10. Ibid., 50–51.

11. Coodley and Sarasohn, *Green Years*, 5, 247–48; J. Buckley, *Gleanings from an Unplanned Life*, 154–56.

12. Masland to Smith, November 7, 1969, box 5, folder 38, FMP.

13. Flippen, *Nixon and the Environment*, 64–65.

14. Masland to Smith, May 7, 1970, box 5, folder 38; Masland to Nixon, November 24, 1969, April 1 and October 28, 1971, box 7, folder 28, all in FMP.

15. Masland to Nixon, telegram, May 1, 1970, box 7, folder 28; Masland to Abbott, June 2, 1970, box 8, folder 6, and August 23, 1973 (quotation), box 8, folder 7, all in FMP.

16. Rome, *Genius of Earth Day*.

17. Drake, *Loving Nature, Fearing the State*, 88; on Train, see Flippen, *Conservative Conservationist*, 96–97; the Saylor quotation is in Rome, *Genius of Earth Day*, 136–37.

18. Masland, "Futile Exercise," letter to the editor, *Carlisle Daily Sentinel*, May 15, 1970.

19. Masland to Smith, April 7, 1970, box 5, folder 38, FMP.

20. Wayburn quoted in Gottlieb, *Forcing the Spring*, 151.

21. Turner, "'Specter of Environmentalism,'" 124.

22. Gottlieb, *Forcing the Spring*, 176–78; Shabecoff, *Fierce Green Fire*, 101–10; Spears, *Rethinking the American Environmental Movement*, 2–15.

23. Wriglesworth, *Distant Neighbors*, 1–52; Masland to Murie, November 7, 1960, and Murie to Masland, November 21, 1960, both in box 4, folder 35, FMP.

24. Kirk, *Counterculture Green*, 6, 11, 16–17.

25. Masland, speech, "Conservation: High Priority," n.d., box 15, folder 198, FMP.

26. Masland to Nader, April 7, 1970, box 7, folder 26, FMP.

27. Turner, *Promise of Wilderness*, 58–59; Frome, *Battle for the Wilderness*, 182–83.

28. Sellars, *Preserving Nature*, 193.

29. Masland to Olson, June 22, 1972, box 5, folder 8, FMP.

30. Olson to Masland, August 12, 1972, FMP.

31. Ibid. See also Backes, *Wilderness Within*, 320–21.

32. O'Neill, *Coming Apart*; Chafe, *Unfinished Journey*, chap. 11; Murray, *Coming Apart*; Lichtman, *White Protestant Nation*, chaps. 6–7; McGirr, *Suburban Warriors*.

33. Lichtman, *White Protestant Nation*, 286, 320; Masland to Abbott, June 2, 1970, box 8, folder 6, FMP.

34. Masland to Abbott, June 2, 1970.

35. Schlesinger, *Disuniting of America*, 11–24.

36. Ibid., 20–21, 24.

37. Masland to Marston, August 31, 1970, box 144, folder 5, OMP.

38. Masland to Abbott, July 29, 1971, box 8, folder 7, FMP.

39. Saylor to Masland, August 4, 1971, box 7, folder 55, FMP.

40. See http://www.nps.gov/bicy/learn/historyculture/miami-jetport.htm; Masland to Nixon, December 6, 1971, box 7, folder 28, FMP; Flippen, *Nixon and the Environment*, 31, 56.

41. Masland to Otis Marston, n.d., box 144, folder 5, OMP.

42. Masland to Mary Abbott, March 26, July 29, and September 23, 1971, box 8, folder 7; Masland to Robert Lovegren, superintendent, Grand Canyon National Park, July 28, 1971, box 21, folder 151; Whittaker, "Concessions Finding," box 2, folder 88, all in FMP; and Haury, Setzler, and Masland, "Report of Special Advisory Board Yosemite Committee, July 2–6, 1971" to Hartzog; Masland to Hartzog, October 19, 1971, both in box 21, folder 152, Hartzog Papers.

43. Masland to Abbott, September 23, 1971, box 8, folder 7; Masland to Lady Bird Johnson, August 3, 1973 and July 16, 1974, box 1, folder 68; Lady Bird Johnson, "Memorandum to Mr. Frank Masland, Team Chairman, Tour of the Southeast Region," September 3, 1971, box 4, folder 39, all in FMP.

44. Masland to Otis Marston, December 17, 1970, box 144, folder 5, OMP.

45. Masland and Haury, "Alaska Report," September 15, 1972, box 15, folder 220, FMP.

46. Masland to Otis Marston, May 17, 1972, box 144, folder 7, OMP; Masland to Haury, January 12, 1972, box 21, folder 153, Hartzog Papers; Masland to Hartzog, August 22, 1972, box 21, folder 154, Hartzog Papers; Haycox, *Battleground Alaska*, 114.

47. Haycox, *Battleground Alaska*, chap. 1, "Antistatism in Alaska"; Masland to Josiah Eisaman, October 30, 1972, box 8, folder 64, FMP.

48. Dennis Hevesi, "George Hartzog, Parks Chief, Dies at 88," *New York Times*, July 17, 2008; Masland to Marston, December 12, 1972, box 144, folder 7, OMP; Masland to Olson, June 22, 1972, box 5, folder 7, FMP.

49. Masland to Peter Duncan, July 8, 1974, box 3, folder 12, FMP.

50. Flippen, *Nixon and the Environment*, 134–41.

51. Masland to Otis Marston, April 26, 1973, box 144, folder 8, OMP; and, all in FMP, Masland to Train, June 15, 1973, September 22, 1975, box 2, folder 36; Masland to Schweiker, November 1, 1974, December 13, 1974, box 7, folder 58. See also Flippen, *Conservative Conservationist.*

52. Masland's correspondence with Dickenson can be found in box 2, folders 16, 17, 18, FMP.

53. Masland to Josiah Eisaman, May 13, 1969, box 8, folder 64, FMP; Masland to Hugh Scott (quotation), October 14, 1969, box 21, folder 149, Hartzog Papers. On Nixon, the NPS, and Watergate, see Masland to Abbott, December 20, 1972, May 18 and August 23, 1973, and October 4, 1974, box 8, folder 7; Nixon to Masland, June 4, 1973, box 7, folder 28, all in FMP.

54. Masland to Nixon, May 4 and October 23 and 29 (quotation), 1973, April 10, May 16, and August 13 and 16, 1974, box 7, folder 28; Masland to Schweiker, May 14 and September 19 (quotation), 1974, box 7, folder 58; Masland to Goldwater May 14 and 21, July 8, and August 8, 1974; Goldwater to Masland, June 7, 1974, box 6, folder 43, all in FMP.

55. Masland to Albright, January 31, 1973, box 2, folder 61, FMP.

56. Masland to multiple members of Congress, September 24, 1973, box 1, folder 84, FMP.

57. Masland to Marston, January 6 (quotation) and December 15, 1971, box 144, folder 6, OMP.

58. Masland to Marston, August 22, 1974, box 144, folder 9, FMP.

CHAPTER 13

1. Masland to Marston, September 28, 1976, box 143, folder 11, OMP.

2. Masland to Haury, November 6, 1975, box 4, folder 18, FMP.

3. Masland to Abbott, September 10, 1975, box 8, folder 7, FMP.

4. Masland to Schweiker, June 2, 1975; Schweiker to Masland, June 6, 1975, box 7, folder 56, FMP.

5. Masland to Abbott, October 1, 1976 (quotation) and August 29, 1979, box 8, folder 8; Masland to Stoddard, December 19, 1978, box 9, folder 102, all in FMP.

6. Haury to Masland, December 2, 1975, box 4, folder 14, FMP.

7. Masland to Daniel Poole, president of the National Wildlife Institute, March 21, 1978, box 2, folder 8; Heiskell to Masland, November 8, 1978, box 4, folder 18, both in FMP.

8. Masland to Schweiker, February 22, 1978; Schweiker to Masland, March 14, 1978, box 7, folder 58, FMP.

9. Dickenson to Masland, November 19, 1981, box 3, folder 20, FMP.

10. Masland to James Watt, August 31, 1981; Dickenson to Masland, December 31, 1981, box 3, folder 20, FMP.

11. Masland to Fred Smith, September 25, 1980, box 5, folder 38, FMP.

12. Masland to Schweiker, January 14, 1980; Schweiker to Masland, January 28, 1960, box 7, folder 58 (b), FMP.

13. Masland to Mary Abbott, July 7, 1980, box 8, folder 8; Masland to the Republican National Committee, October 19, 1979, box 7, folder 47, FMP.

14. See Lichtman, *White Protestant Nation*; Phillips-Fein, *Invisible Hands*; G. Nash, *Conservative Intellectual Movement in America*; Dochuk, *From Bible Belt to Sunbelt*; Lassiter, *Silent Majority*; McGirr, *Suburban Warriors*; Turner and Isenberg, *Republican Reversal*, 56–62.

15. Masland to Smith, December 30, 1980, box 5, folder 38, FMP.

16. Nelson, *Nature's Burdens*, 45.

17. Watt, *Courage of a Conservative*, 123; Decker, *Other Rights Revolution*, 75.

18. Turner and Isenberg, *Republican Reversal*, 45. Coors also established the Heritage Foundation as a conservative think tank. For Coors's background, see Decker, *Other Rights Revolution*, 73–75.

19. Decker, *Other Rights Revolution*, 90.

20. Udall quoted in ibid., 134; Turner "'Specter of Environmentalism,'" 135–36.

21. Hays, *Beauty, Health, and Permanence*, 494.

22. Masland to Abbott, April 15, 1981, box 8, folder 8, FMP.

23. Masland to Watt, May 12, 1981; Watt to Masland, June 1, 1981, box 3, folder 7, FMP.

24. Representative William Goodling (R-PA) to Masland, August 13, 1981, box 6, folder 49, FMP.

25. Hays, *Beauty, Health, and Permanence*, 498–500; Turner and Isenberg, *Republican Reversal*, 62–69, 111 (first quotation); Cannon, *Governor Reagan*, 297–98 (second quotation).

26. Hays, *Beauty, Health, and Permanence*, 513–14; Decker, *Other Rights Revolution*, 128 (quotation).

27. Masland to David Burwell, National Wildlife Federation, August 27, 1981 ("unsuitable"), box 1, folder 84, FMP; Winks quoted in Helvarg, *War Against the Greens*, 112.

28. Friends of the Earth, memorandum, "The National Parks Are Under Assault," May 24, 1982 ("Nazis," "destruction of rural America," and "cultural genocide" quotations), box 3, folder 7, FMP; Hays, *Beauty, Health, and Permanence*, 108. For Cushman's personality and background, see Helvarg, *War Against the Greens*, 101–2, 107.

29. Cushman quoted in Helvarg, *War Against the Greens*, 108; see also Cushman, memorandum to all National Park System Advisory Board and Council members, September 21, 1981, box 3, folder 7, FMP.

30. Masland to Watt, December 22, 1981; Watt to Masland, January 5, 1982, box 3, folder 7, FMP.

31. Masland to Rennell, February 24, 1982, box 5, folder 26 (first quotation); Masland to Ralph Abele, September 14, 1981 (second quotation), box 1, folder 1; Masland to Emil Haury, October 20, 1981, box 4, folder 15, all in FMP.

32. Masland to Pritchard, January 12, 1982, box 4, folder 43, FMP.

33. Masland to Watt, March 9, 1982, box 4, folder 42, FMP.

34. Masland to Watt, July 23, 1982, box 3, folder 7, FMP.

35. Masland to Dennis Hanson (of *Living Wilderness* magazine), June 15, 1982, and July 15, 1982 (quotation), box 2, folder 52; Masland to Emil Haury, September 9, 1982, box 4, folder 15, all in FMP.

36. Goodling to Masland, July 28, 1982; Watt to Masland, August 20, 1982, both in box 6, folder 49, FMP.

37. Masland to Watt, August 26, 1982, FMP.

38. Ibid.

39. Masland to Goodling, September 3, 1982, FMP; Masland to Watt and members of the National Park Service Advisory Board Council, January 29, 1983, with attached essay by Paul Sears, "What Worth Nature?," box 4, folder 41, FMP.

40. Masland to Nancy Rennell, March 23, 1983, box 5, folder 26; Masland to Paul Pritchard, October 28, 1981, box 4, folder 43; Frank Masland to members of the National Park System Advisory Council, May 12, 1983, box 4, folder 41; Masland to Cushman, June 6, 1983, box 3, folder 7, all in FMP.

41. Congress found Gorsuch in contempt for refusing to turn over documents regarding the EPA's enforcement of a 1980 law on cleanup of hazardous waste dumps. Decker, *Other Rights Revolution*, 138, 152.

42. Turner, "'Specter of Environmentalism,'" 124, 131, 138.

43. Spears, *Rethinking the American Environmental Movement*.

44. Undated, unidentified news clipping, box 16, folder 9, FMP.

45. Masland to Reagan, December 3, 1981, February 4, 1982, box 7, folder 44, FMP.

46. Turner and Isenberg, *Republican Reversal*, 11, 20 (quotation).

47. Drake, *Loving Nature, Fearing the State*, 107–8.

48. Ibid., 107–9.

49. Masland to Dickenson, September 16, 1981, August 31, 1982, and September 10, 1982 (quotation), box 3, folder 19, FMP.

50. Masland to Marian Heiskell, August 5, 1981, box 4, folder 18, FMP.

51. Masland to Heiskell, November 5, 1980; Heiskell to Masland, November 20, 1981, FMP.

52. Hartzog, *Battling for the National Parks*, 208–9; Everhardt quoted in Nelson, *Nation's Burdens*, 48.

53. Heiskell to Masland, July [?] 1982, box 4, folder 18, FMP.

54. Foresta, *America's National Parks*, 312n48.

55. Masland to Heiskell, December 8, 1983; Heiskell to Masland, March 5, 1985; Heiskell to Hartzog, July 29, 1986, all in box 4, folder 18, FMP.

56. Masland to Heiskell, January 30, 1984, FMP.

57. Masland to Taylor, November 5, 1985; Masland to Heiskell, March 4, 1985, and other letters, all in FMP.

58. Nelson, *Nature's Burdens*, 210; Graham, *Presidents and the American Environment*, 307.

59. George Will, "The Green Tree Has Replaced the Red Scare," *Los Angeles Times*, April 19, 1990; Helvarg, *War Against the Greens*, x.

60. On the wise-use movement, see Turner, "'Specter of Environmentalism,'" 139–40; Helvarg, *War Against the Greens*, 109–12.

61. Masland, telegram to President George H. W. Bush, August 14, 1991, box 6, folder 23, FMP.

62. Masland, letter to the editor, *Harrisburg Patriot-News*, January 6, 1991, box 14, folder 83, FMP.

CHAPTER 14

1. Masland to William Rusher, April 26, 1983, box 9, folder 28, FMP; Masland, letter to the editor, *Reader's Digest*, April 9, 1975, carton 2, folder 26, Record Group 72, Pennsylvania State Archives. I have borrowed the title for this chapter from Harry M. Caudill's classic work *Night Comes to the Cumberlands: A Biography of a Depressed Area* (Boston: Little Brown, 1963).

2. Masland, letter to the editor, *Carlisle Sentinel*, April 11, 1979, box 14, folder 81, FMP; Spears, *Rethinking the American Environmental Movement*, 134–59.

3. Masland to Robert Bielo, January 5, 1971, carton 2, folder 24, Record Group 72, Pennsylvania State Archives; Masland, letters to the editor of the *Carlisle Evening Sentinel*, May 13, 1976, January 2, 1978, and January 8, 1983, box 14, folder 82, FMP.

4. Masland to Hartzog, September 10, 1971, box 21, folder 152; July 3, 1971, box 21, folder 153, Hartzog Papers; Masland to Clifford Jones, May 21, 1979, box 1, folder 69, FMP.

5. Joseph C. Rumburg to Masland, with attached "Detailed Description of Property," September 6, 1972, box 21, folder 154; Masland to Morton, September 14, 1972, box 21, folder 154, Hartzog Papers.

6. Masland to Goddard, September 17 (quotation) and September 25, 1973, January 24 and July 3, 1974, box 1, folder 47; Masland to David Morine, director of the Nature Conservancy, June 27, July 2, and October 4, 1973, box 1, folder 85; *Harrisburg Evening News*, September 28, 1973; *Carlisle Evening Sentinel*, June 27, 1975, box 16, folder 17, all in FMP.

7. Jones to Masland, December 11, 1979, box 1, folder 69; Masland to McConnell, June 20, 1980, box 2, folder 2, both in FMP.

8. Masland to Danson, December 5, 1986, box 3, folder 12, FMP.

9. Masland to Goddard, November 16, 1972, box 1, folder 47; Masland to Mary Abbott, July 7, 1980, box 8, folder 8; Susan Cary Nicholas, executive director, Nature Conservancy, to Masland, January 29, 1992, box 1, folder 85; Masland to Heiskell, November 17, 1990, box 4, folder 18; Charles Thompson, "Environmental Efforts Prompt Award for Man," *Harrisburg Patriot-News*, December 17, 1990, and "Masland Recognized for Work," *Carlisle Sentinel*, December 31, 1990, box 14, folder 83, all in FMP.

10. Webster, handwritten note to Masland, n.d., box 2, folder 46, FMP; Peter Duncan III, telephone interview by author, September 11, 2018.

11. Masland, oral history interview, September 10, 1982, box 9, folder 1; *Harrisburg Evening News*, July 29, 1965, box 16, folder 8, both in FMP.

12. Masland to William Belknap, July 22, 1969, October 25, 1974, box 8, folder 27, FMP.

13. Mary Abbott to Masland, September 2, 1979; Masland to Abbott, January 14, 1981; box 8, folder 8; Masland to Bill Belknap, December 29, 1981, box 8, folder 27, all in FMP.

14. Masland to Bill Belknap, May 13, 1981, box 8, folder 27, FMP.

15. Masland to Richard Masland, January 4 and May 10, 1984, box 9, folder 43; Masland to Janet Masland, August 8, 1984, box 9, folder 28, FMP.

16. Masland to Edel, September 4, 1985, box 11, folder 40; Masland to Bill and Fran Belknap, December 20, 1984, box 8, folder 27, FMP.

17. Masland to Sherman Gray, June 2, 1986, box 1, folder 19; Masland to Lady Bird Johnson, October 12, 1981, July 21, 1988, box 1, folder 68; Masland to Marian Heiskell, November 17, 1990, box 4, folder 18, all in FMP.

18. Masland to William Edel, September 4, 1985, box 11, folder 40, FMP.

19. Masland to William S. Masland, February 27, 1979, box 9, folder 44, FMP. Samuel Witwer II, class of 1930, was an attorney and Dickinson College trustee.

20. Masland to Danson, September 24, 1985, box 3, folder 12, FMP.

21. The correspondence between Masland and Lisa Kittler may be found in box 8, folder 120; see also Masland to his son David Masland, box 9, folder 28; Masland to grandson Jonathan Masland, box 9, folder 36, FMP.

22. Masland to Jonathan Masland, June 25, 1986, box 9, folder 36, FMP.

23. Masland to Jonathan Masland, May 16, 1988, box 9, folder 36; *Boiling Springs Morning Call*, June 26, 1988, box 16, folder 8, FMP.

24. Peter Duncan III, telephone interview by author, September 11, 2018.

25. Masland, "Conservation," July 6, 1988, privately held, courtesy of Frank Masland IV.

26. Masland to Lisa Kittler, April 2, 1986, box 8, folder 120; Masland to Florence Corey, March 18, 1988, box 8, folder 49, FMP.

27. Masland to Graham, December 12, 1983, box 12, folder 11, FMP.

28. Masland to Kennedy, January 27, 1986, and numerous other letters in box 12, folder 121, FMP; Lichtman, *White Protestant Nation*, 343–45.

29. Masland, "Ravelings from a Carpet Weaver," n.d., privately held, courtesy of Frank Masland IV.

30. The correspondence between Masland and Corey is in box 8, folder 49, FMP; Mark Weinberg, "At 93, He Takes a Bride," *Carlisle Sentinel*, April 28, 1989; "Masland Dead at 98," *Carlisle Sentinel*, August 1, 1994.

31. Frank Masland IV, email to author, May 21, 2018.

32. "Memorial Service for Frank E., Masland, Jr. on August 4, 1994, Allison United Methodist Church, Carlisle, PA," transcript, privately held, courtesy of Frank Masland IV.

33. Andrea Ciccocioppo, "Masland Looks Back over Area Industry and History," *Carlisle Sentinel*, January 4, 2009; "Masland Corporation," https://www.company-histories.com/Masland-Corporation-Company-History.html.

34. Matt Miller, "Industrialist Espouses Conservatism, Conservation," *Harrisburg Patriot-News*, December 28, 1987, box 8, folder 49; Masland to David Masland, October 4, 1983, box 9, folder 28; Masland to Clifford Jones, December 7, 1979, box 1, folder 69, all in FMP; Berry quoted in Bliese, *Greening of Conservative America*, 14.

35. Barry Goldwater to Frank Masland III, January 30, 1968; Lady Bird Johnson to Ginny Boynton, May 6, 2003, folder "FE Bio," both letters privately held, courtesy of Frank Masland IV; Masland to the Boone and Crockett Club, June 16, 1987, box 1, folder 19; Dickenson to Masland, June 16, 1984, box 3, folder 21, both in FMP.

36. Abyssus, "'Fish Eyes' Runs His Last Rapid."

37. "Masland's Inspirational Advocacy," editorial, *Harrisburg Patriot-News*, November 19, 1990.

38. Masland to Russell Dickenson, July 14, 1980, box 3, folder 19, FMP.

BIBLIOGRAPHY

WORKS BY FRANK MASLAND JR.

Interviews and Recollections

Interview by unnamed interviewer, part 1. September 10, 1982. Folder 46, box 14, Frank E. Masland Jr. Papers (FMP), Dickinson College, Archives and Special Collections, Carlisle, PA.

Interview with unnamed interviewer, part 2. November 5, 1982. Folder 47, box 14, FMP.

"My 85th Year." January [?] 1980. Folder 44, box 14, FMP.

"Slightly Autobiographical." February [?] 1984. Folder 45, box 14, FMP.

"Ten Generations." N.d. Folder 149, box 15, FMP.

Unpublished Works

"By the Rim of Time." N.d. Folder 75, box 14, FMP.

"The Goat Run." N.d. Folder 77, box 14, FMP.

"Masland and Sons." N.d. Box 5, manuscript group 008, Cumberland County Historical Society, Carlisle, PA.

Published Works

"Exploring the Colorado: Lees Ferry to Lake Mead." *National Parks Magazine*, May 1964, 4–6, 15.

"First Among the Haves." *American Forests*, February 1968, 6, 42–43.

"Land of the Anasazi: My Travels in Slickrock Country." *Explorers Journal* 40 (October 1962): 13–29.

"National Park System Planning and the Layman." *Sierra Club Bulletin*, June 1960, 4–7, 17.

"Rainbow Below the Rim." *Field and Stream*, April 1949, 61–63, 118–19.

"Running the Colorado Rapids." *Explorers Journal* 35 (December 1957): 1–4.

"A Survey of Ethiopia." *Explorers Journal* 46 (June 1968): 120–26.

MANUSCRIPTS

Abbey, Edward. Papers. University of Arizona Libraries, Special Collections, Tucson.

Abbott, Mary. Papers. Massachusetts Historical Society, Boston.

Belknap, William. Papers. Northern Arizona University Library, Special Collections, Flagstaff.

Goddard, Maurice K. Papers. Pennsylvania State University, Archival Collections, University Park.

Hartzog, George B., Jr. Papers. Clemson University Libraries, Special Collections and Archives, Clemson, SC.

Marston, Otis R. Papers. Huntington Library, Special Collections, San Marino, CA.

Masland, Frank E., Jr. Papers. Dickinson College, Archives and Special Collections, Carlisle, PA.

Masland and Sons Business Records. Cumberland County Historical Society, Carlisle, PA.

Nevills, Norman. Papers. University of Utah Library, Special Collections, Salt Lake City.

Olson, Sigurd F. Papers. Minnesota Historical Society, Manuscripts Collection, St. Paul.

Records of the National Park Service, Advisory Board Files. Record Group 79, National Archives, College Park, MD.

Saylor, John P. Papers. Indiana University of Pennsylvania, Special Collections and University Archives, Indiana, PA.

Scranton, William W. Papers, 1963–1967. Manuscript Group 208, Pennsylvania Historical and Museum Commission, Harrisburg.

Shafer, Raymond P. Papers, 1967–1971. Manuscript Group 209, Pennsylvania Historical and Museum Commission, Harrisburg.

Udall, Stewart L. Papers. University of Arizona Libraries, Special Collections, Tucson.

SECONDARY SOURCES

Abbey, Edward. *Abbey's Road*. New York: Penguin, 1991.

———. *Desert Solitaire: A Season in the Wilderness*. New York: Random House, 1968. New ed., Tucson: University of Arizona Press, 1998.

———. *Down the River*. New York: E. P. Dutton, 1982.

———. *The Journey Home: Some Words in Defense of the American West*. New York: Penguin, 1991.

———. *One Life at a Time, Please*. New York: Henry Holt, 1987.

———. *The Serpents of Paradise: A Reader*. Edited by John Macrae. New York: Henry Holt, 1995.

Abyssus, C. V. [Richard D. Quartaroli]. "'Fish Eyes' Runs His Last Rapid." *Boatman's Quarterly Review* 8, no. 2 (1995): 26.

Adams, Alexander B., ed. *First World Conference on National Parks*. Washington, DC: US Department of the Interior, National Park Service, 1964.

Albert, Richard C. *Damming the Delaware: The Rise and Fall of Tocks Island Dam*. University Park: Penn State University Press, 1987.

Albright, Horace. *The Birth of the National Park Service*. Salt Lake City: Howe Brothers, 1985.

Allin, Craig W. *The Politics of Wilderness Preservation*. Westport, CT: Greenwood Press, 1982.

Andrews, Richard N. L. *Managing the Environment, Managing Ourselves: A History of American Environmental Policy*. New Haven: Yale University Press, 1999.

Backes, David. *A Wilderness Within: The Life of Sigurd F. Olson*. Minneapolis: University of Minnesota Press, 1997.

Barry, John. *The Great Influenza: The Epic Story of the Deadliest Plague in History*. New York: Penguin, 2004.

Beard, Daniel B. *Special Report: Everglades National Park Project, Florida*. Washington, DC: US Department of the Interior, National Park Service, 1938.

Benjey, Tom. *Glorious Times: Adventures of the Craighead Naturalists*. Missoula: University of Montana Press, 2016.

Berry, Wendell. *The Gift of Good Land: Further Essays Cultural and Agricultural*. Berkeley, CA: Counterpoint Press, 1981.

———. *The Long-Legged House: Essays*. Berkeley, CA: Counterpoint Press, 2012.

———. *What Are People For? Essays*. Berkeley, CA: Counterpoint Press, 2010.

Bliese, John R. E. *The Greening of Conservative America*. Boulder, CO: Westview Press, 2001.

Blue, Martha. *Indian Trader: The Life and Times of J. L. Hubbell*. Walnut, CA: Kiva Press, 2000.

Brinkley, Douglas. *Rightful Heritage: Franklin D. Roosevelt and the Land of America*. New York: Harper Collins, 2016.

———. *The Wilderness Warrior: Theodore Roosevelt and the Crusade for America*. New York: Harper Collins, 2009.

Brooks, Paul. "Canyonlands: A New National Park." *Atlantic Monthly*, March 1963, 52–57.

———. *The Pursuit of Wilderness*. Boston: Houghton Mifflin, 1971.

Buckley, James L. *Gleanings from an Unplanned Life*. Wilmington, DE: Intercollegiate Studies Institute, 2006.

Buckley, William F., Jr. *God and Man at Yale: The Superstitions of "Academic Freedom."* Chicago: Henry Regnery, 1951.

Buckley, William F., Jr., and L. Brent Bozell. *McCarthy and His Enemies: The Record and Its Meaning*. Chicago: Henry Regnery, 1954.

Burford, Anne. *Are You Tough Enough? An Insider's View of Washington Power Politics*. New York: McGraw Hill, 1986.

Cahalan, James M. *Edward Abbey: A Life*. Tucson: University of Arizona Press, 2001.

Cannon, Lou. *Governor Reagan: His Rise to Power*. New York: Public Affairs, 2003.

Carr, Ethan. *Mission 66: Modernism and the National Park Dilemma*. Amherst: University of Massachusetts Press, 2007.

Chafe, William. *Unfinished Journey: America Since World War II*. New York: Oxford University Press, 2014.

Cioc, Mark. *The Game of Conservation: International Treaties to Protect the World's Migratory Animals*. Athens: Ohio University Press, 2009.

Clark, Neil. "Fast Water Man." *Saturday Evening Post*, May 18, 1946, 30, 146–48, 150.

Coate, Charles. "'The Biggest Water Fight in American History': Stewart Udall and the Central Arizona Project." *Journal of the Southwest* 37 (Spring 1995): 79–101.

Colwell, David G. *The Bitter Fruits: The Civil War Comes to a Small Town in Pennsylvania*. Carlisle, PA: Cumberland County Historical Society, 2001.

Coodley, Gregg, and David Sarasohn. *The Green Years, 1964–1976: When Democrats and Republicans United to Repair the Earth*. Lawrence: University Press of Kansas, 2021.

Cooke, Edward. "Patterns of Voting in Pennsylvania, 1944–1953." *Pennsylvania History* 27 (January 1960): 69–87.

Cronon, William. "The Trouble with Wilderness." *New York Times Magazine*, August 13, 1995.

Decker, Jefferson. *The Other Rights Revolution: Conservative Lawyers and the Remaking of American Government*. New York: Oxford University Press, 2016.

Desert Magazine. "Nevills Plaque Is Dedicated." October 1952, 5–7.

DeVoto, Bernard. "Let's Close the National Parks." *Harper's Magazine*, October 1953, 49–52.

Dochuk, Darren. *From Bible Belt to Sunbelt: Plain-Folk Religion, Grassroots Politics, and the Rise of Evangelical Conservatism*. New York: W. W. Norton, 2011.

Donehoo, George P. *A History of the Cumberland Valley in Pennsylvania*. Harrisburg, PA: Susquehanna History Association, 1930.

Drake, Brian Allen. *Loving Nature, Fearing the State: Environmentalism and Antigovernment Politics Before Reagan*. Seattle: University of Washington Press, 2013.

———. "The Skeptical Environmentalist: Senator Barry Goldwater and the Environment Management State." *Environmental History* 15 (October 2010): 587–611.

Dulles, Foster Rhea, and Melvyn Dubofsky. *Labor in America: A History*. 4th ed. Arlington Heights, IL: Harlan Davidson, 1984.

Dunlap, Thomas R. *Faith in Nature: Environmentalism as Religious Quest*. Seattle: University of Washington Press, 2004.

———. *Saving America's Wildlife: Ecology and the American Mind, 1850–1990*. Princeton: Princeton University Press, 1988.

Durand, P. A., and J. Fraise Richard. *History of Cumberland County, Pennsylvania*. 1888. Reprint, Harrisburg, PA: Heritage Books, 2008.

Everhart, William C. *The National Park Service*. New York: Praeger, 1972.

Farb, Peter. "Disaster Threatens the Everglades." *Audubon Magazine*, September–October 1965, 302–9.

Farber, David. *The Rise and Fall of Modern American Conservatism: A Short History*. Princeton: Princeton University Press, 2010.

Federal Writers' Project of the WPA, comp. *Pennsylvania: A Guide to the Keystone State*. New York: North American Book Distributors, 1940.

Fixico, Donald L. *Termination and Relocation: Federal Indian Policy, 1945–1960*. Albuquerque: University of New Mexico Press, 1990.

Flippen, J. Brooks. *Conservative Conservationist: Russell E. Train and the Emergence of American Environmentalism*. Baton Rouge: Louisiana State University Press, 2006.

———. "Mr. Hickel Goes to Washington." *Alaska History* 12 (Fall 1998): 1–22.

———. *Nixon and the Environment*. Albuquerque: University of New Mexico Press, 2000.

Foresta, Ronald A. *America's National Parks and Their Keepers*. Washington, DC: Resources for the Future, 1984.

Fox, Stephen. *John Muir and His Legacy: The American Conservation Movement*. Boston: Little, Brown, 1981.

Fradkin, Philip L. *Wallace Stegner and the American West*. New York: Knopf, 2008.

Frome, Michael. *Battle for the Wilderness*. Salt Lake City: University of Utah Press, 1997.

Galbraith, John Kenneth. *The Affluent Society*. Boston: Houghton Mifflin, 1958.

Gessner, David. *All the Wild That Remains: Edward Abbey, Wallace Stegner, and the American West*. New York: W. W. Norton, 2015.

Goldberg, Robert Alan. *Barry Goldwater*. New Haven: Yale University Press, 1995.

Gottlieb, Robert. *Forcing the Spring: The Transformation of the American Environmental Movement*. Washington, DC: Island Press, 2005.

Gould, Lewis L. *Lady Bird Johnson and the Environment*. Lawrence: University Press of Kansas, 1988.

Graham, Otis L., Jr. *Presidents and the American Environment*. Lawrence: University Press of Kansas, 2015.

Hartzog, George B., Jr. *Battling for the National Parks*. Mt. Kisco, NY: Moyer Bell, 1988.

Harvey, Mark. "Defending the Park System: The Controversy over Rainbow Bridge." *New Mexico Historical Review* 73 (January 1998): 45–67.

———. *A Symbol of Wilderness: Echo Park and the American Conservation Movement*. Albuquerque: University of New Mexico Press, 1994.

———. *Wilderness Forever: Howard Zahniser and the Path to the Wilderness Act*. Seattle: University of Washington Press, 2005.

Haury, Eric Penner. *Edward Bridge Danson: Steward of the New West*. Flagstaff: Museum of Northern Arizona, 2011.

Haycox, Stephen. *Battleground Alaska: Fighting Federal Power in Alaska*. Lawrence: University Press of Kansas, 2016.

———. *Frigid Embrace: Politics, Economics, and Environment in Alaska*. Corvallis: Oregon State University Press, 2002.

Hays, Samuel P. *Beauty, Health, and Permanence: Environmental Politics in the United States, 1955–1985*. Cambridge: Cambridge University Press, 1987.

———. *Conservation and the Gospel of Efficiency*. Pittsburgh: University of Pittsburgh Press, 1999.

———. "From Conservation to Environment: Environmental Politics Since World War II." *Environmental Review* 6 (Fall 1982): 14–41.

———. *A History of Environmental Politics Since 1945*. Pittsburgh: University of Pittsburgh Press, 2000.

Healy, Robert. "Interparty Competition in Pennsylvania, 1954–1968: A Historical and Political Perspective." *Pennsylvania History* 37 (October 1970): 352–80.

Helvarg, David. *The War Against the Greens: The 'Wise-Use' Movement, the New Right, and the Browning of America*. Boulder, CO: Johnson Books, 2004.

Hoffer, Ann Kramer. *Twentieth Century Thoughts: Carlisle, the Past Hundred Years*. Carlisle, PA: Cumberland County Historical Society, 2001.

Huffman, Thomas R. *Protectors of the Land and Water: Environmentalism in Wisconsin, 1961–1965*. Chapel Hill: University of North Carolina Press, 1994.

Hundley, Norris, Jr. "Clio Nods: *Arizona v. California* and the Boulder Canyon Act—A Reassessment." *Western Historical Quarterly* 3 (January 1972): 17–51.

Ise, John. *Our National Park Policy: A Critical History*. Baltimore: Johns Hopkins University Press, 1958.

Iverson, Peter. *Diné: A History of the Navajos*. Albuquerque: University of New Mexico Press, 2002.

Jackson, Donna R. *US Foreign Policy in the Horn of Africa: From Colonialism to Terrorism*. London: Routledge, 2018.

Jacoby, Karl. *Crimes Against Nature: Squatters, Poachers, Thieves, and the Hidden History of American Conservation*. Berkeley: University of California Press, 2001.

Johnson, Rich. *The Central Arizona Project*. Tucson: University of Arizona Press, 1977.

Kallman, Diane. "German POWs in Carlisle." Master's thesis, Pennsylvania State University, 1989.

Kennedy, David. *Freedom from Fear: The American People in Depression and War*.

New York: Oxford University Press, 1999.

Kirk, Andrew G. *Counterculture Green: The Whole Earth Catalog and American Environmentalism*. Lawrence: University Press of Kansas, 2007.

Koppes, Clayton R. "Efficiency/Equity/Esthetics: Towards a Reinterpretation of American Conservation." *Environmental Review* 11 (Summer 1987): 127–46.

Lassiter, Matthew. *The Silent Majority: Suburban Politics in the Sunbelt South*. Princeton: Princeton University Press, 2001.

Liartis, Christopher. "The Spanish Flu in Cumberland County, 1918." *Cumberland County History Journal* 13 (Summer 1996): 17–22.

Lichtman, Allan J. *White Protestant Nation: The Rise of the American Conservative Movement*. New York: Atlantic Monthly Press, 2008.

Life. "The John Birch Society: Patriotic or Irresponsible, It Is a Subject of Controversy." May 12, 1961, 124–30.

Linenberger, Toni Rae. "The Navajo Unit: Colorado River Storage Project." Denver: US Department of the Interior, Bureau of Reclamation, 1998. https://www.usbr.gov/projects/pdf.php?id=86.

Louter, David. *Windshield Wilderness: Cars, Roads, and Nature in Washington's National Parks*. Seattle: University of Washington Press, 2006.

Lytle, Mark Hamilton. *The Gentle Subversive: Rachel Carson, "Silent Spring," and the Rise of the Environmental Movement*. New York: Oxford University Press, 2007.

Mackintosh, Barry. "NPS Advisory Board: A Short History." April 1999, updated March 2004. https://www.nps.gov/articles/npsab-history.htm.

Macleod, David I. *Building Character in the American Boy: The Boy Scouts, YMCA, and Their Forerunners, 1870–1920*. Madison: University of Wisconsin Press, 1983.

Maher, Neil M. *Nature's New Deal: The Civilian Conservation Corps and the Roots of the American Environmental Movement*. New York: Oxford University Press, 2008.

Mahoney, Richard D. *JFK: Ordeal in Africa*. New York: Oxford University Press, 1983.

Marston, Otis Reed, and Tom Martin. *From Powell to Power: A Recounting of the First 100 River Runners Through the Grand Canyon*. Flagstaff: Vishnu Temple Press, 2014.

Masland, Frank, IV. "Descendants of John Masland of Annesley." https://masland.org/genealogy/descendants-john-masland-annesley/.

———. "'Weavers and Warriors': The Story of the Masland Family." https://masland.org/weavers-warriors/.

May, Gary. "Passing the Torch and Lighting Fires: The Peace Corps." In *Kennedy's Quest for Victory: American Foreign Policy, 1961–1963*, edited by Thomas G. Paterson, 284–316. New York: Oxford University Press, 1989.

McCloskey, Michael. "Wilderness at the Crossroads." *Pacific Historical Review* 41 (August 1972): 346–61.

McConnell-Sidorick, Sharon. *Silk Stockings and Socialism: Philadelphia's Radical Hosiery Workers from the Jazz Age to the New Deal*. Chapel Hill: University of North Carolina Press, 2017.

McGirr, Lisa. *Suburban Warriors: The Origins of the New American Right*. Princeton: Princeton University Press, 2001.

McGurty, Eileen. "From NIMBY to Civil Rights: The Origins of the Environmental Justice Movement." *Environmental History* 2 (July 1997): 307–23.

Mengak, Kathy. *Reshaping Our National Parks and Their Guardians: The Legacy of George B. Hartzog, Jr.* Albuquerque: University of New Mexico Press, 2012.

Milazzo, Paul Charles. *Unlikely Environmentalists: Congress and Clean Water, 1945–1972*. Lawrence: University Press of Kansas, 2006.

Miles, John C. *Guardians of the Parks: A History of the National Parks and Conservation Association*. Washington, DC: Taylor & Francis, 1995.

———. *Wilderness in National Parks: Playground or Preserve*. Seattle: University of Washington Press, 2009.

Millard, Candace. *The River of Doubt: Theodore Roosevelt's Darkest Journey*. New York: Doubleday, 2005.

Miller, Char. *Gifford Pinchot and the Making of the Modern Environmental Movement.* Washington, DC: Island Press, 2001.

Moon, Samuel. *Tall Sheep: Harvey Goulding, Monument Valley Trader*. Norman: University of Oklahoma Press, 1992.

Morrison, Ernest. *J. Horace McFarland: A Thorn for Beauty*. Harrisburg: Pennsylvania Historical and Museum Commission, 1995.

———. "Maurice Goddard: The Commonwealth's Conservation Czar." *Pennsylvania Heritage* 27 (Fall 2002): 32–37.

———. *A Walk on the Downhill Side of the Log: The Life of Maurice Goddard*. Mechanicsburg, PA: Pennsylvania Forestry Association, 2000.

Murray, Charles. *Coming Apart: The State of White America, 1960–2010*. New York: Crown, 2012.

Nash, George H. *The Conservative Intellectual Movement in America Since 1945*. Wilmington, DE: Intercollegiate Studies Institute, 1996.

Nash, Roderick. "The American Cult of the Primitive." *American Quarterly* 18 (Fall 1966): 517–37.

———. *Wilderness and the American Mind*. 3rd ed. New Haven: Yale University Press, 1982.

National Parks Magazine. "Secretary of the Interior Fred A. Seaton Creates Arctic and Two Other Wildlife Ranges in Alaska." January 1961, 17.

National Recovery Administration. *Code of Fair Competition for the Carpet and Rug Manufacturing Industry*. Washington, DC: US Government Printing Office, 1934.

Needham, Andrew. *Power Lines: Phoenix and the Making of the Modern Southwest.* Princeton: Princeton University Press, 2014.

Nelson, Daniel. *Nature's Burdens: Conservation and American Politics, the Reagan Era to the Present.* Logan: Utah State University Press, 2017.

Nicol, C. W. *From the Roof of Africa*. New York: Knopf, 1971.

Noer, Thomas. "New Frontiers and Old Priorities in Africa." In *Kennedy's Quest for Victory: American Foreign Policy, 1961–1963*, edited by Thomas G. Paterson, 253–83. New York: Oxford University Press, 1989.

Oakes, David. "Family Affair." *Central Manufacturing District Magazine*, August 1953, 22–31.

Olson, Sigurd. "Why Wilderness?" *American Forests*, September 1938, 395–97, 429.

O'Neill, William L. *Coming Apart: An Informal History of America in the 1960s*. Chicago: Ivan Dee, 2005.

Opie, John. *Nature's Nation: An Environmental History of the United States*. New York: Harcourt Brace, 1998.

Paterson, Thomas G., ed. *Kennedy's Quest for Victory: American Foreign Policy, 1961–1963*. New York: Oxford University Press, 1989.

Pearson, Byron E. *Saving Grand Canyon: Dams, Deals, and a Noble Myth*. Reno: University of Nevada Press, 2019.

———. *Still the Wild River Runs: Congress, the Sierra Club, and the Fight to Save Grand Canyon*. Tucson: University of Arizona Press, 2002.

Phillips-Fein, Kim. *Invisible Hands: The Businessmen's Crusade Against the New Deal*. New York: W. W. Norton, 2009.

Porter, Eliot. *The Place No One Knew: Glen Canyon on the Colorado*. San Francisco: Sierra Club, 1963.

Reilly, P. T. "Norman Nevills: Whitewater Man of the West." *Utah Historical Quarterly* 55 (Spring 1987): 181–200.

Reuling, Nancy Streator. "Nancy Streator Reuling: The Passenger's Experience in the Late 1940s." Interview by Roy Webb, September 1990. *Boatman's Quarterly Review* 11, no. 4 (1998): 24–28.

Richardson, Elmo R. *Dams, Parks, and Politics: Resource Development and Preservation in the Truman-Eisenhower Era*. Lexington: University Press of Kentucky, 1973.

———. "The Interior Secretary as Conservation Villain: The Notorious Case of Douglas 'Giveaway' McKay." *Pacific Historical Review* 41 (August 1972): 109–33.

Righter, Robert W. *The Battle over Hetch Hetchy: America's Most Controversial Dam and the Birth of Modern Environmentalism*. New York: Oxford University Press, 2005.

Roberts, Elliott. "Frank Masland, Fellow." *Explorers Journal* 50 (June 1972): 110–11.

Rome, Adam. *The Bulldozer in the Countryside: Suburban Sprawl and the Rise of American Environmentalism*. Cambridge: Cambridge University Press, 2001.

———. *The Genius of Earth Day: How a 1970 Teach-In Unexpectedly Made a Green Generation*. New York: Hill and Wang, 2013.

———. "'Give Earth a Chance': The Environmental Movement and the Sixties." *Journal of American History* 90 (September 2003): 525–54.

Rothman, Hal K. *The Greening of a Nation? Environmentalism in the United States Since 1945*. Fort Worth: Harcourt Brace, 1998.

Runte, Alfred. *National Parks: The American Experience*. 2nd ed. Lincoln: University of Nebraska Press, 1987.

Sale, Kirkpatrick. *The Green Revolution: The American Environmental Movement, 1962–1992*. New York: Hill and Wang, 1993.

Schlesinger, Arthur M., Jr. *The Crisis of the Old Order, 1919–1933*. Boston: Houghton Mifflin, 1957.

———. *The Disuniting of America: Reflections on a Multicultural Society*. Rev. and enl. ed. New York: W. W. Norton, 1991.

Schulte, Steven C. *Wayne Aspinall and the Shaping of the American West*. Boulder: University of Colorado Press, 2002.

Schwar, Harriet Dashiell, and Stanley Shaloff, eds. *Foreign Relations of the United States, 1958–1960, Africa*. Washington, DC: US Government Printing Office, 1992.

Scranton, Phillip. *Figured Tapestry: Production, Markets, and Power in Philadelphia Textiles, 1885–1941*. Cambridge: Cambridge University Press, 1989.

Sellars, Richard West. *Preserving Nature in the National Parks: A History*. New Haven: Yale University Press, 1997.

Shabecoff, Philip. *A Fierce Green Fire: The American Environmental Movement*. New York: Hill and Wang, 1993.

Shivik, John. *The Predator Paradox: Ending the War with Wolves, Bears, Cougars, and Coyotes*. Boston: Beacon Press, 2014.

Smith, Thomas G. "The Canyonlands National Park Controversy, 1961–1964." *Utah Historical Quarterly* 59 (Summer 1991): 216–42.

———. *Green Republican: John Saylor and the Preservation of America's Wilderness*. Pittsburgh: University of Pittsburgh Press, 2006.

———. *Stewart L. Udall: Steward of the Land*. Albuquerque: University of New Mexico Press, 2017.

———. "Warren Ost and the Formative Years of a Christian Ministry in the National Parks." *Journal of Presbyterian History* 98 (Fall–Winter 2020): 48–65.

———. "Worshipping at the Grand Canyon: The Shrine of the Ages Chapel Controversy." *Journal of Arizona History* 53 (Autumn 2012): 221–52.

Speakman, Joseph M. *At Work in Penn's Woods: The Civilian Conservation Corps in Pennsylvania*. University Park: Penn State University Press, 2006.

Spears, Ellen Griffith. *Rethinking the American Environmental Movement Post-1945*. New York: Routledge, 2021.

Spence, Mark David. *Dispossessing the Wilderness: Indian Removal and the Making of the National Parks*. New York: Oxford University Press, 1999.

Staveley, Gaylord. "Norman Nevills." *Boatman's Quarterly Review* 17, no. 1 (2004): 26–43.

Stegner, Wallace, ed. *This Is Dinosaur: Echo Park Country and Its Magic Rivers*. New York: Knopf, 1955.

Stevenson, Charles. "The Shocking Truth About Our National Parks." *Reader's Digest*, January 1955, 45–50.

Stoll, Mark R. *Inherit the Holy Mountain: Religion and the Rise of American Environmentalism*. New York: Oxford University Press, 2015.

———. *Protestantism, Capitalism, and Nature in America*. Albuquerque: University of New Mexico Press, 1997.

Stone, Barbara. "The John Birch Society: A Profile." *Journal of Politics* 36 (February 1974): 184–97.

Sturgeon, Stephen C. *The Politics of Western Water: The Congressional Career of Wayne Aspinall*. Tucson: University of Arizona Press, 2002.

Sutter, Paul S. *Driven Wild: How the Fight Against Automobiles Launched the Modern Wilderness Movement*. Seattle: University of Washington Press, 2002.

Sutterfield, Ragan. *Wendell Berry and the Given Life*. Cincinnati: Franciscan Media, 2017.

Swain, Donald C. *Wilderness Defender: Horace M. Albright and Conservation*. Chicago: University of Chicago Press, 1970.

Swanson, Donna. "From Depression Street to Prosperity Avenue: Turning the Corner with Roosevelt in Cumberland County." *Cumberland County History Journal* 7 (Winter 1990): 83–95.

Taliaferro, John. *Grinnell: America's Environmental Pioneer and His Restless Drive to Save the West*. New York: Liveright, 2019.

Time. "Education: The Man Who Confessed." October 10, 1955.

———. "Organizations: The Americanists." March 10, 1961.

Train, Russell E. *Politics, Pollution, and Pandas: An Environmental Memoir*. Washington, DC: Island Press, 2003.

Turner, James Morton. *The Promise of Wilderness: American Environmental Politics Since 1964*. Seattle: University of Washington Press, 2012.

———. "'The Specter of Environmentalism': Wilderness Environmental Politics and the Evolution of the New Right." *Journal of American History* 96 (June 2009): 123–47.

Turner, James Morton, and Andrew C. Isenberg. *The Republican Reversal: Conservatives and the Environment from Nixon to Trump*. Cambridge: Harvard University Press, 2018.

Washburn, Wilcomb. *The Cosmos Club of Washington: A Centennial History*. Washington, DC: Cosmos Club, 1978.

Watkins, T. H. *Righteous Pilgrim: The Life and Times of Harold L. Ickes, 1874–1952*. New York: Henry Holt, 1990.

Watt, James G. *The Courage of a Conservative*. New York: Simon and Schuster, 1985.

Webb, Roy, ed. *High, Wide, and Handsome: The River Journals of Norman D. Nevills*. Logan: Utah State University Press, 2005.

Weisiger, Marsha. *Dreaming of Sheep in Navajo Country*. Seattle: University of Washington Press, 2009.

Westin, Alan F. "The John Birch Society." *Commentary*, August 1961. https://www.commentarymagazine.com/articles/the-john-birch-society.

White, Lynn, Jr. "The Historical Roots of Our Ecological Crisis." *Science*, March 10, 1967, 1203–7.

White, Richard. *The Roots of Dependency: Subsistence, Environment, and Social Change Among the Choctaws, Pawnees, and Navajos*. Lincoln: University of Nebraska Press, 1983.

Wiecks, Michael. "The 1918 Influenza Epidemic in Cumberland County, Pennsylvania." *Cumberland County History Journal* 24 (Summer–Winter 2005): 3–37.

Winks, Robin W. *Laurance S. Rockefeller: Catalyst for Conservation*. Washington, DC: Island Press, 1997.

Wirth, Conrad L. *Parks, Politics, and the People*. Norman: University of Oklahoma Press, 1980.

Witmer, Linda. *The Indian Industrial School, Carlisle, Pennsylvania, 1879–1918*. Carlisle, PA: Cumberland County Historical Society, 2000.

Woodhouse, Keith Makoto. "Regulating Off-Road: The California Desert and Collaborative Environmentalism." *Modern American History* 2 (November 2019): 321–43.

Worster, Donald. "John Muir and the Modern Passion for Nature." *Environmental History* 10 (January 2005): 8–19.

———. *A Passion for Nature: The Life of John Muir*. New York: Oxford University Press, 2008.

Wriglesworth, Chad, ed. *Distant Neighbors: The Selected Letters of Wendell Berry and Gary Snyder*. Berkeley, CA: Counterpoint Press, 2014.

INDEX